ADVANCE PRAISE FOR
OPENING THE INNER WORLD

"I had heard of the 18th century philosopher, Emanuel Swedenborg, and people had told me that some of his ideas were similar to IFS, but I had never studied him. So, it has been fascinating to read this dialogue between IFS therapist Bob Falconer and two of the world's experts on Swedenborg. It also feels a bit surreal to have IFS compared so favorably to such an influential philosopher.

"When we invite clients to focus on their parts, they often seem to enter a separate but real inner realm where they interact with one another, which is what I've studied the past forty years. Swedenborg seems to have spent much of his life exploring that realm and other, more spiritual ones. While some of his reports on those explorations are more challenging for me to translate than for the three authors, I delight in others that show how he was traversing the same territory as I have been, and clearly he encountered and has a lot to say about Self, but did it almost 300 years earlier. And, for those interested in the spiritual side of IFS, he points to worlds we have yet to explore."

Richard C. Schwartz, PhD, Founder of Internal Family Systems Therapy

"A fascinating conversation between three spiritual archaeologists—one an eminent scholar-practitioner of IFS, two who are erudite followers of Emanuel Swedenborg—on the architecture of the inner world, the cosmology of the spiritual world, and the process by which these two worlds are realigned through healing and authentic spiritual experience."

Frank Rogers Jr., Professor of Spiritual Formation & Narrative Pedagogy at Claremont School of Theology, Co-Founder and Co-Director of the Center for Engaged Compassion, Author of *Cradled in the Arms of Compassion: A Spiritual Journey from Trauma to Recovery*

"Read and understand Swedenborg through the lens of IFS and contemporary scholarship! This reading brought a Swedenborg that is accessible, relevant, and fascinating. This is a book I will annotate and return to for additional insights."

Dr. Donald Davies, MD, Psychiatrist

OPENING THE INNER WORLD

Opening the Inner World

Spiritual Healing, Internal Family Systems, and Emanuel Swedenborg

by

Chelsea Rose Odhner, Robert Falconer, and Jonathan S. Rose

SWEDENBORG
FOUNDATION
Royersford, Pennsylvania

Library of Congress Cataloging-in-Publication Data

Names: Odhner, Chelsea Rose author | Falconer, Robert, 1948- author | Rose, Jonathan S., 1956- author
Title: Opening the inner world : spiritual healing, internal family systems, and Emanuel Swedenborg / by Chelsea Odhner, Robert Falconer, and Jonathan S. Rose.
Description: First edition. | Royersford, PA : Swedenborg Foundation, [2025] | Includes bibliographical references and index.
Identifiers: LCCN 2024047717 (print) | LCCN 2024047718 (ebook) | ISBN 9780877853671 paperback | ISBN 9780877857396 ebook
Subjects: LCSH: Swedenborg, Emanuel, 1688-1772 | Spiritual healing | Psychotherapy--Religious aspects | Psychotherapy--Methodology
Classification: LCC BX8748 .O36 2025 (print) | LCC BX8748 (ebook) | DDC 203/.1--dc23/eng/20250505
LC record available at https://lccn.loc.gov/2024047717
LC ebook record available at https://lccn.loc.gov/2024047718

Printed in the United States of America
Typesetting and cover desgin by Karen Connor
Index by Rae Schneider
Author photos of Chelsea Rose Odhner and Jonathan S. Rose by Gillian Rose Hyam
All author photos edited by Gillian Rose Hyam

Swedenborg Foundation • 70 Buckwalter Road
Suite 900 PMB 405 • Royersford, PA 19468
www.swedenborg.com

CONTENTS

AUTHORS' PREFACE

The following conversations explore the intersection of the Internal Family Systems (IFS) model and Emanuel Swedenborg's vast writings on the spiritual nature of existence. Even as you explore these two models, don't confuse the teacher for the Teacher. One thing both perspectives have in common is a keen awareness of the value of systematic models and the risk of them—that they may be used to supersede the real, lived experience, rather than to draw it out in the mind of the learner. That is why we are presenting this material as conversations rather than a didactic flow of information. What we are describing are landscapes to be explored in your own consciousness. We hope these words lift off the page and guide you to new realms within your imagination. The excitement and joy of these meetings is what we most want to shine through.

You will find the material marked with headings that specify the subject matter covered. We have ordered the conversations so the information flows through a useful sequence, but you will find the conversations themselves are natural and accessible, as if you are sitting with us and joining the conversation yourself. The chapters have a cyclical nature to them; each one deepens the subjects explored and adds to them.

At the outset of the conversations captured within this book, Chelsea had recently met Bob, but Bob and Jonathan had never met each other. Chelsea was the instigator in bringing these two minds together—one with decades of experience and teaching in the Internal Family Systems model, pushing the envelope of that model with his work on unattached burdens and his theory of porous mind; and the other with a lifetime of study of Swedenborg's works and a PhD in Latin. Chelsea, as facilitator and a bridge between the two models, is an IFS Level 1 trained coach and bodyworker and a lifelong student of Swedenborg's teachings.

Whether you are coming from an IFS background, a Swedenborg background, or are new to both, we hope you will be enriched through these dialogues, hearing fresh takes on what is both old and new.

Additional Notes

- In this work, although we cover an introduction to both IFS and Emanuel Swedenborg's writings, neither is comprehensive, and we encourage people to research both via other sources.[1] For example, we never spell out the steps of unburdening according to IFS, but we do touch on the topic at various points.
- Throughout the work, we make many references to Swedenborg's works. In several instances, we quote his texts; in many others, we simply cite a book title and section number. Customarily, section numbers are used to refer to Swedenborg's works instead of page numbers because the former are uniform across different editions and translations. We have used in-text citations to reference Swedenborg's works, while all other citations are footnoted.

---

1 For introductions to Emanuel Swedenborg's thought, see Emanuel Swedenborg, *New Jerusalem*, trans. George F. Dole (West Chester: Swedenborg Foundation, 2016) and Emanuel Swedenborg, *Survey / Soul-Body Interaction*, trans. Jonathan S. Rose and George F. Dole (West Chester: Swedenborg Foundation, 2022). See Richard C. Schwartz, *No Bad Parts: Healing Trauma and Restoring Wholeness with the Internal Family Systems Model* (Boulder: Sounds True, 2021) for an accessible introduction to Internal Family Systems.

- To pursue any reference further, all of Swedenborg's published theological works are available online in free downloadable form at swedenborg.com/emanuel-swedenborg, and his entire theological corpus is searchable at newchristianbiblestudy.org/advanced-search and browsable at newchristianbiblestudy.org/swedenborg.

- The Internal Family Systems model and Emanuel Swedenborg each have a particular use of the word "self." We have capitalized all instances of Self as the concept in Internal Family Systems.

- Although what is shared here is the result of recorded conversations, the language has been edited for written text; citations have been added for references made during the live discussions; and charts or diagrams have been added to aid the reader.

INTRODUCTION

Chelsea: Let's introduce ourselves, saying who we are and what brings us to this project, and then we can get into a dialogue. I am excited because you both are relatively new to the others' area of expertise.

We will be covering the basics of IFS and Swedenborg's worldview. I also want to be sure to touch on why we are here, why we are pursuing this project, and why we want to bring Swedenborg and IFS together in the first place. So that might factor into our introductions of ourselves.

I will start off by introducing myself, and then I will pass it to one of you. I was raised with Swedenborg's writings in one of the few church organizations in America that draw on Swedenborg's theology as a religious, confessional framework. I moved away from that in my early twenties with an interest in the experience of faith and spirituality of all people, religions, and cultures around the world. My interest took me to explore Eastern faiths and Southeastern philosophy. I came back to Swedenborg and read the New Century Edition (NCE) translation of Swedenborg's works, which was newly underway. When I took away all the filters that had been put on it through my religious upbringing, what I found was just really useful information that helped me with what I was struggling with in my own life. It helped me make sense of what felt like a whole mess of consciousness inside.

At the same time, I have an interest in healing modalities in general. I'm a licensed massage therapist and have always been fascinated by the connection of our mind or spirit with our body. I am interested in how to listen to the life energy in our bodies and curious about what it is all for; how to work with it in a positive way to relieve people's suffering, and support people in living whole, authentic, fulfilling lives connected to joy.

My path led me to working for the Swedenborg Foundation as well as finding Internal Family Systems. I am lit up about connecting what I see in IFS with the framework that Swedenborg describes and bringing it down to a practical level to really help people make sense of their own minds and find agency, liberation, and joy.

So that is a quick riff from me and where I'm coming from. How about you, Bob or Jonathan?

Jonathan: I can go. I, like Chelsea, was born into the Swedenborgian tradition. The total number of Swedenborgians on the planet I think hit a high point around the year 1900, with 15,000 people. So it has always been small, yet somehow, I am the eighth generation in this. My ancestors have been in this for a long time. Like Chelsea, I too grew up with this framework and then kind of turned my back on it for a while. Never totally, but I felt like I had been kind of duped or that the way that I had been taught it was simplistic. I joined a rock band and toured around Canada.

What I found playing in these clubs, though, was that the thing that I didn't need and didn't want I really felt would help these people. It was some clarity. I was busy turning my back on this thing and then realizing, wait a minute, this could really help people. And so through that process, I came back to it for myself.

I studied Latin and got a PhD in Latin from Bryn Mawr College in Pennsylvania. It was so different to be able to read Swedenborg in the original Latin, to read the first editions, compared to reading translations that were done in the late 1800s, over a hundred years after the originals were first published. Most translations widely available in English before the New Century Edition were translated in kind of a stilted English by people without much in the way of credentials; people at the time were eager to have translations made but it's a small group, so you use whomever you can, and you do your best.

So I had quite a different experience starting to read the material for myself from facsimile first editions. The color and the sense of humor really stood out to me. I realized there were things that were not being properly conveyed in the old translations. That was very invigorating to me.

I had studied Swedenborg in school and had come to a point at which I felt like I knew the whole territory; I had read everything. But when I came back to it, and was reading in Latin, it was much more like I had the eyes of a child and was in a state of wonder. I love the word *curiosity* that comes up a lot in Bob's book *The Others Within Us*,[2] which I understand is core to the Internal Family Systems model. That was the spirit in which I read Swedenborg's works. It was like I used to be a surveyor, and I could tell you how the whole forest worked, and now I'm going, "Wow, that leaf is cool; I never noticed how it's a little purple on the underside."

I was coming to a very different understanding. Part of what I wanted to do was join Swedenborg's effort to tell the world about his experiences and what he learned from them. So I got involved in the NCE translation project, which is an ambitious project; just phase one is twenty-seven volumes.

I have been doing that since 1997, just past twenty-five years, and it's been great. What I tell people sometimes is that I feel like I get a spiritual sunburn from reading Swedenborg eight hours a day. I often have this mental image of being at the front of the plane. The passengers have a little window beside them while I feel that, just by being in the seat I'm in, I can see this

---

2 Robert Falconer, *The Others Within Us: Internal Family Systems, Porous Mind, and Spirit Possession* (n.p.: Great Mystery Press, 2023).

vast expanse. What drives me is the desire to share what I see. A big part of my personal mission, which I realize has really been a lifelong quest of mine, is to be able to differentiate between what people *say* Swedenborg says and what he *actually* says.

Obviously, that's an endless quest. Swedenborg talks a fair amount about "the truth for its own sake," loving the truth for its own sake. I feel as though that got under my skin at some point.

With regard to healing, I knew the Swedenborg-influenced psychologist Wilson Van Dusen personally, quite well. I was very influenced by him and his work *The Presence of Spirits in Madness.*[3] In my late teens or early twenties, I was absolutely riveted by it. What an unbelievable book. And what a use of Swedenborg—what an interesting way of taking Swedenborg and marrying that to therapy. That amazed me. And then later on, I got to know Jerry Marzinsky and his work in weaving together Swedenborg's works with his therapeutic approach.

For many, many years I have felt that Swedenborg is a gold mine for therapeutic approaches. Sometimes I feel like one paragraph of his works could turn into an entire modality. There's so much potential in it.

I am an ordained minister, but seldom preach at this point. I was chaplain of a college for eight or ten years, so I did counseling of that type, but I have no counseling degree; no technical training. What I do have is an interest in the whole area of what can help people quickly and effectively.

Bob: Me too. I'm Bob Falconer, and I'll start with why I really want to be part of these conversations. This is a little bit heretical, but I tend not to stay inside the box: I think all healing is fundamentally spiritual. And cognitive behavioral therapy is not spiritual. It's like putting little Band-Aids on a wound and a little padding so you don't get smashed too much. But any significant

---

3 Wilson Van Dusen, *The Presence of Spirits in Madness: A Confirmation of Swedenborg in Recent Empirical Findings* (New York: Swedenborg Foundation, 1972).

healing must be spiritual (and you have to pretend it's *not,* to be acceptable in American academic circles).

The whole idea of Self in the IFS model is a profoundly spiritual concept, but it's phrased in a way that makes it seem not spiritual. And I think that's very intentional to sneak spirituality in so that it can be at least marginally acceptable.

I also came to Swedenborg through Van Dusen.

And those books of his, *The Presence of Other Worlds*[4] and *The Presence of Spirits in Madness*—great material. They connected spirituality and healing—these realms that are almost fighting each other. And that is so important to me. As long as these two things are separate from each other, fighting each other, it weakens both of them.

Anthropologists, most of them—the good ones—won't use the phrase "mental illness" because that's a culturally created concept. If you start talking about mental illness in a tribe, you've put something on them that isn't theirs. So instead they talk about "idioms of distress." I think the Western academic therapy world has blinders on that are causing immense suffering and preventing therapists from doing what they're supposed to do.

So I saw the coming together of Swedenborg and a reputable big-time major psychologist (Van Dusen) as a huge milestone, but there hasn't been anywhere near the echoes or ripples out of that which I think there should be. It was a pebble in a pond. And there's Jerry Marzinsky, and there's me, and there's a few other people following this, but so many others are still avoidant of acknowledging the spiritual aspect of healing. My wife is Korean, so I'm very connected to Korean culture, and this stuff is very alive there. Brazil is much more accepting. Mexico is much more accepting. I taught in Pakistan; they're much more accepting. To connect therapy to spirituality is to bring the West

---

4 Wilson Van Dusen, *The Presence of Other Worlds: The Psychological and Spiritual Findings of Emanuel Swedenborg* (West Chester: Swedenborg Foundation, 2004).

up to the level of the rest of the world. That is why I am interested and really excited about doing this. My sense is that Swedenborg somehow escaped the European curse and was able to see a little farther, and that is perhaps why books, such as D.T. Suzuki's *Swedenborg: Buddha of the North*,[5] have been written.

My own history: I come from one of the really—I think the word "evil" is appropriate, and I know we will talk about how Swedenborg views evil later on—families. It was churchgoing Presbyterian. On the outside it looked good, if you didn't look closely, but sadistic sexual abuse of me and my brother by my father and mother was happening on the inside. And my father often had these live-in men who were his gay lovers and also child abusers. So it was often gang rape. Both of my parents were addicts. Mom, more prescription pills; dad, hardcore heavy drinker. My brother died by suicide when we were teenagers; he had also started abusing me. He was a couple years older. My mom was institutionalized a few times and dad was murdered a few years later when I was twenty-one.

By all odds, I should be dead like my brother, or in prison.

Chelsea: Whew, that's intense. I'm so sorry you experienced such horrendous suffering.

Bob: Yeah. For a long time, I was suicidal, and I made this list in my mind: "Well, if you're really going to kill yourself, you ought to try A, B, C, D, E, and F before you do." And a lot of these things were sort of substantive, like get a master's degree in psychology and have a comfortable, secure place to live. And it took a while. As I started checking them off the top, I added more to the bottom. I am not recommending this as a therapeutic technique.

I went through every form of therapy known to humanity, or at least most of what was available at the time. Many of them

---

5 Daisetz Teitaro Suzuki, *Swedenborg: Buddha of the North* (West Chester: Swedenborg Foundation, 1996).

are very destructive and poisonous, fueled by the narcissism and messianic ambitions of their founders. We could spend the whole time tearing down false gurus, but I think that would be useless.

But I do parts work. There are many traditions of parts work, and I think IFS is the pinnacle or surfer on top of the wave of parts work. We are made up of parts. We are not one unified thing. The idea of a mono-mind is a myth, and it is a very toxic one that really limits our thinking. I think that, for several reasons, IFS is perhaps the most sophisticated and powerful of the parts-work models. And its founder, Dick (Richard Schwartz) has been an evangelist. He has been incredibly dedicated for forty years to spreading this model. For most of those years, he has spent more than two hundred days a year on the road, giving workshops and lectures everywhere.

So, that is another one of the reasons why his stuff is unbelievably popular now. And I personally have taught in Korea, Pakistan, Australia, Mexico, Spain, Poland, and Canada, and I have clients from all over the world. I even had a client from New Caledonia, and I had to get the atlas out to find out where that was. It is a little island, not far from Australia, that is a possession of France. So I think that's enough for a beginning introduction here.

Why IFS and Swedenborg

Chelsea: I want to share some thoughts that came to me while hearing you both speak. Connecting it back to my journey, I was taught so much about Swedenborg; it was loaded in my brain from a young age. But as I grew up and engaged with it, I felt that everything Swedenborg said was worthless unless it came down to the level of my life and actually helped me. No one in my circle of life—in my community—was really turning the information into a practice, like here's how to use it; here's how to make use of this amazing information. And so in the absence of that, I found such a community in the yoga circles in my neighborhood. These happened to be yoga practitioners who were really interested in the philosophical lineage traditions; not an overly Westernized aerobic yoga for external well-being, but like, let's study the scriptures. Let's practice the meditations, and here's why—because we are these beings of consciousness. And here's how you get to know your own consciousness, and here are the obstacles that are going to come your way, and so here's how you make this a practice.

The practices of yoga as a spiritual path made sense to me because they were something I could use. That was my introduction to really feeling like *this* is what Swedenborg is missing. Swedenborg has a lot of great ideas, but nobody was bringing it down to the level of practice and application to one's consciousness in a deeply embodied way.

I want to second what you shared, Bob, that Internal Family Systems really is amazing as the best of the tools that we have right now for looking inside and making sense of what's arising as a therapeutic approach.

What I think sets it apart is that IFS doesn't just tell you what's going on in there, but rather functions like a guide, saying, "Okay, you get to this crossroads, go this way, do this, apply this principle, then apply that principle." So you have this approach that lets you find success and make inroads for the healing opportunity that otherwise is too much of a jumble of noise to know where to go or how to start.

To me, IFS and Swedenborg together give you a form of practice set in an expansive framework for understanding consciousness. They give you both the larger context and help you at the level of knowing whether to turn right or left, so to speak, when you meet the next part in yourself.

I notice a parallel between Swedenborg and Dick Schwartz. I created and hosted the *Inside Off The Left Eye* podcast, where we studied the historical context of Swedenborg's works. In the episodes, we dug deep into *Swedenborg's Dream Diary*[6] and

6 Lars Bergquist, ed., *Swedenborg's Dream Diary*, trans. Anders Hallengren (Royersford: Swedenborg, Foundation, 2024).

Spiritual Experiences[7] to get at what was going on in Swedenborg's head as he was first having his spiritual experiences in his early fifties.

Swedenborg is coming from a Lutheran background where he's not even allowed to question the doctrine, and yet, he is like, "What's really going on in our spirits?" He also had roots in Swedish folk practices that were mindful of the presence and influence of angels and spirits.[8]

There is a moment when the recognition begins to dawn on him that the world—spiritual reality—is way bigger than his little circle of Lutherans in Europe. It is his introduction to the idea that there are spirits on or associated with other planets.[9]

The thing about Swedenborg is, he was willing to say, "Oh, maybe I don't know." He had this intellectual humility to acknowledge that things were bigger than he knew. He was willing to step into uncertainty and have his mind expanded and be opened to a deeper reality. And he *was* a scientist. A similar thing is what struck me about Dick Schwartz and made me willing to lend my trust to the IFS model. When I hear Dick speak and I read his books about IFS, knitted into it is an intellectual humility to be like, "We're not going to pretend that we know what the heck we're dealing with when we work with clients. They know better what's true about their subjective experience, and let's actually trust that." Doing that repeatedly, you get led

---

7 John Durban Odhner and Kurt Nemitz, trans. *Emanuel Swedenborg's Diary, recounting Spiritual Experiences during the years 1745–1765*, 4 vols (Bryn Athyn: General Church of the New Jerusalem, 1998–2013).

8 Cyriel Odhner Sigstedt, *The Swedenborg Epic: The Life and Works of Emanuel Swedenborg* (New York: Bookman Associates, 1952), 7–8, and Sarah Odhner, "Emanuel Swedenborg | GCED | Childhood 1688–1709," YouTube video, 11:26, September 6, 2016, https://www.youtube.com/watch?v=3O4vhrqdpjk.

9 Chelsea Odhner, "When Swedenborg First Spoke to Spirits from Other Planets," produced by Chelsea Odhner, *Inside Off The Left Eye*, January 17, 2021, podcast, MP3 audio, 42:19, https://inside-offthelefteye.simplecast.com/episodes/when-swedenborg-first-spoke-to-spirits-from-other-planets.

into deeper reality. So the quicker we can admit we don't know what's really going on, the sooner we can actually be let into truer realities, realities that could actually help us and serve us in our life.

Jonathan: I want to file an amended report! Many years ago, I went for a while to Bethesda, Maryland, to a Center for Family Process that was run by Ed Friedman, a rabbi who was helping all these Christian preachers be better Christian preachers. I read his books and got very interested in Bowen's Family Systems therapy—not a formal education. I was drawn to the concepts in there, of thinking of the family system, the identified patient, and these kinds of ideas. And then someone I know who's a therapist said, "Well, now they have this Internal Family Systems theory." And I remember thinking, "Well that's amazing, because Swedenborg talks about how each one of our thoughts and feelings is in the human form," which is a concept that blew my mind that we'll explore later (see pp. 76–77). So I was hearing about IFS, but I never read anything. I didn't know who was doing this or anything until I read your book, Bob, *The Others Within Us*.

People have wondered, if you think God was looking for someone to convey a revelation (not that that's really how it works), why Swedenborg? Why somebody in Sweden? One of the answers that a colleague of mine came up with, which I thought was very interesting, is that Swedenborg was embedded in the Christian world, so he could comment on that. His father was a Lutheran bishop. There were only about thirteen bishops in the country at that time, and one of them was his father. So Swedenborg could comment on Lutheranism and Christian theology with some authority.

He was in the thick of it—a nobleman, and serving in the government. And yet, as you say, Chelsea, he was only a few miles away from the Sámi people with shamans. And Swedenborg writes about them. Not much, but he has a passage in a relatively small, unpublished work called *The Fiber* in which he talks about the Sámi people who could go into what he called an "ecstasy energumene," a self-induced ecstasy or out-of-body experience, in which their body becomes more or less lifeless, functioning "in the operations of their soul alone," and they come back able "to reveal thefts and declare desired secrets."[10]

He was interested in this. What physiological state are you in when you're not there? When you've left your body? So he writes a page and a half about it, and it shows that he was aware of the Sámi people and some of the things that they would do. In general, Sweden in his time period was very conscious of the influence of spirits. You still had the idea of the Tomten, and Swedish lore had spirits. If you take the tour of the Falun Mine, they will still tell you there was a woman who was the spirit of the mine, and she would warn people when there was going to be a collapse, or when they were going to strike gold and such things. So Swedenborg's context was Christian, but it was also on the edge of an animistic kind of religion.

One last point I want to make is that I really like the idea that Bob references in his book called radical pragmatism: that you can sit down with people and find out what works. If it doesn't work, you don't keep doing it. Just kind of crawling on your hands and knees rather than coming in with a great organized theory of everything. And so, as a comment about this book itself, I have a concern of not wanting to make it an explanation—"Well, here, I'll tell you why that works that way"—because that would be against that same spirit. But in a spirit of exploration, there are some interesting concepts drawn from Swedenborg that could be applied within a therapeutic setting, and I'm excited to share and explore those with you both.

---

10 Emanuel Swedenborg, "The Fiber" in *The Economy of the Animal Kingdom, Considered Anatomically, Physically, and Philosophically, Transaction III*, trans. Alfred Acton (Bryn Athyn: Swedenborg Scientific Association, 1976), 339.

Bob: Thanks, Jonathan. I want to add something to your point about why it was someone in Sweden and how the folk traditions were still alive in Swedenborg's time period. The 1400–1500s are often called the "golden age of the demonic" in history that culminated in the frenzy of killing off the witches. I have come to interpret the frenzy of killing off the witches as the dominating structure's attempt to destroy the last European shamanic traditions.

It was extremely successful in Western Europe. It was not as successful in the East—Hungary, Romania, Macedonia—where they have ecstatic dances that go all the way back to the Dionysian dances of ancient Greece. So I think that might also be true of the north with Swedenborg in Sweden, that some of the native traditions that have a shamanic root of direct contact with spirits and an experiential basis for spirituality were still alive—alive enough. They hadn't been successfully snuffed out. How bad was the witchcraft persecution in Sweden? Was it milder than it was in central Europe? Or was it pretty horrible? My assumption is that it wasn't so bad.

Chelsea: It was not so bad.[11]

Bob: Was Swedenborg persecuted for his spiritual ideas?

Chelsea: Swedenborg was a nobleman himself and would dine with the royal family on occasion. Certain people in the Lutheran church, though, were adamantly opposed to his doctrines. His works were on trial at the end of his life in what's known as the Gothenburg trial. He was tried, and it failed because the

11 Peter T. Leeson and Jacob W. Russ, "Witch Trials," *The Economic Journal* 128, no. 613 (2018): 2066–2105. According to their research, Sweden had less than 1 percent (0.8) of the total number of witch trials in Europe between the years 1300 and 1850 (353 trials out of a population of one million, with no deaths) (Table 1). Nearly 75 percent of all witch trials occurred in only five countries: Germany, Switzerland, France, England, and the Netherlands (2079).

allegations were insubstantial.[12] But at the time there were people who wanted to snuff out the influence of his ideas, to stop them from spreading, even though they hadn't ever read them.

The trial failed, but certain Lutheran bishops wanted to campaign to try to wipe out his influence and eradicate it.[13] As I understand it, whoever was at the head of this campaign finally just gave up, because he found that, as it turned out, so many Lutheran ministers had already totally imbibed Swedenborg's teachings.[14] The Royal Court was interested and fascinated by Swedenborg's spiritual experiences during his lifetime.[15] People would visit him to learn more about them. So it was an interesting mix of a certain attack and antagonism toward his ideas, but then also this interest. His perspective gained some traction in Sweden, even though it did have to eventually go underground after his lifetime.

Jonathan: Yes. When he had been publishing his books for fifteen years and they weren't getting enough traction, he made a deliberate campaign of telling people about his spiritual experiences; and not just spiritual experiences, but telling people how their recently deceased loved ones were doing in the spiritual world.[16] People were very interested and would seek him out. Recently, his works have been declared a "world memory" by

---

12 Carl Theophilus Odhner, *Annals of the New Church: With a Chronological Account of the Life of Emanuel Swedenborg*, vol. 1, 1688–1850 (Bryn Athyn: Academy of the New Church, 1904), 109, 111, and Chelsea Odhner, "The Danger of Enjoying Evil and the Gothenburg Heresy Trial," produced by Chelsea Odhner, *Inside Off The Left Eye*, May 23, 2021, podcast, MP3 audio, 55:04, https://inside-offthelefteye.simplecast.com/episodes/the-danger-of-enjoying-evil-and-the-gothenburg-heresy-trial.

13 Odhner, *Annals*, 1:111. Odhner, *Annals*, 1:142.

14 Odhner, *Annals*, 1:142.

15 Jonathan S. Rose, introduction to *The Shorter Works of 1763* by Emanuel Swedenborg, trans. George Dole (West Chester: Swedenborg Foundation, 2020) 88–91.

16 Rose, introduction to *The Shorter Works of 1763*, 62.

UNESCO, and in 2010 there was funding through the Swedish government to have a whole conference about him, which I attended. It was held at the Swedish Royal Academy of Sciences.

Swedes themselves still seem unsure of how to hold Swedenborg; what to do with him. They are proud of his scientific achievements but somewhat embarrassed by his spirituality. You must know, Swedenborg sat for years on the Board of Mines, which was in charge of mining in Sweden. Mining was the backbone of the Swedish economy. It was an important function. I had long thought it was simply engineering, and settling disputes, but there was a paper at the conference honoring Swedenborg about how the Board of Mines was a hotbed of spiritism. Almost all the people on the Board of Mines were spiritists. It's interesting to think that many of those leading noblemen were very engaged with this stuff. I haven't heard much about the persecution of witches in Sweden though, specifically, but this seems to relate.

Bob: Mircea Eliade, an intellectual hero of mine, wrote a great book called *The Forge and the Crucible*.[17] It's about mining and metal smelting as a spiritual practice. Throughout Africa, metal smelting is a center of spirituality. The forge and the crucible were considered sacred rituals. I wonder if there was a similar culture for mining in Sweden in Swedenborg's day.

Jonathan: As I said, Swedenborg's father, Jesper Svedberg, was a Lutheran bishop. Stories are still told about him that are wild folktales. But the fact that these wild folktales exist about this Lutheran bishop points to the persistence of a sense of the spirit world in Sweden in Swedenborg's day. There is one story about how Jesper's driver was driving him home in the carriage on a snowy evening—a five-mile journey—and the wheel fell off and the carriage crashed. What to do? The bishop says,

---

17 Mircea Eliade, *The Forge and the Crucible*, trans. Stephen Corrin, (London: Rider & Co., 1962).

"Don't worry, I've got this handled. Just drive on, drive on!" And so they drive on and everything goes okay, and they get to his house. Then, when they get out, they look and, as the story goes, the devil himself is wrapped around the axle. So as it's told, the bishop got the devil to be the fourth wheel.

The legend goes on and says that the devil was so mad about it that two weeks later, he burned the bishop's house to the ground. And the bishop's house did burn down. Such an interesting supernatural tale.

Bob: It's very fascinating. The exciting thing to me that we are doing in this book is presenting Swedenborg with a lens from way over here, and the modern psychotherapy world in a language from way over here, and seeing how they're reflecting the same underlying reality. As we sort through the language, the underlying reality gets clearer. Like something with light shone on it from two directions. You can see all the details a whole lot better.

Chelsea: Yes! And why would we do that? Because it can be useful; it can make people's lives better and make us better at helping people have better lives.

We're writing this book, not just to get people to think, but to wonder, "How can this be useful?" Our interest is to operationalize these ideas; to make them functional. I hope people will play with them and explore whatever that reality is that it's all pointing to.

To that end, we'll address what might be roadblocks for people to enter into this material as we go along, but there's one that's worth touching on right now at the outset.

Bob: The whole word "Christianity."

There are many people who start gagging if you say that word. When I've tried to talk to people about Swedenborg, the thing that's gotten more people curious is Suzuki's book, *Swedenborg: Buddha of the North*—not any Christian comments.[18]

Chelsea: To address this, we can have Swedenborg speak for himself with regard to Christianity. He's having to wrestle with his own Christian baggage (not that he would put it in those terms), and he's adamant about the need to get out from under dogmatism so we can actually connect to what's spiritually real with us right now.

Jonathan: Here's a great passage for that. *Divine Love and Wisdom* 374:

> Another reason these things have not been seen and therefore recognized [speaking of how there is a spiritual reality connected to our physical one] is that we have displaced from our field of vision all the matters of religion that we refer to as "spiritual" by the dogma, prevalent throughout Christendom, that theological matters, "spiritual" matters, as defined by the councils and by some leaders of the church, are to be believed blindly because (so they say) they transcend understanding. This has led some people to believe that anything spiritual is like a bird that flies beyond the air into the ether, beyond the reach of our eyesight. In fact, though, it is like a bird of paradise flying so close to our eyes that its lovely feathers brush the pupils, willing to be seen.

And then he adds, "'Our eyesight' means our intellectual sight."

Bob: The divine is an exotic bird, not on the other side of the planet—she's brushing your eyes with her wing tips!

---

18 Suzuki, *Swedenborg: Buddha of the North.*

I have a quote that relates to this: "Theology is the corpse of revelation."[19] Swedenborg takes us back to direct experience, to revelation.

I think Swedenborg was enough of a scientist to be able to reintroduce spirituality to modern healing. Until about 1800, healing was primarily still spiritual. I think it's super important that psychotherapy be re-spiritualized.

19 Robert Falconer, *When Going Through Hell . . . Keep Going: Trauma, Healing, Spirit, and Internal Family Systems* (n.p.: Great Mystery Press, 2024), 32.

OPENING THE INNER WORLD

1
INTRODUCTION TO INTERNAL FAMILY SYSTEMS AND EMANUEL SWEDENBORG

Let's start with the origin stories of IFS and Swedenborg, and overviews of their key concepts. These introductions will lay an initial foundation for our later discussions. We will explore everything we touch on here more deeply further on, like an overture for the whole production.

Origin Stories of Internal Family Systems and Swedenborg

Chelsea: I want us to start by talking about what each of these approaches found: Swedenborg through his path and Internal Family Systems through its evolution as a model, and then your own work in it, Bob, specifically.

As an opener on Swedenborg, he was born in 1688 in Stockholm, Sweden, and died in 1772 in London, England, at the age of eighty-four. After studying at Uppsala University (1699–1709), he journeyed to England, Holland, France, and Germany to study with leading scientists in Western Europe. He then apprenticed as an engineer under the Swedish inventor

Christopher Polhem (1661–1751). He was ennobled by Queen Ulrika Eleonora (1688–1741), which gave him an active seat in the Swedish House of Nobility. He was an active participant in the Swedish government throughout his life.

During a transitional phase from 1743 to 1745, in his mid-fifties, he underwent a spiritual awakening, which opened his perception to a dual consciousness of this life and the life after death. He went on to publish eighteen theological titles that draw on the Bible, philosophical reasoning, and his own spiritual experiences.

There are records that he was having spiritual experiences even from a young age, though.[20] He was always observing his own consciousness and was curious about it. At the point right before his spiritual awakening, he was an anatomist. He was really interested in trying to find "the seat of the soul" in the body. He was writing a multi-volume work called *The Soul's Domain*,[21] about the soul in the body, right before he transitioned to writing spiritual literature. Then the second-to-last work that he published was called *Soul-Body Interaction*.[22] This quest to find the seat of the soul, to understand consciousness, was a throughline in his life.

His curiosity led him into states of mind beyond his imagination until it awoke in his consciousness a connection to spiritual realms that lasted for the rest of his life. His interest in finding the seat of the soul and the curiosity that he brought to that feels very similar to the approach of Internal Family Systems and its willingness to plumb the depths of the unconscious, to step beyond our waking, talking life.

---

20 Sigstedt, *The Swedenborg Epic*, 5.

21 Emanuel Swedenborg, *The Economy of the Animal Kingdom, Considered Anatomically, Physically, and Philosophically*, trans. Augustus Clissold, 2 vols (Bryn Athyn: Swedenborg Scientific Association, 1955). A more accurate translation of the title of this work is *Dynamics of the Soul's Domain*.

22 Emanuel Swedenborg, *Survey / Soul-Body Interaction*, trans. Jonathan S. Rose and George F. Dole (West Chester: Swedenborg Foundation, 2022).

In IFS, you might say, "I'm not feeling great," and then, as you bring curiosity to what is arising in yourself, you go into a deeper level of consciousness, an awareness of this inner realm where you can have dialogues with your parts; and then it can go even further as described in Bob's book *The Others Within Us*. I see a parallel there, between Swedenborg and the IFS model.

So let's start with Swedenborg. Passing it to you, Jonathan.

Jonathan: A lot of people see Swedenborg as a scientist—he was a polymath, renaissance man, learning all these different things, especially about anatomy and the brain—who then had a spiritual awakening and dropped all that science stuff and got interested in the Bible and the afterlife. But Anders Hallengren, a Swedenborg scholar from Sweden, has argued that there's more of a throughline, which was that, from an early age, Swedenborg was interested in thoughts and feelings and where they come from. And this is long before Jung and Freud, obviously; in fact, some people say that the reason for Swedenborg's popularity in the nineteenth century was that he was *psychology* before it got going, because he was talking about thoughts and feelings and where they come from. There's a draft work that is lost, but he mentioned it in a document to his brother-in-law. The New Century Edition refers to it as *Lost Draft Method of Analyzing Feelings*,[23] which he wrote when he was only twenty-six years old, long before his spiritual awakening.

So I think, in a way, the connection between the physical world and spiritual world—the soul, the brain, the body—was a lifelong interest for him. Partly what he was interested in was, "What is this whole thing?" He really came to believe that the human mind is thoughts and feelings—that is our soul, that is our spirit, and it transcends death.

---

23 Jonathan S. Rose, Stuart Shotwell, and Mary Lou Bertucci, eds., *Emanuel Swedenborg: Essays for the New Century Edition on his Life, Work, and Impact* (West Chester: Swedenborg Foundation, 2005), 448.

Bob: Okay. I think Dick came to this stuff—and most people in therapy-land come to this stuff—from a very different point of view. It's not this vast curiosity. It's more, "Oh, here's this suffering person in front of me. What can I do?"

And I've adopted that point of view too, and I've made it a discipline because I am intensely curious, but when there's someone in front of me suffering, it's my contract and my responsibility to help relieve their suffering and not to use their suffering to advance my research agenda. It takes ongoing effort on my part not to do that.

The things you were saying, Chelsea, about "not knowing," are so important. The reason Dick could discover, or invent—really, he would say discover—IFS is because he was *not* trained in individual therapy. He didn't have a whole raft of theories he had to get rid of. He didn't have this whole framework to look at the world. He was only trained in Family Systems. He often tells the story of how he was doing a study, and in it were a bunch of families with kids with bulimia—kids who eat way too much and then make themselves vomit. His belief—he was a professor and wrote the leading textbook on Family Systems therapy of the day,[24] which is still being used—was that if you rearrange the family system, everything's going to be fine. He did an outcome study to prove that this stuff worked, and it didn't work. He sort of jokingly said, "Well, the kids didn't know they were healed." They kept starving themselves to the verge of death and eating a great deal and vomiting.

From a place of ignorance, he brought a lot of focused curiosity to what was going on for them. So I think that *not knowing* was key to his learning what was going on. It's stunning—actually listening to the client. Now, this is a horrible indictment of Western therapy, but that was radical. You listen to these people and believe what they're saying, instead of coming up with

---

24 Michael P. Nichols and Richard C. Schwartz, *Family Therapy: Concepts and Methods* (New York: Gardner Press, 1984).

some fancy theory to explain it away (I'm afraid some of my snarky parts are sneaking in here!).

My basic point is that it comes from ignorance. It all comes from being ignorant and not having the education in all the current theories of the day.

Overview of the Internal Family Systems Model

Bob: I want to lay out in a relatively concise way the basic view of what a human is from an IFS point of view. I studied the history of religions a lot, and we would talk about this as "the anthropology of that religion"; how they saw humans as a spiritual being.

Parts

So the basic idea is that we're made up of parts. We're not one whole mono-mind. That's a terrible myth and very, very damaging. We're much more like a basketball team or a baseball team than a tennis player.

We need all these parts, and we don't want to mush them together. It's like in an orchestra; you want the violins to be violins. You don't want everyone sounding like a piano. You need all these different things. Take artificial intelligence and computers—you need all these separate subroutines which are relatively encapsulated and sparsely interlinked, or otherwise they're not subroutines. So you've got all these parts of people, and they are natural, healthy, and beneficial.

Before Dick's time, most people saw them as the product of trauma. And that's because of how people were noticing these things. They were noticing them in extremely traumatized people. But now it's clear that they're not; this is how we're made, and it's a good thing.

There's also direct evidence. Infants recognize human faces. And what they've done is made these stick-figure drawings of a human face, with a little smile and two eyes, and maybe a nose. Infants will orient themselves to that in their first days of life. They'll turn their face and look at it. And they've even done these experiments with how much of that you can mess up before they won't orient to it—won't recognize it as a face. There is a pre-programmed module that does human facial recognition inside an infant—that's a part!

And this other researcher, Thomas Berry Brazelton, observed that there are four or five discrete states in infants.[25] Usually they're considered emotional states, but they're parts!

Noam Chomsky writes about deep grammar[26]—there is a language-learning module that typically turns on at a certain time, and then, unfortunately for some of us, turns off when we're teenagers. So there are all these parts; these modules of the mind.

This is not new at all. Plato had a multiple model of mind. In one of the dialogues, Socrates is sitting there talking with this other guy, and he says, "Well, the very fact that we can have arguments in our head and say to ourselves 'I want to do this.' 'No, I don't.' 'Yes, I do.' 'No, I don't.' That proves we're multiple." It's so obvious that it's trivial. They go on to discuss something else. But this myth of the mono-mind keeps coming back, and it's really poisonous. We're made up of parts.

Parts come in several varieties. This was also not new with Dick. He refined it. Another therapist named Pia Mellody, who was an addiction specialist, had the same basic insight. Dick calls them protectors and exiles. Pia Mellody called them "adult-adapted, wounded children," and "wounded children." The broad concept is that there are parts who were badly hurt; and the pain they were given was so overwhelming that they had to be hidden away—locked in a basement, encapsulated—so that

---

25 T. Berry Brazelton and Bertrand G. Cramer, *The Earliest Relationship: Parents, Infants and the Drama of Early Attachment* (Addison-Wesley: 1991).

26 Noam Chomsky, "Deep Structure, Surface Structure, and Semantic Interpretation" in *Foundational Issues*, vol. 1 of *Semantics: Critical Concepts in Linguistics*, ed. Javier Gutiérrez-Rexach (United Kingdom: Routledge, 2003), 154–196.

the person could survive. This happens in childhood; it also happens during combat. This is a repeated dissociative mental process that is actually wonderful. It saves people's lives. It's not a disease; it's a resource.

So there are the hurt ones who are kept in a basement somewhere. And then there are these protectors who are trying to keep that wounded one from being triggered; or they're reacting when that one *is* triggered.

Dick says—and this is, as far as I know, new with Dick—that protectors come in two flavors: managers and firefighters. Managers are proactive. They come before the exile gets triggered, and their whole job is to keep that part safe, where it won't be triggered, so the flames of that overwhelming emotion won't come roaring up. Managers tend to be socially acceptable: overwork, perfectionism, internal criticism, all that kind of stuff. Managers.

Firefighters tend to come up after that exile has been triggered and the flames of that overwhelming emotion are burning the whole system. Firefighters just want to put that out. They don't care about collateral damage. And they're almost never socially approved: addictions are the classic firefighters. Overspending. Overwork can be a firefighter. It depends on how it's used. A lot of things can be used either as a firefighter or as a manager. Alcohol can be used as a manager or a firefighter. So you have to explore with each person.

Most people have a firefighter pyramid. They can do moderate stuff, like eat too much at lunch if they were distressed in the morning, and that's enough. But as it gets worse, they go up and up and up. Well, they have three or four martinis on their way home. They watch porn all night, then they start snorting coke; maybe they start cutting themselves.

The top of the firefighter pyramid is almost always the same. That's suicide. In IFS, we view suicide as some part in there saying, "If this pain gets absolutely unbearable, I can stop it. I will save you. I'm here." That gives us a very different attitude toward suicide. It's not an enemy. We don't make "no suicide" contracts, except in states where you're required by law to make them. In that case we say, "Well, we're going to work really hard to stop you from killing the body, but we can really appreciate what you're doing here." It really works. Pragmatically, this works.

Parts are what populate our inner world. They're real beings with full personalities and good intentions for the system. They get frozen in time. You can have parts stuck in the past from when you were a two-year-old, and those frozen-in-time parts don't know how old you are in the present. They can appear to be non-human, but Dick says the spirit in them seems to eventually be human. Parts can communicate with us, oftentimes through our bodies.

There was a quote from Swedenborg you shared with me, Jonathan, that fits in perfectly here. *Secrets of Heaven* 4800:

> Very few can believe that spirits and angels live in communities, and that everything in a person corresponds to those communities. Few can believe that the more communities there are, and the more members in a community, the better and stronger the correspondence, because there is strength in unanimous numbers.

That's multiplicity. We're communities; we're not an individual.

Burdens

So we've got this two-layered thing of parts: exiles down here, layers of protectors above. All these parts are good. What makes them a problem is they've got burdens on them. You get these exiles who were really hurt in childhood and they're carrying all this terror, self-hate, shame, or overwhelm. You get burdens off these parts, and they're the most tender, the most sensitive, the most innocent. The most playful. None of these parts are bad. They all have treasures in them. The suicidal part is often the most loyal, dedicated being you could imagine inside a person. None of them are bad.

Parts are not their burdens. Parts get a lot of gunk stuck to them, and that's not who they are. That's a major problem with most therapies. We think the angry part is anger, and we just want to get rid of it. That doesn't work.

Jonathan: My wife was just asking me the other day about IFS and saying, "So the parts are all good." And I said, "Well, as far as I can figure out, the parts are all good, but the burdens are not." The burdens can be suicidal or drug addicted, but that's not the part's true essence. You can experience the part without that.

Bob: Dick has said, "This world is the school, and the burdens are our lesson plan." That's the curriculum, dealing with all that.

Self

Then Dick discovered there's something else inside. He discovered it in his clients. He actually listened to them—like I said, revolutionary. Anyway, they would all come across this thing, and when Dick would ask about it—"What part is that?"—client after client would say, "Oh, it's not a part really, it's different." This different, "not a part" part seemed to be wise and kind; it always came with the same basic characteristics. No matter how traumatized a client was, this wise and kind "not a part" part would eventually emerge. Dick came to call this presence "Self" with a capital S because that's what people usually referred to it as. Every client he worked with would say something along the lines of, "Oh, that's not a part, that's myself." But he gave it a capital S to distinguish it. Dick has come to think that this is the most important aspect of his description of humans.

He characterizes the Self by 8 Cs: curiosity, compassion, creativity, connectedness, courage, clarity, confidence, and calm.

I personally don't think Self is calm. I think Self is full of light. He even admits it—I'm going off topic a little—he said the first time he met Self was in peak experience flow-moments during athletics, when you're performing at your absolute maximum. That's not calm!

So there's Self, and parts, and parts come as protectors and exiles.

Jonathan: It's cool to hear you describe all this. As Chelsea mentioned earlier, Swedenborg left a journal in Swedish, unpublished at the time of his death. It's known as his dream diary, or *Journal of Dreams*. It chronicles his experiences during his spiritual awakening. Part of his process was noticing that his thoughts would argue with each other.

Bob: That sounds like what IFS calls polarizations. There are ways to work with polarized parts; parts who are at odds with each other.

Jonathan: It's amazing to think about what that must have been like for Swedenborg. What vocabulary did he have to articulate what he was going through? It wasn't something people talked about. He seemed very surprised that his thoughts were arguing with each other.

Chelsea: I happened to be at the Swedenborg House in London, which is the home of the Swedenborg Society, and they had a pamphlet that they had produced a while ago on everything Swedenborg says about "double thoughts."[27] He writes about it a lot in his dream diary. I took a picture of one page; it's just a bunch of different excerpts. One from *Spiritual Experiences* 484 says, "I've been endowed with a double thought, one being the inmost, the other interior. So that while I have been in the company of evil spirits, I could at the same time be in the company of good ones and could thus perceive of what quality were the spirits who desired to lead me." Another reads:

---

27 Swedenborg Society, *Double Thoughts* (London: Swedenborg Society, 2010).

> It was wonderful that I was able to have at one and the same time two thoughts quite distinct from one another. The one for myself, which occupied entirely the thoughts of others. And at the side of this, the thoughts of the temptation in such a manner that nothing was powerful enough to drive them away. They held me captive so that I did not know whither to flee for I carried them with me. (*Dream Diary* 69)

Bob: This is IFS. I've never heard this phrase "double thoughts" before. This is something that really fits well with IFS. In the history of multiple personality in the psychology of the West, they first got to dual personality and then they went, whoops, it's not just two.

Have you seen Henri Ellenberger's book *The Discovery of the Unconscious*?[28] Magisterial. He spent his whole life researching psychology in the nineteenth century and early twentieth century. I don't think anyone's going to match that volume for scholarship for a very long time to come.

He traces this stuff about the dual personality. Also Hermann Hesse's *Steppenwolf*.[29] Steppenwolf knew before he got into the Magic Theater, "Oh, I'm two people. I'm the mild-mannered professor and I'm the wolf." He knew that. And then he gets that book from the Magic Theater, and he starts reading. He says, "Well, it's good you know you're two, but you're not two. You're thousands."

And that was the doorway into his mystical enlightenment.

Jonathan: I think Swedenborg started with that idea of two and definitely came along the way to, like, oh no, there's a lot.

---

28 Henri F. Ellenberger, *The Discovery of the Unconscious: The History and Evolution of Dynamic Psychiatry* (New York: Basic Books, 1970).

29 Hermann Hesse, *Steppenwolf*, trans. David Horrocks (United Kingdom: Penguin UK, 2012).

Bob: So that dream diary might be closer to the realm of modern-day therapy stuff.

Jonathan: Some people have looked at it from that angle. Several editions of it exist that are interesting with commentaries on the different dreams, what he sees in the symbolism, and what he seems to be going through psychologically.[30]

The Locus of Healing

Bob: Going back to IFS, the locus of healing in IFS is *not* the relationship between the therapist, out here, and the client. That's important. The real locus of healing is the relationship between the client's Self and the client's parts. We, or the ones of us who've done this for a while, do everything we can to back off, and instead foreground that relationship. We ask, "How do you feel toward that part? How is it for the part to receive your care?" That's where real, profound healing can occur.

Dick describes Self as a particle and a wave, or field. And I've even heard him theorize that if you get up into that Self, as a field, there might only be one Self that we all participate in.

To complicate things further, he also says that every part is made up the same way we are. Every part has parts and Self. It's fractal—which makes me think of a few concepts in Swedenborg's writings I've heard of like the "grand human" idea and thoughts being human, which I know we'll get into later (see pp. 54, 76).

In IFS, the basic pattern of therapy is to help a person get to a place where they are in Self-leadership, where Self is leading their system and the parts are unburdened, so their true nature can shine forth. And we want an orchestra. We don't want mush. We don't want to put all this in a blender.

---

30 See Wilson Van Dusen, *Emanuel Swedenborg's Journal of Dreams: The Extraordinary Record of the Transformation of a Scientist into a Seer*, trans. J. J. G. Wilkinson (New York: Swedenborg Foundation, 1986).

Another important thing here from a therapeutic point of view is that we don't teach grounding skills at all in IFS. We don't do any of that because if there's some part in a person who's all agitated and totally freaked out who shows up in the therapy room, and you start doing a grounding technique, what message does it give to that part? "Go away. You're not welcome here. We can't handle you. Shut up." That's absolutely the wrong message. So we say, "Oh, hi, anxious part. Welcome. Please come in. We want to get to know you. Don't go away." This is very different.

There can be exiled protectors as well; protective parts who get exiled. So it's not all vulnerable little nice guys. For example, women have been culturally trained to exile anger.

There are nested systems, nested isomorphic systems. Parts have parts, and parts have a Self. They have the entire structure of a human. And you can go down one more level. You can keep going forever. I think it's parts all the way down. You can go in the other direction, too. A person is a part of a family system. A family is a part of a community. You can go in either direction. It's all isomorphic in either direction. It doesn't seem to end. There's a wonderful saying that has taken various forms, but the gist of it is that a guy is asked, "What's the world? What does the world rest on?"

The guy answers, "Oh, the world rests on the back of a tiger."

"What does the tiger stand on?"

"An elephant."

"What does the elephant stand on?"

"A turtle."

"What does the turtle stand on?"

He says, "It's turtles all the way down."

Jonathan: I read a book about international diplomacy and it is fascinating the extent to which you can totally think of Russia as one person and China as one person. They have a relationship with each other. You can think of the whole world as having the Russia part and the China part, and how they're interacting with the US part. It was interesting to read from a diplomat that it sounded like you could actually use that approach—that it's helpful to think that way, even though it aggregates tens or hundreds of millions of people into one thing. But you can usefully think of it that way. There's an interaction there.

Bob: That goes the other way too. I think an idea that comes from politics is very useful in psychotherapy: the idea of colonization and colonialism. I think the Native American therapists are the ones who brought this to the fore.[31] But if you think about what the ego does, often what the managers do inside our heads is that they try to colonize the rest of the mind. They put out their messages and try to dominate it and colonize the unconscious and get control, and get spirit all walled up in nice little neat containers. I think it's exactly the same process.

Jonathan: They try to put in a whole level of government above the government that was already there.

Bob: Going back to the concept of Self for a minute, Dick says Self cannot be damaged even in the worst trauma. That's a life-saving message for guys like me. Who you really are can't be damaged or even dirtied. No matter how bad the storm is down here, the sun is not affected, and you are the sun. Pema Chödrön is generally attributed as saying something like that. She says, "You are the sky. Everything else—it's just weather."

The Self is undamaged; it can't be damaged. That's very radical. And I think it's also fundamentally a spiritual perspective. And the Self heals; it's the aspect of us that can heal our parts.

Jonathan: If we were just a body walking around having experiences, we would be totally damageable, and the damage would

---

31 David R. Hodge, Gordon E. Limb, and Terry L. Cross, "Moving from Colonization toward Balance and Harmony: A Native American Perspective on Wellness," *Social Work* 54, no. 3 (2009): 211–219.

be what we are. The idea that there's some part that's pure no matter what else goes on—that's transcendent.

Bob: Does that fit with Swedenborg?

Jonathan: Perfectly. He says it point blank in *Spiritual Experiences* 2487 (emphasis added):

> *The innermost and very inward parts of a person cannot be harmed, but only the inward ones.*
>
> Since the first human being up until now the Lord has preserved the very inward human parts so they would not be corrupted. This he has done by means of the innermost parts, because these are such that they *cannot be corrupted*. But their inward parts, on the other hand, have been corrupted.
>
> This can be grasped in a spiritual mental image by means of forms, by those who are able to understand what very inward and innermost forms are like. They are such that they can be attached to anything whatever that can possibly exist in the world, can be twisted toward all things, but still conspire from the individual points as centers toward the state of integrity. For while they can most easily be attached to evil and distorted things in the inward parts, yet *from their ability to return to their state of integrity*, which the Lord preserves and constantly restores, *they are not harmed*.

Bob: Dick talks about how once parts open inner space, when the clouds part back, the Self exudes energy—it radiates, pulsates, vibrates. He compares it to prana and qi and the Hebrew word for spirit that also means breath, *ruach*.

Dick sees Self as radiating this. Is there a concept parallel to qi or prana in Swedenborg's work?

Jonathan: He definitely talks in similar terms about after you are reborn. He sees rebirth as an ongoing, eternal process of development. But when you reach the point when love takes over, he has several beautiful things to say about how transformative that is. The humility, the understanding, the perspective. He says you really are alive for the first time. So he does associate it with life.

Chelsea: What comes to mind for me is what he calls "spiritual substance." Spiritual substance is the spirit that is alive in our body. The spiritual substance has its own kind of movement to it. It's the whole nature of spiritual substance that is what's connecting us to other people, and to the spirits and angels. And it's on account of the nature of spiritual substance that we receive spiritual light and spiritual warmth as life from the divine. The warmth is love, and the light is wisdom; in his terms, light and heat in this world correspond to the spiritual realities of love and wisdom. So spiritual substance is always streaming into us from the divine, which appears like a sun in the spiritual world. That is our whole life, and we're made of it. In a word, he calls it inflow (*Soul-Body Interaction* 2). That's what's coming to my mind as the closest thing to prana, qi, or the radiance of Self.

Bob: That seems to line up well, how love is warmth and wisdom is light. That could be the qi, the radiance of Self, all of that; all of that lines up quite well.

Jonathan: He describes a long battle that goes on between what he calls the inner self and the outer self. But when the outer self gets on board and is more subservient, there's this kind of peace and joy, and this life and lightness. He talks about it in terms of waking up. He says that when you go through this process, because a lot of it is interior, you may not feel it in a really loud way in your outer self. But it's there. He says a lot of it filters down as just a quiet sense of calm and peace, and like, everything's okay now. But he says after death, that energy gets magnified.

He talks about people after death, particularly when they come into their inner state, if their inner state is good, saying that it's like waking up out of a sleep. So I think there are things that relate to that kind of transformation. I think he was someone who had very much experienced that. He was surprised his friends couldn't tell how much had changed in him because he felt completely different, head to toe, on the inside. He comments on the fact that they didn't even seem to notice that he was a completely different person:

> But to the end that everyone may believe this, I can earnestly declare by God that I have experienced it so clearly that I am sure there could not be a clearer sensation in these matters. This has lasted now for a period of almost eight months. During this time, by the Divine Grace of the Messiah, my mind has been governed by spirits of His heaven, with whom I have spoken throughout that entire period by day, almost without interruption.
>
> At such times, these spirits streamed into my mind, bringing spiritual light together with the mental images themselves and the least points of thought, and even the actual words themselves, *which no bystander was able to hear*. Their inflow was so plain that I knew I was not thinking anything at all, not the least thing, that was not thus consciously streaming in. I could not produce even one idea by my own effort, even though I was conceded the appearance that I could. Yet all the while, during a period of five months, I was going around as before with friends in my country and with others socially, and *no one noticed that such a heavenly association existed*. (*Spiritual Experiences* 5a, emphasis added)
>
> Even if I am in the company of other people, I speak exactly as anyone else, so that *no one yet has been able to tell any difference in me from my old self*, or from another person. (*Spiritual Experiences* 82a, emphasis added)

Unattached Burdens, Guides, and Legacy Burdens

Bob: There is one other thing I have to talk about. Some things in people are not part of their personal lives. They are not part of their personal histories. These things are in their mind, but they are not part of them. The one that's sort of obvious, and pretty much everybody has to accept these days, is called legacy burdens. It's stuff you've inherited from your family, your ethnic group, whatever. And the classic example is how Holocaust survivors' descendants show a distinct syndrome of effects, even entire generations later.

Now there is hard science behind the study of epigenetics, which did not exist when I was in school. Part of the stuff that's in our minds that's not part of us is inherited from our ancestors. Everybody has to admit this. I just want to cite one experiment because—there's this thing about the Western academic world: if you can do it with rats, it's real.

We can do this with rats.

Two guys, Dr. Dias from Emory and Dr. Ressler from Harvard, designed these experiments.[32] Dias thought that where he came from, which was poor Hispanic slums in Atlanta, Georgia, that mental illness and addictions ran in families. He wondered if there could be something more than just behavioral transmission. So he devised what I think is a brilliant experiment. He took male rats, only the male rats, and exposed them to a smell, which is quite pleasant. It's sort of like cherries or almonds. It's a chemical. And he would pair that with a shock until they had a conditioned startle response whenever they smelled this nice smell. Then he took semen from the male rats and impregnated female rats who had never been exposed to this smell, and who'd never met the male rat. Then when they had the pups, he tested the pups, and the pups had the startle response to that chemical. This startle response went on for generations. That is not a behavioral transmission.

Legacy burdens are a big part of the inner geography of IFS. There is recognition that all these things are in there that are not part of us. It's very parallel to Jung: you go inside, and the first things people usually encounter are the personal unconscious

---

32 Brian G. Dias and Kerry J. Ressler, "Parental olfactory experience influences behavior and neural structure in subsequent generations," *Nature Neuroscience* 17, no. 1 (2014).

and the complexes, and then the shadow, but when you go further into the archetypal realm, it is no longer yours. It's not even human; it's otherworldly.

Jonathan: Swedenborg describes hereditary evil in a very similar way. He made the point that people inherit tendencies to different kinds of evil from their ancestors and their parents most directly. He says that no one is culpable for what they inherit, but since we have a tendency toward those things, we tend to act them out at some point. And then we've made it our own. That sequence, that pattern, can be broken by what he calls "regeneration."

Bob: Legacy burdens are real. That's one category of things that are in our minds that are not part of our minds. The other one that is quite controversial—and that's the one I've focused on—is what IFS calls "unattached burdens" or UBs. They used to call them critters. These are energies that are in our system. We don't know where they come from.

Most cultures call this spirit possession. Dick was nervous about my using the term "spirit possession" in the subtitle to my book because he was afraid it would lose him academic respectability.[33] I like to put it this way: there is a basic bio-psychological dynamic that we have records of in pretty much every culture we know about and every era of history; the metaphor used to describe this is spirit possession. It can have profound effects for good or ill, and it deserves our study. It's one of the most widely spread cultural features.

This is where I go a little beyond IFS, and I think it might be where I fit in with Swedenborg the best. Not only is the mind multiple, it's also porous.

Things come in; things go out. Thoughts are not ours. They come in; they go out.

---

33 Richard C. Schwartz, foreword to *The Others Within Us*, by Robert Falconer (Great Mystery Press: 2023), xiii–xx.

We'll discuss the whole idea of porosity and how crucial that is in future conversations (see p. 169). Suffice it to say for now, I think our belief that we have this impervious citadel mind is a poison that underlies many of our modern disasters and problems.

Chelsea: This seems like another feature of how IFS makes a point to listen to the client, and in the same way a person might say, "Oh, that's not a part, that's my Self," that's how you've come across this phenomenon as well. It's not that you're saying, "Hey, maybe there's spirit possession going on here" in a client. You're saying, "Oh wait, what is this person telling me? And let me actually listen."

Bob: Yes. It is also super important that I learn the client's language. I don't want to be teaching them these IFS terms. I never would mention the IFS names unless the client really wants them. I do not mention any of this stuff.

Jonathan: You know better than I do that so much of therapy has seemed to be, "Let me tell you: this is your inner child," or whatever. As if it's just about conveying this knowledge rather than learning from the client.

Bob: Knowledge alone doesn't do anything. If I'm working with someone of the Islamic faith, I talk about jinn, because that's their name for spirit, and they have a whole bunch of beliefs about it. And I respectfully try to learn that. I try to use whatever language the clients bring me.

There is a magnificent story about Dr. Milton Erickson, who was one of the greatest healers of the last century. Throughout most of his career, he was involved with inpatient treatment of psychosis—in his early career, before he became a very famous guy. And this one guy was standing in the hallway, and he would just talk word salad—nonsense that sounds as though it might be a language. He'd been doing this for years. The nurses would take him to bed, give him a meal, and he'd stand in the hallway and talk word salad. Totally in his own world for years. Dr. Erickson goes up and stands beside him and studies the word salad and starts transcribing parts of it and has it typed up. He studies it, and he learns it. And then he goes and stands next to the guy and starts talking word salad back to him with the same kind of rhythm and stuff. Only two, three days later in the middle of his word salad, the guy turns to him and says, "Cut it out, Doc," and then is right back in word salad.[34] But that's all it took! Just learning the man's language broke a multi-year, total isolation. To me, that's respect. So I really, really try and listen to what my clients are telling me and get my arrogant little theories well back.

Swedenborg's Anthropology of the Human

Chelsea: So, Jonathan, would you then speak to Swedenborg's model of the human?

Jonathan: It's wonderful to listen to you, Bob. It's a real privilege. The fact that you have spent a lifetime trying to help people and understand what this geography is and what's going on inside people is so great. In my world, I'm looking at Latin, studying the language, and translating and editing Swedenborg's works, so trying to summarize what Swedenborg says about what a human is—trying to put together a picture—is a bit of a different process, but let me see.

The Human Form

Swedenborg says that the soul or the spirit is in the complete human form; that when we die, we lose nothing. Our consciousness transitions. This was his experience of many years

34 Milton H. Erickson, "The Use of Symptoms as an Integral Part of Hypnotherapy" in *American Journal of Clinical Hypnosis* 8, no. 1 (1965): 57–65.

of duality, being in the afterlife and in this world at the same time. There'd been so much discussion about the questions, "Is the soul in the pineal gland?" or "Is it in the heart or is it in the liver?" or "Where is it?" And he said: it's everywhere. Any part that doesn't have it in it just dies. It's contiguous with your whole form.

The Layers of Our Being

We are multi-layered beings. That's terribly, terribly important to Swedenborg. He writes in New Testament terms about there being an inner self and an outer self (see Ephesians 4:22–24; Colossians 3:9–10; 2 Corinthians 4:16; Romans 7:22–23). But he acknowledges that this is a gross simplification of what's really going on. There's an inner self within the inner self, and another inner self within that, and so on. So when you were talking about fractals, I get very much of a fractal feeling studying Swedenborg. I don't know how people thought about this stuff before fractals came along to give us a container for these kinds of thoughts.

Our Innermost, Undamaged Part

There is a part in us that's the highest and purest part. Swedenborg's words sometimes fail him as he's trying to put into language what he is experiencing directly. He says it's just a highest or an innermost something (*Heaven and Hell* 39). It's just a something which is absolutely undamageable. No matter what you've been through.

> Let me disclose a particular secret about the angels of the three heavens that people have not been aware of until now because they have not understood levels. It is this, that within every angel—and within every one of us here—*there is a central or highest level, or a central and highest something*, where the Lord's divine life flows in first and most intimately. It is from this center that the Lord arranges the other, relatively internal aspects within us that follow in sequence according to the levels of the overall design.

> This central or highest level can be called the Lord's gateway to the angels or to us, his essential dwelling within us. . . . It is why we can receive intelligence and wisdom, and talk rationally. It is also why we live forever.
>
> However, what is arranged and provided by the Lord at this center does not flow into the open perception of any angel, because it is higher than angelic thought, and surpasses angelic wisdom. (*Heaven and Hell* 39, emphasis added)

I'll mix Swedenborg with my own analogies to try to communicate it. I think in terms of computer programming: everybody who writes a program leaves a back door for the programmer so you can get back in there, and the back door for God is this highest part of us. It's the closest to God and cannot be wrecked. You can think of it like a modem, where this divine energy flows in. That's what allows God to be connected with everybody, no matter what's happened to them or what they're going through, or how evil or good they are. It comes through that highest level.

The Will and Intellect

Swedenborg talks a lot about the mind, and it's quite, quite complicated. But within these different levels—we'll talk in terms of two levels—one very important thing to say is that they have two sides to them; I think of it like the left and right half. But given the analogy of the human body, he says it's basically like the circulatory system; the heart and the lungs. Swedenborg ties in the lungs with the nervous system, because he talks about the fact that if you're unconscious, your heart can still be beating, but your conscious mind is gone—like if you get the wind knocked out of you, or the state you're in in the womb. The heart and lungs correspond to what's been called the will and the intellect—the two parts of the human spirit—a really basic duality there.

The will and the intellect are what we might call the heart and the mind. Love belongs to the will, whereas understanding belongs to the intellect. I've often thought of what he says about love as also being values. The Swedish word *väljer*, which is cognate with value, is to choose. It's the choice. The will is the part of us that can make a choice of purpose or a strategy. So when he's talking about love, I think he's talking about the *choice* of, "I wish to love my fellow beings in this way," or "this is how I want to contribute to others."

He goes against his time period very strongly with this. He's seen as a forerunner of the Romantic movement, against the enlightenment, because of the primacy that he puts on love.[35] Again, using my own analogies, think of the ideal of a Spock on *Star Trek*, or Sherlock Holmes, who will just set all that emotion nonsense aside and can supposedly enter this glorious world of pure thought because you have this ideal of a sparkling intellect. That insane fantasy was something that Swedenborg went against a lot. Even though he was an extremely well-educated European white male, he said really the heart is in charge. The will is the real you. It may be harder to access, because it's easier to see what you're thinking than it is to feel what you're feeling, but it's in the driver's seat.

And he talks a lot about how feelings will manifest in your thoughts, and then you can kind of see what's going on. But don't be fooled into thinking that you are your thinking; your thinking totally comes from your will, your heart, your values. That's the real you in the court of the mind. The heart is in charge. The intellect can advise—it can make suggestions, and it can give information. It does not make decisions. It's not in charge. And it gets run over a lot.

He says that the intellect is such that it can be lifted up into a kind of light. He talks a lot about the light and heat of the spiritual world. Heat having to do with love, and light having

---

35 Bernhard Lang, introduction to *Heaven and Hell* (West Chester: Swedenborg Foundation, 2000), 45–49.

to do with wisdom or truth, as we said. The intellect can be lifted up into a light that's higher than where your heart is. Our heart could be not very developed yet, but we're salvable because our mind can go someplace that our heart can't go yet. And the mind can guide us, even though it doesn't make the final decision. It can be lifted up even into the light of heaven and can have a kind of transcendent perspective.

Swedenborg's Pairing of Essential Aspects of the Divine	
Love	Wisdom
Heart	Lungs
Circulatory system	Nervous system
Right	Left
Will	Intellect
Heat	Light

The Inner and Outer Self

Then, in terms of the inner and outer self, he writes about how a lot of people in his day thought of the inner self as being your mental and emotional states, and your outer self as just being your physical body. He said, no, I'm not even talking about that. The outer self is the *you* that you present to the world. It's your most conscious part of yourself. In other words, you're closest to it, and it is closest to the flesh, so you mostly know what's happening on that level. But there is an inner level, and the two are independent. He cites things from Paul's epistles about how our inner self and outer self can be and will be at war with each other (see Romans 7:22–23).

When you talk about different parts, Bob—absolutely. He makes the same argument you cited earlier of being able to see what you're thinking and wonder, "What am I thinking? Or why would I say that? What am I doing?" (see *Divine Providence* 104:2; *Secrets of Heaven* 5127:2). Those kinds of things show that there's a higher level looking down on that lower level. And there are multiple levels. It's not simply that there's one unit that can look at the other unit. It's that the two units can entirely disagree. And he called them, which the New Testament does too (see 2 Corinthians 4:16), "the inner man," (*homo* in Latin, just a generic term) meaning that there's an entire self in the inner level and an entire self in the outer level. And they don't have the same agendas. They have their own memories. They have their own everything. And for much of our lives, they're at war with each other. It's kind of a life and death struggle for dominance.

> There is an inner and an outer person as distinct from each other as heaven and the world. They must become one if the person is to be truly human. (*Heaven and Hell* 356:15)

Bob: Excuse me, Jonathan, do both the inner self and the outer self have their own heart, will, and intellect?

Jonathan: I believe they do, yes. I don't find that Swedenborg overtly speaks of an inner and outer will and intellect, but he does speak of inner and outer desires, inner and outer thought processes, and an inner memory that is completely separate from our outer memory.

Bob: Is the outer self how we are in the external world?

Jonathan: What a great question.

Chelsea: Yeah. It's not an easy answer.

Jonathan: Yeah. Certainly by the way Swedenborg uses the term "the outer self" sometimes. When he talks about hypocrites or flatterers, he might say the outer self is what they present to others. And then the inner self is what they're really thinking about when they're by themselves and they don't feel self-conscious.

What Is Inner Organizes What Is Outer

One of Swedenborg's key concepts, which again, is in the Bible, is that it's a radically honest world after death (Luke 8:17; 12:2–3; *Heaven and Hell* 505, 507; *Divine Providence* 224:3; *Revelation Unveiled* 294:1). So who you really are on the inside comes out. So the thing that's really effective for change is this kind of innermost-to-outer process—the divine inflow, just like Self in IFS, coming in and becoming central. He talks a lot about organizing things in our minds. So when the inner thing flows in, it is as though you're under new management and it says, "This is valuable, these things that I've learned. This is worthless. That's not great. This is bad. Make this central," and so on. The huge change that we need to go through, the rebirth that the Bible talks about, is quite a substantial rearrangement of who and what is in charge.

Bob: Do you guys know about predictive coding? It's a theory of perception. A lot of the psychedelic researchers believe psychedelics work by modifying this. Basically the idea is there's raw sensory data coming up, and there are a bunch of predictions about what data has any value. These predictions are all based on valuing, which is this idea of choice and purpose. What is of value? What is going to be meaningful? Many of these predictive coding schema have six or twelve gates. If it doesn't seem significant enough, it doesn't get through, so your value structure or your love actually determines the universe you live in. It determines your perceptual universe.

Jonathan: This is very much Swedenborg's message. One example he gives is from the Bible, when Joseph is unrecognized by his brothers, and they're all astounded when he seats them all in the right order of their age at the table to eat because, as far as they know, he's just some Egyptian overlord or something. But he gets them all in the right order (Genesis 43:33). And Swedenborg has a field day with how Joseph represents love there, and he's organizing all the thoughts—the brothers—all these truths and insights and saying, "Okay, you're down at that seat, and you're over here." This is the order they all go in (*Secrets of Heaven* 5704). I love that because I find that even when I'm doing a simple thing, like preparing to give a talk, the first thing I'll do is draft what I call the pieces, because these various pieces have been floating in my head. Here's one, here's another, here's another, and so on. And then I try to get into that mode of letting love or purpose organize. "Well, this would be central. This other thing, it's cute. It's funny. I could use it or not use it; this is really important; that's really peripheral to what I'm talking about here. That's maybe another talk." That's the function of that will or love or purpose—to organize.

Bob: You've got a value system built into how you perceive the world. The question is not whether you have one or not; it's whether or not you're conscious of it.

The Importance of Choice

Jonathan: And so basically there are battles between the inner and outer self, and there's a part of us that has a choice. Really, all we are is a choice. So we're kind of witnessing the battle; in some of his analogies, we need to pick up a sword and fight for one team or the other. So if we join up with that outer self, the spirituality goes away. And that's what we are. We're just an external person, and self-centered.

Chelsea: I just want to connect choice to what Swedenborg says about freedom for a moment. When we are in what we love, when we get to express our love, that is when we feel like we have freedom, because we're getting to express our love; but love also wants to accomplish something. Love, apart from wisdom, has no power. It can't get done the thing it wants to get done. So it needs means, a channel, and a form, which it gets through wisdom—in partnership with our intellect—and then it finally gets to do something. He says love and wisdom together are nothing apart from their manifestation, apart from being able to come down into action and result. So us using our choice in that flow is a big part of our process here.

Three Basic Categories of Love

Jonathan: Swedenborg organizes things in terms of categories of love: love for God; love for the neighbor; and then love of the world, which has to do with money and possessing things; and then love of self, which is egotistical or even narcissistic the way he describes it. It's not like taking good care of yourself. It's the view that "everybody exists to serve me"—that kind of attitude. And those last two loves need to be subordinated to the other two; they are identified in his system with the outer self. When those more altruistic, compassion-based loves dominate, they perfect you. When that happens, even the love of self on the outer level becomes a good thing. The love of the world and love of self become good things if they're prioritized in the right order.

In *True Christianity* 394, he writes, "There are three universal categories of love: love for heaven; love for the world; and love for ourselves." He describes what these three mean, that,

> Love for heaven means love for the Lord, and also love for our neighbor. Love for heaven could also be called love for usefulness . . . . Love for the world is love for wealth and possessions . . . . Love for ourselves is not only a love for respect, glory, fame, and status but also a love for seeking and getting high positions and becoming a leader. (394)

The House of the Mind

One helpful way Swedenborg gives to think about all of this is the idea that our minds are like a three-story house. It's an amazing description because he says that in our basement, there are demons or evil spirits living down there; on the main floor are people of the world, and on the top floor are angels. If we get our floors in the right order, then we can go up and down at will, which he presents as crucial. If your basement is your most important part, it's hard for you to get upstairs because it's at the wrong part of the house; your house is in effect upside down.

He says that the goal is to be an angel among the angels, or when you go downstairs to the main level, to be an angelic person among the other people of the world. Or if you go into the basement, to be a person of the world and to tame and reprove the evil spirits down there. It's very Christian eighteenth-century language, but it's fascinating that he would describe the mind as having all these beings in it. And ideally, you'll function at a higher level than whichever level you're on. You're coming down from above onto that level. We'll dig deeper into the dynamic between the levels later on (see pp. 78–86).

He describes these levels in the same section on the categories of love (*True Christianity* 395). He says,

> These three categories of love are in each one of us from creation and by birth; when they are prioritized in the right way they improve us, but when they are not prioritized in the right way they damage us. At present it is enough to mention that these three loves are prioritized in the right way when our love for heaven plays the part of the head; our love for the world, the part of the chest and abdomen; and our love for ourselves, the part of the lower legs and feet.

Then he immediately says,

> As I have mentioned several times before, the human mind is divided into three regions. From our highest region we focus on God; from our second or middle region we focus on the world; and

> from our third or lowest region we focus on ourselves. Because our mind has this structure, it can be lifted up or can lift itself up to focus on God and heaven; it can be spread out or spread itself out in every direction to focus on the world and its nature; and it can be lowered down or can lower itself down to focus on the earth and hell. In these respects physical sight emulates mental sight—physical sight too can look up, around, and down. The human mind is like a three-story house with stairs that provide transitions between levels. There are angels from heaven living on the top floor, people of the world on the middle floor, and demons on the bottom floor. People for whom these three categories of love have been prioritized in the right way can go up or down whenever they want. When they go up to the top floor, they are like angels among the angels there. When they go down to the middle floor, they are like angelic people with the people there. When they go even farther down, they are like worldly people with the demons there—they give the demons instructions, confront them, and tame them.

And he says, "When these three categories of love are properly prioritized in us, they are also coordinated in such a way that the highest love, our love for heaven, is present in the second love, our love for the world, and through that in the third or lowest love, our love for ourselves." We all get organized in that way.

Bob: Houses in dreams are a classical symbol of the person's personality structure. So when people have these dreams of a house, it's very often about their personality structure.

Jonathan: What does it say that I often dream that I'm in houses that are falling down?

Bob: Actually, that can mean that you're changing rapidly.

Jonathan: There you go. That's good.

And Swedenborg also says, when he's talking about Biblical imagery or dream imagery, that the house in particular represents our will. It's really the core of who we are. Then sometimes when he talks about the house as being the whole mind, the memory or your outer self might be like a front hall where you can interact with people, but then you've got your private chambers, which is where what really goes on inside you happens, which you may not show the world.

Swedenborg's Cosmology

Jonathan: In Swedenborg's cosmology, there is a whole heaven and a whole hell, and the only people in the spiritual world are people who used to live in this material universe and have now passed on. He does not believe in reincarnation per se (see p. 223). In other words, life here is "one and done." You're born here and die here—you can't turn a pickle back into a cucumber—once you go through the process, you're in the afterlife and you stay there.

Through the choices that you've made in this world, and also the choices you make when you're in the "world of spirits"—which is a kind of clearing house midway between heaven and hell—you really decide: Okay, you've got all these different aspects to you. What's your favorite? What comes out on top? What's the main thing? What's your dominant or ruling love? What's the most important thing to you? And there's every effort to turn people around to help them to heal. But there are some people who decide, no, I'm just with the darkness. It matches what's in my heart, and I can breathe there. So that's how you end up with these beings in hell. There are multiple levels of hell, and some are worse than others.

Bob: In Dante, I think it is the deepest—the moderate levels of hell are fire and burning realms, but the deepest levels are all ice and freezing. Is it like that in Swedenborg?

Jonathan: Interesting. In a way, Swedenborg has it both ways. He talks about how heaven is in touch with reality. And so the light and the warmth that you feel in that realm are real. Hell is kind of an upside-down world, so the fire, the hellfire that the Bible talks about, is really these lusts or passions. If your chief desire, what you love, is to torture people, that's like a burning that you just can't resist. When it's useful, the light and heat of heaven will flow in, and then that will reveal what anything there is really like. When that flows in, evil spirits are just freezing. But when that light and heat withdraw, they are comfortable again.

He says they're like an iceberg (see *True Christianity* 385). He had done a lot of sailing in the North Sea, and he says you shiver when that iceberg goes by; it chills you to the bone. Some of these beings that he encounters are like that. There's a profound cold that radiates from them. So they have their own sort of itchy heat but in the presence of true love, it's freezing.

The Spiritual and Physical World Connection

Bob: William Blake believed that the sun was a conscious being. Where's Swedenborg on this idea that all these other things are conscious beings too?

Jonathan: One thing that he says quite a lot is that if you could see the physical world as it is in itself, you would see that there is a deadness to it. But he says that it's nevertheless full of the spiritual world. The spiritual world is what makes every flower, every blossom happen. In *True Christianity* 12:9, he says, "Everything occurring in nature is produced by God himself through the spiritual world."

There was a lot of materialism in the world in his day, and in science in particular. There were people who believed that the sun was the origin of the world and everything in the universe and all this wonderful life. And so he was going against that to say the sun is just a ball of fire. There's a spiritual sun in the spiritual world that animates the physical sun and animates all of nature and all human beings. He even goes so far as to say that it's because of the spiritual world that human beings have the body temperature that they have; that's from an inflow of heat from the spiritual world that animates us. He says that you look out and you think, well, the trees are blooming now because it's warmer than it was, but that's just because physical circumstances got to the point where that new growth became possible, while in wintry conditions, the spiritual life is still flowing in, but the vessel or whatever you want to call it, is not able to respond to that energy right now.

I'm very drawn to the idea that the physical planet is alive. I'm so stunned by everything that's been found out in the last thirty or forty years about the life in plants and how they respond to and help each other. So I think partly Swedenborg was perhaps overstating the deadness of this world a bit to fight against materialism by saying it's not just the sun; there's this other layer flowing through physical matter. But he also says that even inanimate objects such as stone, metal, and sand have something analogous to free choice (*True Christianity* 491, 499).

Bob: I thought that he had said that if it wasn't for the constant inflow from spirit or God, nothing would exist.

Jonathan: That's right. That's correct. He repeats this phrase several times that I think was prominent in philosophy from his time. I don't think he coined this, but that "continued existence is a perpetual creation." Things are created every moment. And I think there again, he's speaking against the deists who believe that God wound up the clock, and then it's just going to run and whatever happens, happens.

I like the potential for healing with this idea, since if your body's being created every moment, yes, there's a continuity with the past, but it could change, too. And if it weren't for that inflow from the spiritual world, nothing would be happening.

Chelsea: One of the main things that Swedenborg describes about how the spiritual world is connected to the material world is through *correspondences.* Correspondences is a term he applies to describe the inflowing from the spiritual into the physical; the connection is accomplished through correspondences. He writes that the correspondence can be more misaligned or aligned. When this world becomes aligned with the spiritual world, then the correspondence is as good as it can be and that's when you have this amazing amount of inflow happening between the spiritual world and this world. But we can be off kilter with spiritual reality, and in that case there's still a correspondence but it's not as aligned.

What It Means To Be Distinguishably One

Forwarding Swedenborg's thought to what we understand now, to me, the whole idea of consciousness is such a resonant term with how Swedenborg describes the divine. He describes the divine as the spiritual sun that is full of light and heat, which is love and wisdom. That is consciousness itself. The "I am"; the one being. And it's not just love and wisdom as two separate things, but Swedenborg describes them as being distinguishably one.

There's this eternal interplay between love and wisdom, which, in yogic scriptures, is described as a pulsation, *spanda*; this eternal dance between Shiva and Shakti. It's amazing to think about consciousness, love and wisdom itself, having a correspondence with light and heat in the physical world. I think that there's so much you could explore in terms of how that correspondence is playing out, when you understand there's this love and wisdom interplay happening spiritually, and then wonder how what's happening on the physical level is a reflection of that. That alignment is gaining more depth the more and more we understand the nature of light and heat and the electromagnetic spectrum. Light and heat are one thing, but they are distinguishably one.

Bob: I think the idea you mentioned of "distinguishably one" is super important. That's a big bridge between IFS and Swedenborg, because you could say parts are distinguishably one. I think that's a key to how it can all be one and you can have multiplicity, and they're not contradictory. That's a helpful way to understand the relationship between parts and Self.

Chelsea: Parts and Self being distinguishably one in a similar way with how love and wisdom are one aligns even more because Swedenborg says that love itself is unity. It is one thing, and it is always and forever one thing. It creates unity out of diversity. But truth by nature is multiplicity. Truth by nature is infinite. Truth is all the infinite ways that love can be expressed in form. You can almost line up Self as love and parts as truth, which are vessels for love. Love needs truth and truth needs love. They both go together. This dynamic aligns with how we have a Self who holds this unity—a wholeness—out of the multiplicity of parts who are all the different aspects of ourselves or our subpersonalities.

Bob: That's magnificent. I love it. Yeah. There's another level to that. As Dick says, Self is both a particle and a wave, or now he's saying, which I think is even better, Self is a particle and a field.

So as a particle, Self is a single entity; we each have our own Self, but in a bigger sense, we are all part of a field of Self. We're all different waves in this. If you take that level of Self, it is wanting everything to become one, but in a distinguishably one way, which is such a useful term.

What you're saying also lines up brilliantly with Iain McGilchrist's analysis of the hemispheric function of the brain. The right hemisphere would be like love; it perceives everything as one united thing. Everything is always in context. It sees the big picture, it sees value, and it scans the whole world. Whereas the left brain picks out individual things—understands things by slicing them up into smaller, smaller pieces, and is more language oriented and all these other things. And he says that we need both.

Chelsea: It's remarkable that Swedenborg is the first person we know of, predating even the field of neuroscience itself, to make that hemispheric distinction—that there are two hemispheres of the brain that have the love and wisdom pairing. He writes about it in *Secrets of Heaven* 644, published in 1749, and he also writes about it in *Divine Love and Wisdom* 384 and 432, published in 1763. So we had Paul Broca and Carl Wernicke in the 1860s and 1870s,[36] and Roger Sperry and Michael Gazzaniga in the 1960s,[37] but you had Swedenborg saying so back in the mid-1700s![38]

Jonathan: He talks about the hemispheres quite a lot. He also talks about the cerebrum as opposed to the cerebellum, which is another pairing with a similar relationship. And what it brings to mind is where Swedenborg says that you can shape individual sounds, but the fact of sound is uncreatable; in other words, there's this vibration everywhere that allows sound to happen. And you could never get rid of that; that's infinite and eternal. He uses the term "uncreate" to mean it was built in from the beginning.

Chelsea: Swedenborg is acknowledged in the field of neuroscience for having had this advanced understanding. We made a video for the *Off The Left Eye* YouTube channel on what Swedenborg writes about the brain, and in the video, we had to put together a quick summary about it. People don't know what to

---

36 Nina F. Dronkers, Maria V. Ivanova, and Juliana V. Baldo, "What Do Language Disorders Reveal About Brain–Language Relationships? From Classic Models to Network Approaches," *Journal of the International Neuropsychological Society* 23, no. 9–10 (2017): 741–754.

37 Michael S. Gazzaniga, "The Split Brain in Man," *Scientific American* 217, no. 2 (1967): 24–29.

38 Emanuel Swedenborg, *Secrets of Heaven*, vol 1 (West Chester: Swedenborg Foundation, 2008), 414, n. 356.

make of it, but they can't deny that Swedenborg was describing things that weren't discovered for another hundred years. He describes neurons before that was a coined term. He made up his own word for them: cerebellula![39]

Bob: Iain McGilchrist has a book on this called *The Master and His Emissary*.[40] He's astoundingly brilliant. His books are difficult and very long. His feeling is that the left brain, with its particulate multiplicity focus, was supposed to be the emissary for the holistic visionary right brain, but it's usurped and taken over. That's what's wrong with our culture, and it's killing us. If we don't get a balance back, we're going to destroy ourselves and the planet.

---

39 *Off The Left Eye*, "The Spiritual Link Between the Human Brain and Consciousness," *Swedenborg and Life*, YouTube video, 26:32, November 16, 2020, https://www.youtube.com/watch?v=Iu8VeM1Dm0A, 4:51.

40 Iain McGilchrist, *The Master and His Emissary: The Divided Brain and the Making of the Western World* (New Haven: Yale University Press, 2019).

2
GOING INSIDE: INNER SENSE CULTIVATION

Now that we have given an overview of the basics in both the IFS model and Swedenborg's worldview, we turn our attention to what each perspective says about how to sense these inner realities in our minds, and how the inner realm operates.

The Realness of Our Imagination

Bob: I'm a big fan of Henry Corbin and his whole idea of the "mundus imaginalis"—that there's this imaginal realm, which has a reality that in his view is more real than the physical world.[41] He aligns it with the Sufi mystics' "beyond Mount Qaf" as a realm of the psyche. I think that's where we go when we're doing the inner work of IFS—this sort of visionary inner work. My first hypothesis would be that this would match Swedenborg's spiritual realm, because I'm assuming that's a realm of nonphysical things.

---

41 Henry Corbin, *Swedenborg and Esoteric Islam*, trans. Leonard Fox (West Chester: Swedenborg Foundation, 1995).

Jonathan: Yes. Where our minds live all the time, according to Swedenborg, is in the world of spirits, which as I said before is midway between heaven and hell. It's where we "wake up" after we die, but our consciousness is already connected to that realm right now. He describes the world of spirits as a world full of imagery. It's kind of fascinating the way he talks about it. He says that when angels, in a higher realm, are having substantive conversations, people will see horses and chariots or trees or pigs or whatever—it becomes manifest at that level. It's like a level of symbolism.

He describes seeing a building called the Temple of Wisdom (see *True Christianity* 387). That was one such building full of symbolism. He mentions buildings there that have a largely symbolic function, so that you can walk through and experience the inner meaning.

He describes there being three heavens, but the world of spirits is also multi-leveled, so you have angelic spirits there who are angels in training, so to speak, and you have evil spirits who are not yet processed (see *Heaven and Hell* 421–431 and *Divine Love and Wisdom* 140). It strikes me that that's a lot of what you're talking about in the work that you do, where you send unattached burdens to the light. The people who are in the world of spirits, according to Swedenborg, haven't made up their minds yet. They're not set.

When people go toward the light, in the sessions you've shared in your book *The Others Within Us*, what you experience might align with evil spirits who have been in the world of spirits but have not anchored themselves to hell yet. Some go toward the light, like you say, and others decide to go down.

It's very interesting to think of the world of spirits in relation to IFS. It's definitely nonphysical. In an IFS session, someone's just sitting there with their eyes closed, and yet this amazing healing is going on. I was very struck by what you said before: that all healing is spiritual. That really rings true to me. And so I think with no more equipment than our imagination, we can go there. It seems quite easy to just go there and start seeing things in that realm.

Bob: It occurs to me that the nature of the inner self might line up with what Muslims call the unseen world, and the outer self might line up with what they call the seen world.

Jonathan: Yes. That aligns well because Swedenborg often says that people are not generally aware of their inner self. It's there, and it's active, but they're not consciously registering it in the same way unless it shows up in a feeling or a thought lower down in the chain.

Chelsea: Swedenborg also says that when our eyes are open on the outer level, things seem dark on the inner level, but when things go dark on this outer level, the inner sense pops open (see *Other Planets* 135).

Jonathan: He talks about meditative states where your senses are relatively quiet, or you're in the hypnagogic state on the edge of sleep—your awareness of the inner realm opens up.

Bob: One of the things I like about Islam is that one of their names for God is the Real. So the whole inner, unseen world is the real, which totally turns the Western paradigm on its head.

Chelsea: I love that.

Jonathan: Swedenborg would wholeheartedly agree that it's much more real than this world.

So again, the world of spirits, where our inner self already resides, is this intermediate level between heaven and hell where we go to be processed when we die. People spend shorter or extensive amounts of "time" there. What's striking to me is that the work that he describes happening there sounds like therapy! He says there are these schools, but they're not schools of cognitive development. They're more about behavioral change.

Both heaven and hell flow into the world of spirits. And like I said, the world of spirits is where our minds live. While we're in this world, we really are there. We're spirits, wearing flesh, and so we can hear angels and spirits, so to speak, in the form of our thoughts and feelings all the time, whether we realize it or not.

Bob: So when we're alive, we're living in the world of spirit.

Chelsea: Yes, and Swedenborg often writes the term as plural: the world of spirits.

Jonathan: Yes. And we're seldom conscious of it—depending on how thin our veil is, so to speak. But that's where we are. After we pass on, we're right where we are; our physical senses shut down and our spiritual senses are awakened, and then we can actually see what's going on and meet the people we've been interacting with mentally or emotionally.

When this started for him, Swedenborg was so shocked. He believed that only God knows your thoughts; he totally came from the belief of the mind as its own little island—that everything that happened in his interior space was 100 percent himself. And the first time some spirit commented on his thought, it was profoundly shocking and unsettling to him.[42]

It absolutely rocked his world. And he writes that at certain points, early on, he really thought, "This is going to be so annoying because I have zero privacy here. I mean, if they know everything I'm thinking and feeling—" really, thought and feeling comes from them! It was experimentally demonstrated to him that if you take these people—the spirits—away, he would stop having a certain thought (see *Secrets of Heaven* 6321 and 6191).

Even when he is having dreams, he can talk to these angels, and he can't even tell whether he is dreaming their conversation

42 Bergquist, *Swedenborg's Dream Diary*, 242.

or if they're talking about his dream, or what. It's all so connected. And yet, there's still that level shift I was describing called correspondences: they might be talking about abstractions, but it manifests as a story about animals in the woods, or it comes down in some format that's unique to his own experiences.

Chelsea: Here are a couple things Swedenborg says about it in *Heaven and Hell* 356:15.

> Heaven's light is the light the inner person is in, and the world's light is the light the outer person is in. Heaven's light is what is essentially divine and true, the source of all intelligence.

And about correspondences in particular:

> There is a responsiveness between the things in the inner person and those in the outer, so that things from either side appear in a different guise on the other side—so different that they cannot be identified without a knowledge of correspondences.

Jonathan: So Swedenborg learned that the spiritual world, and the world of spirits in particular, is where our thoughts and feelings come from, which was not the answer he was expecting. Just think, if he had this lifelong interest in knowing where thoughts and feelings were—this was not the answer that the scientist thought he was going to get to that question. He writes that he got used to it after a while though. The funny thing is that when he finally realized that his thoughts and feelings were coming in from elsewhere, he felt more alive! A lot of other people engaged with him about this in both worlds, asking (in my own words), "Well, aren't you just the hole in the donut? Isn't there, like, nothing left—you just know, 'Oh, this is flowing in and that's flowing in'?"

A very important concept to him, though, is that, yes, it's flowing in, *but you have a choice*. In a way, you just *are* the choice (see *Divine Providence* 308). You're the chooser. So you say no to this and yes to that. And he says he never felt as alive as when he started to realize where these things were coming from. He talks about when he was going through his transition—waking up to the spiritual realm in his early fifties—he would have bizarre experiences. For instance, suddenly a bad mood would roll in. And he'd wonder, where is that coming from? It all made more sense to him when he realized how it was all flowing in from spirits in the spiritual world who were with him.

I used to think, after reading Swedenborg a lot, that there must be some evil spirit right here with me since I was thinking *this*, or there must be some good angel with me because *this* was coming in. But he writes that in the spiritual world you can communicate at vast "distances," so don't be thinking they're right in you. Those signals can cross vast spiritual distances, so to speak.

But he talked about the fact that—in modern analogies, I picture this being like an elevator going up and down—certain thoughts and feelings would be so noisy when he was in the basement of himself, at that lowest level. Then you just go up and whoa, it's all quiet. These different levels have a very different kind of signature in terms of the nature of the thoughts that you're having and the nature of the feelings.

His experiences seem to have led him to become a connoisseur of where each thought and feeling were coming from. He writes about the fact that part of his process was to learn and study this. Once he was having a thought, say, "Okay, who said that? Who was it?" The next step would be to go talk to them. Find out where they live, what they're all about. And if it's not something he wants around him, tell them no. Reject their input. It's pretty astounding.

Bob: Could I ask another question here? You said *who* sent the thought. So it's clearly a personalistic view—that these are persons.

Jonathan: That's right. But he says since most of the time they want to destroy us, it's very important that evil spirits do not know who we are, even as they influence us. So there's a certain restriction that he talks about where when they're with you, they hack into your mind and take on your whole memory, and they think *they* are *you*. They have access to all your memories; to any language you know. They can express things in the languages that you know.

He describes one conversation I read about recently that's rather comical, where someone came into him and said, "I've always been here. I've been part of you from the beginning." And he said, "No, you haven't. You just got here." And then the spirit realizes, "Oh yeah, you're right. No, I just got here. You're right." This is a paraphrase, obviously; the actual quote reads as follows:

> Some spirits came climbing up saying they had been with me from the start, since they did not know better. Because I proved the opposite to them, though, they eventually admitted they had just arrived. They said they could not have known any better, since they had immediately adopted the entire contents of my memory. (*Secrets of Heaven* 5859)

So, it's a defense mechanism. What a great burglar alarm if someone broke into your house but the alarm that you have set up is a kind of force field so when they break in, they think it's their house. They're not going to ransack the place, because they think it's their own!

Chelsea: Right! Even though they know all that information, they don't know the *you* who they think they are. It's like the personally identifying information is redacted. At least it seems that way from what Swedenborg writes.

Jonathan: Yeah. That's right. There are some passages where it sounds like they do know who they're with. But as a general rule, they don't, because it would be really bad for us if they did. In his case, of course, they broke through to where he'd have spirits who were trying to get him to kill himself and things like that. Every time he saw a knife, they would urge him to stick it into himself, for example (see *Spiritual Experiences* 4530). So in his case, the connection became more obvious. He writes though that although his experience was so dangerous, he felt absolutely protected by the Lord. It sounds like the protection of Self and curiosity. If you can be in that state, with abundant Self-energy, you can be present to some pretty wild stuff.

He says that at one point there was a crazy vampire spirit who believed that by eating Swedenborg's blood, the spirit could come back to life, because he realized, "Hey, you're a flesh-and-blood person." So he's biting him on the neck, and Swedenborg is inured to it. He's not reacting; he is not terrified, and finally the guy stops (*Spiritual Experiences* 1289–1290).

Bob: Would you equate the spiritual realm with Corbin's *mundus imaginalis?*

Jonathan: Swedenborg definitely says that the imagination is one of the building blocks in terms of human development. Children first need to just get their senses hooked up. So they're getting information; then they need to build their imagination. And then that leads to what he considers higher-level functioning, like intuition. He talks a lot about the highest level having this perception, as he calls it, which sounds to me like an intuitive understanding, where you don't reach an insight through cogitation; you just see it. And so I think what you're describing may be in that realm where you see things. When I've done counseling sessions—when I've been on either side of the couch, so to speak, I've been struck how sometimes what seems like just a metaphor will form, but you can just go and go and go with that. In other words, it's just fraught with meaning. The more you think about it, you think yes, it's a sailing ship, and do you need to weigh anchor? Or, where are you going? Where's the wind coming from? You can keep explaining the image and getting more lessons from it. And I think that relates to what Swedenborg calls correspondences; that that ship is a great way to think of things because it has all these layers. There's something *real* about the image.

Chelsea: Something that Swedenborg describes about the spiritual realm, which I think lines up with the *mundus imaginalis*, is that in this material world, people often wonder, "What does it mean that this feather just dropped across my path?" Or, "I saw the clock as 11:11. What does that mean?" We have this instinct to find meaning in all the little details of our life, and yet we live in this material world that runs on physics. But Swedenborg says that instinct is because that *is* what's true in the spiritual world, on the spiritual level. Everything has meaning. All the things around where an angel or spirit resides represent everything about themselves. So if there's a forest to the one side, and there's a pond beside it, with a certain kind of tree—everything represents something, and it is specifically a mirror of the angels and spirits who are in that world. All of spiritual reality there is an extension of the minds and hearts, the will and understanding, of all the angels and spirits.

He says that angels can walk around and perceive the inner meaning of all of those elements. They can see, "Oh, I know why you look this way," or "There's this thing in your environment because of this aspect of yourself." I think that's the world that opens up to us when we go inside in IFS.

There's no step between a certain thought or feeling and it having some sort of representation, some sort of correspondence on that level. That's just the way that spiritual substance behaves.

The reason for this is because all spiritual substance is made up of love and wisdom. Heat corresponds to love, and light corresponds to wisdom, as we said. So you might wonder, how does it work, that an angel's environment is a perfect reflection of who they are? But it's just that it all has to do with the quality of love and wisdom in each angel or spirit's will and understanding. And then that's what is ordering the communities in the spiritual world and creating the whole look and feel of the different places.

That's a fascinating parallel with parts—to consider that it's the parts in us who create the inner landscapes we interact with when we go inside; and those landscapes are a reflection of the quality of love and wisdom—or in the case of a burden, the falsity and evil—that each part has in its environment.

I feel like in IFS sessions, I experience correspondences in real time. I start by talking about some outward, external thing in my awareness, like, "Well, I get really upset when this happens." So the therapist says, "Okay, let's get to know that part." So, I turn my attention inward and where I end up doing the work on the inside, I would not have been able to predict the concerns and feelings of the part we connect to. In many cases, by the end of the session I can barely remember what outer level thing connected me to the parts in the first place, but they are directly connected. You cross that veil; when Swedenborg describes correspondences, he says how what appears on each level is so distinct. What I love about IFS is, it really takes you from that one level into the other one. You're in that one guise, and then you go to its corresponding guise on the inner level, and you do work there in heaven's light. It's remarkable.

Jonathan: As a footnote to that, Swedenborg says that the earliest people on this planet even saw that that same property of the spiritual world penetrated into their vision of this physical world. They saw everything as alive, and he likens that to the way that children with their toys believe they are alive. (There's no way to convince a little kid that this thing is just a stuffed animal. I mean, come on, look at it!) Swedenborg claims that that was a quality that we used to have even down in the material world—being able to see that layer of meaning in everything, seeing the spiritual life in it.

Bob: This brings up something that I think is a crucial issue. I think of it in terms of the locus of healing. Where does healing actually occur? As I said earlier, the locus of healing in IFS is the relationship between the Self and the parts, forming that two-way relationship. That's definitely primary. It's not the relationship between the client and the therapist. That's one answer to this question of where the locus of healing is. And what I'm thinking of in terms of Swedenborg is that the locus of healing is this spiritual world. I'm not sure how well that lines up. Another point that Corbin or one of his students made is that imagination is not at all what we ordinarily think of it as; it's a mode of perception, like sight or hearing for the inner world.

Two other things also fit well. The first is the Romantic poets' idea of imagination. They very much had this idea that imagination was incredibly important. For William Blake, it was more important than the physical. They were also onto something very much like this.

The second is from two scholars who work together—an anthropologist and a psychiatrist. The psychiatrist's name is Luh Ketut Suryani. She's Balinese. The anthropologist is Michele Stephen from Australia. Together, they developed the idea of the autonomous imagination.[43] They make no reference to Corbin, or to the Romantic poets. They came up with it on their own. They were studying how the Balinese healers—the balians—get their powers. They said the balians get their powers by learning to operate and move in the realm of the autonomous imagination. Now are they talking about Swedenborg's world of spirits, or what?

They've got these fairly detailed descriptions of the characteristics of this, but they even came up with this larger theory that nobody has tested yet. They say shamanic initiation is not about the shamans healing from initiatory madness; it's about their learning how to navigate in the world of the autonomous imagination.

With Swedenborg's idea of the world of spirits being where healing happens, we've got the spiritual world as the locus of

---

43 Stephen, Michele, and Luh Ketut Suryani, "Shamanism, Psychosis and Autonomous Imagination" in *Culture, Medicine and Psychiatry* 24, no. 1 (2000): 5–38.

healing, and that lining up with the *mundus imaginalis*. It's all sort of coming together.

Jonathan: What's striking to me about what you just said is that Swedenborg was of course writing at a time when, as far as I know, there was nothing like therapy. That came a century or more later. And yet, what he describes people going through in the world of spirits is that they get kind of boiled down to their inner essence, you might say, and they go into their inner state and then they come back into their outer state, like the one they had in the world, and then back into their inner state, then into their outer state. And he says when some people are in their inner state, they're wiser and more beautiful. Some people are more deranged and then they go back to their more sober self, and then they're back into their irrational self.

This process is to help people make choices; to help people see who they are. But it sounds a lot like it has to do with kind of an unveiling of who you are and what spiritual connections you have.

I've thought for some time about how therapy as a modality came about since Swedenborg's time, and it seems like it's a taste of the world of spirits while you're still here. You're doing some of that work. And clearly in shamanistic cultures, which predated Swedenborg by thousands of years, they are doing something like this all the time. But I think that your average potato farmer back in Swedenborg's day pretty much had to wait until they passed on to get that work done in the spiritual world. But now there are all these modalities where people can do this work and address things. And he talks about people in that world working through crimes they've committed in this world and a whole number of things.

In one process, he witnesses a grown man who enters a childlike state and is working things out with his parents.[44] I'm using that term—I don't think he uses the term "works it out,"

44 See *Spiritual Experiences* 3146.

but he's interacting with the parents and seeing things in a different light. And so it sounds to me like the sort of work Swedenborg witnessed in the other world in his day has now come down here more.

But that's still where you do it, even if you're still alive in this world; that's still the locus of healing. And, by the way, I think it's very Swedenborg-esque of you to think about the locus of healing. He likes to think about questions like, "Where does religious devotion live in the spirit? Is it in the inside, or the middle, or the outside?" And he'll spend years thinking, "Where is that?" And after a lot of observation, he decides that it's at the deepest level in people. So I like that thought of, "Where is it?" because it's useful to know! I mean, if you're on the wrong plane or something, you can't get that work done.

Bob: Dick says that a lot of people thought he was doing hypnotic stuff when he would have people go and meet parts. He says that he does not do hypnosis.[45] Well, I think that's not exactly accurate.

Milton Erickson showed conclusively that you do not need a formal induction to induce profound trance states; profound alterations of consciousness. If you watch an IFS session, the clients are in profoundly altered states of consciousness. Dick never discusses altered states of consciousness. He never discusses hypnosis. But I think that's more a limitation and a choice of language. Consensus reality is a trance state, and one with a whole lot of problems. It's very illusionary. Dick says he goes into this inner world, and that it is the same place shamans have been visiting for thousands of years.

Changes we make in the inner world are very potent. You go into this inner world, and it can have big effects, even on our physical wellness. I think the inner world is more real, closer

---

45 Richard C. Schwartz and Martha Sweezy, *Internal Family Systems Therapy*, 2nd ed. (New York: The Guilford Press, 2020), 265–280.

to cause than the external physical world. I think Swedenborg might agree with that.

Chelsea: Absolutely!

The Somatic Level of the Inner World

Chelsea: It would be good for us all to learn how to navigate the realm of the autonomous imagination. So let's shift now to discuss how to do that from the IFS and Swedenborg viewpoints.

The fractal nature of things extends to the body, according to Swedenborg's writings. The model of our mind is the model of the divine with everybody, and then that same model is mapped on our bodies and is in the human form. So the way that cells and organ systems all work together is a picture of the mind and a picture of heaven.

Swedenborg says heaven is in the human form. He talks about angels and spirits belonging to communities, like we discussed, but that they are mapped on our bodies, so that our physical body, and literally the anatomy and physiology of it, is an image of heaven. He gets very specific. He says things like, "They were a part of my teeth," or "They were a part of the intestines," or "It was connected to my kidney."

It's not abstract. It's not a metaphor. He's saying, the spirits were in my kneecap. He describes how the communities of angels and spirits are connected to all those different parts of our body via correspondences. Evil spirits seem connected to what can go wrong in those areas. They flow in and relate in some way to the physical ailments we can have.

The way Swedenborg describes connecting to spirits in his body is almost the same, word for word, as the way IFS describes connecting to parts. They both describe where they are within or around the body.

Swedenborg is rarely explicit about his method, but we can glean some idea of it from the way he describes his spiritual experiences. There must be some purpose or usefulness in identifying how the spirits are connected to his body, because whenever he's describing them, he'll first put it in these geographical and anatomical terms: "They were under me and to the left side."[46] And evil spirits often cause him pain in various areas of his body.

Jonathan: Especially trying to dial back to the eighteenth century and imagine what it was like when these books came out. He really does not take any great pains to explain what the heck he's talking about. He is already way into weird-land, because he is talking about all these spirits. And I think that time period was more open to that than maybe our own is in some ways. But then now you really killed it because you said, "They were above the liver, just out in front."

"They were near the left eye, or the jaw, the teeth, the knees," and so on.

"I saw a spirit. He attached himself to my left hip, and then he moved up a little bit toward my ribs." To people, it has to be like, "Why are you telling me this?" I've wondered myself sometimes, why is he saying this? It took me a long time to realize that I think he's using his body as a map, so you know where you are on that map. He realizes his body is the map. And so that's how he's able to orient.

He orders everything that way. It's very curious. He will often bother to tell you which ear a spirit was talking in.

It seems almost like a technology that we don't know how to use yet. He is providing all that information. But it certainly suggests that far from being sort of disembodied and floating around in a world of pure visualization or something, he's more in touch with his internal organs and with how his body's doing, and feels how these spirits cause a toothache and those other ones made his bones ache, or when these ones were near, he couldn't pee. And then they went away, and he could pee again. He says things like that all the time.

---

46 Swedenborg, *Heaven and Hell*, 90, n. 22.

I don't know what to make of it, but what you say, Bob, in your IFS work has made it seem very helpful seeing where that connection is and what's there, because it's telling you something. It's data; it's information.

Chelsea: How does the somatic level show up for you in your clinical work, Bob? Are parts being connected to different parts of the body meaningful for you? Is it functional to the process?

Bob: The most important thing here is, I must remain the village idiot. Because all these people—people used to try and make dream dictionaries, right? You see this, it means this. That doesn't work. Something showing up in this person, right here, that has a very specific meaning for this person, you get really curious and explore that thing. The somatic position in the body usually is important. If you really get curious about how that shows up in the body, there are tremendous amounts of information that open up. It's often a wonderful gateway to do inner sense cultivation; a doorway to profound perception to get them focused on that one spot of the body.

Now, there's another way that psychological material shows up in the body. And this is in terms of illness. A person has a bunch of predispositions or weaknesses, and parts will learn how to push those buttons. For example, Dick has asthma and migraines, and he has said that a whole bunch of his parts know how to trigger those.

He says that he could walk into a dusty room and get an asthma attack, or some part could be angry at him, and he'll get an asthma attack. That's a whole different mechanism by which what I think Swedenborg would call the interior world interacts with the physical world.

Jonathan: When people are being processed on arrival in the spiritual world, Swedenborg says that angels perform a sorting function. They look at the person's hands and their bodies, and they listen to their voice. That's how they tell who they are.

And not only who they are, but they can see their whole history. "Okay, you've been through this, and you've been through that."

This kind of thing can happen in this world, too! I know of someone who had an accident where he got some toes chopped off by a boat when he was young. A woman he met on the other side of the country from where he is from, who was a total stranger to him, said, "I can tell from your voice that you had an accident with your toes when you were young." She was able to read it in his voice. It was just astonishing.

Swedenborg says a ton about the correspondences of the body, and even goes into what kind of spirits the bones are, what kind of spirits certain membranes are, or the infundibulum or the ventricles in the brain—really everything. But I have to say that a lot of them don't sound like that much to write home about; when he describes some of these body parts, the spirits are pretty dense, and they don't really care about this or that. Or there are some—which might be like me right now!—who love to talk, but they don't really have anything to say. It's not all glowing praise. But I think that relates to this subject because I imagine Swedenborg would say there's a corresponding reason that a certain kind of spirit is attached to a certain person's kidney. It is a psychological map as well as a physical map. So there's a quality of irritation and criticism that goes with the bladder, or there are similar things about the kidneys. They're always filtering. And so they're always evaluating (see *Secrets of Heaven* 5381–5384). And then there are very peaceful parts of the brain that just listen to both sides of what's going on (*Secrets of Heaven* 4048).

He would certainly say every organ in the body is meaningful. I think that's why he bothers writing down all these strange things about these spirits that were near the liver and these ones that were near the elbow.

Chelsea: How there is meaning to the parts of the body seems very similar to dream interpretation. People want to catalog it. From Swedenborg's perspective, for both topics, it all has meaning, but it is all entirely personal. I think that relates to what you were saying, Bob, where it's like, don't write it off; there's a reason, there's meaning and purpose here, and it's precise. It's so precise to your spiritual development, to your journey. So don't just absorb what somebody else tells you.

All the power is in a person reflecting and saying, what does this mean to me? Or what does this hold for me? What is the history? What is my shoulder holding? It's going to be different than what somebody else's shoulder is holding. But the nature of our bodies is that there's going to be some similarities there, and that's fine, but the power is in understanding the personal relevance to one's own journey. I find it so interesting how that applies to dreams as well as it does to our bodies.

Jonathan: It makes me think of one situation where angels were having a conversation about an absorption with earthly truth, and it manifested in Swedenborg's dream as a certain person that he knew who had that characteristic (*Secrets of Heaven* 1981). It would've been somebody different for somebody else (*Spiritual Experiences* 4151). It might have been an animal or something completely different. The correspondences map onto what we've already got in our memories from our experiences.

Chelsea: One other fundamental thing to bring up here is that Swedenborg says we have a spiritual body. We have a physical body, but we also have a spiritual body. The spiritual body is connected to our physical body, but it's distinct. When we leave our body, or when our life in this world ends, we have a spiritual body that is the totality of who we are. It holds everything. It holds all of our history. It's why angels can look at your hands, they can hear your voice, they look at your body, and it is a picture of all of you; it reveals everything about who you are.

When we're working in IFS, and we're doing this kind of insight or reflection and interoception on the body, there might be a physical thing that has some influence on the situation, but I think primarily we're working with somebody's spiritual body in that moment. I feel like that's how you would have parts who can manage to trigger asthma or something. The spiritual body is somehow the conduit that connects the two.

The Body as a Picture of the Mind

Bob: I have a couple more things I want to mention. One is the idea you brought up about the body as a picture of the mind. Is the body a picture of the inner self or the outer self? I was sort of assuming it was a picture of the inner self.

Jonathan: It's a picture of all the above, if that's not a cop-out. In other words, I think about the fact that in reflexology, your whole body is mapped onto your feet. And so sometimes when you've got something going on with you, somebody can do reflexology or a massage on your feet, and it will help you with your digestive system or with something apparently completely unrelated. In a similar fashion, I think of this physical body that we're wearing as the feet of our spirit. This whole thing is like a foot that connects with all those higher parts.

So when you put them together, there's a sense in which the inner self is like the head and the outer self is like the rest of the body. But if you looked at the inner self in itself, it would have a whole inside and outside, and all the rest of it. And obviously the flesh has all those different parts. What I've been struck by through our conversations thus far is the beautiful oneness of it all. I've been thinking a lot about oneness and multiplicity, and how oneness comes together out of the other. Because if you simply describe certain aspects of IFS, with all the parts, and the parts having parts, you can start to think, well, this is hopeless. There's too much complexity. It's a mathematical equation you couldn't possibly solve. And yet the astounding thing is that you can have that experience of the Self sitting down with everybody and having a tête-à-tête and changing the relationship with the parts.

Chelsea: In regards to how the body can simultaneously represent the inner self and the outer self, I'm reminded of what Swedenborg writes about the brain. He writes that,

> It was shown what the form of heaven is like in its lowest realm. It resembled the patterns of folds seen in human brains. A perceptible view of its flow or circular motion was granted to me, the demonstration lasting several days. From this experience I could tell that the form of the brain matches the pattern of movement in heaven. The deeper parts of the brain, invisible to the eye, match the deeper structures of heaven, which are totally incomprehensible. The angels said this shows that we were created to reflect the structure of the three heavens. So the image of heaven is imprinted on us in such a perfect way that we are a miniature heaven at its smallest scale, which is why we have a correspondence with the heavens. (*Secrets of Heaven* 4041)

That pattern of the movement in the heavens makes me think of how now we are able to use MRIs to look at the way different parts of the brain light up, and how different brain waves match the different states of consciousness that we can get into, like in meditation. It's really interesting.

So he says that our bodies have mapped in them the ideal—heaven—the alignment with the inner self. Yet at the same time, our bodies are very much affected by our physical environment, and our thoughts and feelings have a way of manifesting in our body through the way we carry ourselves, our way of being. So our body holds and is an expression of both the inner and outer self.

Swedenborg underscores the role that the brain and nervous system play in our connection to the spiritual world.

> Only through humankind is there a descent from the heavens into the world, and an ascent from the world to the heavens. The brain and its inner depths provide the means of descent and ascent. (*Secrets of Heaven* 4042)

The body is the domain of our conscious awareness of the interplay between the inner and outer self, and Swedenborg describes a specific role that the brain plays in this.

> The brain, like heaven, exists in an environment of purpose, useful purpose. Anything that flows in from the Lord embraces as its aim the salvation of the human race. This is the goal that reigns supreme in heaven and therefore in the brain as well.
>
> After all, the brain, where the human mind resides, has a goal for the body—that the body serve the soul, enabling the soul to be happy forever. (*Secrets of Heaven* 4054)

What I take away from this is that there is an intention that is alive in the body. The intention as described by Swedenborg aligns with the Self. IFS has described that if you had to put an agenda to the Self, it's our healing. Self has an instinct for healing. And that's what I hear Swedenborg saying: that instinct is in us, in our tissues, even as "the issues are in our tissues" too, as the saying goes.

Jonathan: Hardwired into us, as they say. Healing is the default setting.

Bob: There's a saying in IFS that when Self is present, healing will happen. I think many people don't take that seriously enough. They think they have to go back to technique or do some snazzy thing; but if they can get all their parts to unblend from them so that Self can be present, so they can relate to their own parts and whoever they're with from Self, healing happens.

Jonathan: Your being impacts the other person. It's not an active manipulation or something; it is just a presence.

Chelsea: Swedenborg talks about the brain and the body as if the brain is something else. It's kind of funny that we make that distinction because our brain *is* our body. So when you think about the interconnection of the brain and the body, and take in what he's saying in that quote, that intention, or purpose, is alive throughout our whole living, breathing body.

This next quote might shine a little light into why Swedenborg talks about the brain and the body in this way.

> Our life is found in its primary forms in our brains and in secondary forms in our bodies. "In its primary forms" means in its beginnings, and "in secondary forms" means in the things that are produced and formed from these beginnings. "Life in its primary forms" means the will and understanding. It is these two functions that occur in their primary forms in our brains and in their derivative forms in our bodies. (*Divine Love and Wisdom* 365)

You get a taste there about how he brings it back to the will and understanding, the will and intellect. And he says *that* is who we are. And then that shapes our brains, and it shapes our bodies.

Bob: When he says brain, does he really mean mind, or does he separate mind from brain?

Chelsea: He separates mind from brain.

Jonathan: He does separate mind from brain, and yet he thinks the mind and the spirit live in the entire body, as we talked about before. But it's as though you cross through the veil when he talks about those beginnings in the brain; it really sounds like we're in another realm, in that unseen realm we were just talking about.

Spiritual Senses

Chelsea: One final thing to touch on about somatics, which will help us segue into our exploration of how we can use this information to enter that inner realm, is how Swedenborg says we have spiritual senses. Our spiritual senses are the same as our physical ones, only on the spiritual level. They mean something in a spiritual way. He says the way that our eyes work is that our eyes are these specialized things that can pick up the light that's coming in, and so then we can see, and we know how to interact with this light coming in. Our smell is because we interact with the scents that are coming at us, and touch, and so on.

In every case, our senses are these receptors. And so our spiritual senses are receptors for spiritual things. As the spiritual counterpart to light, our spiritual eyes receive wisdom and understanding, so seeing in the spiritual world is understanding things; smell is being able to perceive the quality of things. And he goes through the whole list of those spiritual counterparts.

Correspondence of the Outer Senses[47]	
Touch	A desire for goodness
Taste	A desire to know
Smell	A desire to perceive
Hearing	A desire to learn
Sight	A desire to have understanding and wisdom

So in our spiritual body, we have all of the spiritual senses.

In terms of the evolution of therapeutic modalities and being able to go inside, Swedenborg talks about the fundamental nature of our free choice. We are receiving all this spiritual input all

47 *Secrets of Heaven* 4404. See the interchapter material in *Secrets of Heaven* volumes 6 and 7 for a more in-depth discussion of the correspondence of the individual senses.

the time, inwardly, just like how our physical senses are receiving input outwardly; what we do with it is what makes us who we are—that choice.

How to Open the Veil to the Inner World

Bob: How do we safely access the inner world? How do we open up this sensitivity? My belief has come to be that the only safety is really to increase that internal awareness.

But in other times, it seems to be that the only safety is shutting down that internal awareness. So controlling that internal awareness permeability is a big issue.

Chelsea: Swedenborg talks about the importance of the outermost level. He talks about the material world being the foundation for everything else—that heaven can't exist apart from this. It's core to divine creation. So to me, our embodiment is key to our safety and to opening up that awareness. It ends up being such a useful tool.

However, people, on account of trauma, leave their bodies; we shut off our awareness of our own bodies. Among other things, I work as a massage therapist, and people can think that they are doing one thing with their bodies, and they are completely wrong. I was working on a woman whose arm was stiff as a board. I asked, "Can you relax your arm?" She said, "I am relaxed." In that case, I knew we had some work to do.

So having an awareness of our own body is the portal to then becoming aware of the inner levels. Our attention can slowly deepen from feeling something on the surface to deeper sensitivity. You can start by paying attention. What does it feel like inside my arms? Can I feel my heartbeat? You can do a body scan. This is the entry level, and it grows from there.

But you have to develop enough safety—a sense of being held in love—for facing what comes up when you first try to dip your awareness into your body; that takes a lot of support because it can be genuinely terrifying for our parts. But that's going to start opening that pathway.

I love that IFS is a body-centered psychotherapeutic approach. The sensations you're feeling in your body turn out to be parts. They're trailheads, and you can start having conversations with those parts. And they're going to talk back to you. It's a natural process. When you turn your senses inward, Swedenborg says that is when your inner senses just open up. It's not work; it just happens.

Embodiment is a crucial role of this outermost level. It's a portal to our inner awareness. It's amazing to me that connecting to the present moment of our senses in this world *is* the means of having neurological safety and opening awareness to the inner world.

Bob: That makes me think of all this stuff about the importance of interoception as the doorway to healing.

Jonathan: What you're saying, Chelsea, reminds me of this line in *Secrets of Heaven* 322. "Life consists in sensation because without it, there is no life, and the quality of sensation determines the quality of life, as anyone can recognize."

Breathing is another pathway he talks about. His own breathing would change and that would help him. Interestingly, what he says helps a lot is going through a crisis. Suffering and going through pain. It breaks up the view that the outer world is all there is. It can awaken you to something else. As soon as our preoccupation with outer worldly things recedes, the inner world is right there. It's pressing to be seen and to be received. If we cooperate at all with a little bit of breathing, a little bit of body sensation, that's going to help.

Chelsea: Putting it in a single word from Swedenborg is the word "reflection." He says we have to reflect on ourselves. And so even when he says sensation, it's about reflecting on your sensation. I think that connects to the cultural zeitgeist right now of awareness. Awareness itself is what brings healing.[48] It's a Buddhist mindfulness approach; there are studies on it, and it lines up with IFS and Self. You need to practice awareness, and the rest is spontaneous.

It's manifest. It's just what is. As soon as you wake up, that's what you're seeing. IFS talks about the constraint release model, which we'll talk more about later (see p. 124), and that's what Swedenborg is describing too. Removing the barriers lets it in. Some of those barriers are being so caught up in outward thinking. So even on the sensory level, you can start to reflect on the question, "What am I feeling in my body?" Just that simplest question can open you up.

Bob: I think an absolutely core issue in IFS that's ignored, because it's so basic, is unblending, which we'll discuss more in detail later (see pp. 153–155). Separating enough from a part so you can be there with it—that's reflection. You can't do any work without that. You're stuck. I know people who use IFS in divorce mediation, and they say that all they're doing is helping people unblend. They're getting the people to unblend from their protectors so there can be some Self in the room, and that's plenty. But we tend to ignore that in IFS and sort of assume it.

What you're saying about reflection agrees perfectly with what the consciousness study people call metacognition.[49] Being aware that we're aware; that second level. There's another form of psychotherapy that calls this "mentalizing," which I think is a horrible word.[50]

---

48 Judson Brewer, *Unwinding Anxiety: New Science Shows How to Break the Cycles of Worry and Fear to Heal Your Mind* (New York: Penguin, 2022).

49 Thomas O. Nelson, "Consciousness and Metacognition," *American Psychologist* 51, no. 2 (1996): 102.

50 Giovanni Liotti and Paul Gilbert, "Mentalizing, Motivation, and Social Mentalities: Theoretical Considerations and Implications for Psychotherapy," in *Psychology and Psychotherapy: Theory, Research and Practice* 84, no. 1 (2011): 9–25.

Jonathan: I also wrote the word "willingness." In a way, Swedenborg's view is that the universe is trying to get us to do this. If you just kind of say yes, if you open to it, it comes forth.

Chelsea: So much so that Swedenborg says you can be willing for the wrong reasons, and it's still going to work for you. It still works.

Bob: Does he discuss pragmatic things about how you can tune in to the inflow, open to it more, and get the gunk out of the stream bed, so to speak?

Jonathan: I think it's mainly a function of focus. Noticing when you're overly focused on outward concerns and shifting your attention helps. To the extent that you can move those things that get in the way aside, the other is always trying to flow in. Swedenborg seems to emphasize that rather than breathe this way or sit this way, work on the obstacles that you are aware of; get them out of the way. And we're aided in that, as I've said before, by spiritual crises. Difficult times we go through actually shake up those attachments and make us less adamant about whatever we're holding on to so tightly.

Chelsea: Swedenborg is so simple about it. He says, if we do our part, then the divine's doing the divine's part. All we have to do is be this little switchboard, where we're just deciding whether we want to do this or that. Like that simple verse, "Cease to do evil, learn to do good" (Isaiah 1:16–17). It's up to us to make some decisions on the outermost level—how are you behaving? What are you saying? We take these actions on the outside, and the divine and all of heaven is going to completely transform us on the inside. We don't have to be involved in all the inner workings if we don't want to be; it's enough if we're just, like, "Well, am I going to hit this person in this moment? Or maybe decide to do something else, like try to see the situation from their perspective."

I personally am somebody who is so interested in the interoception world. Swedenborg says, "All you have to do is this," but clearly he's doing so much on the inside, having these huge experiences. So it's available to us, but it's not necessary. If you want to go there, you can go there and have a lot of fun. He doesn't really have a methodology for it because he is so focused on how it's enough to just reflect on your own intentions and decide what you want to align with and ask for the divine's help. It's not in our power to really do much. It's more about us opening up to the divine inflow.

Jonathan: There's something he calls the stream of providence, which I think other people were talking about in his time; the gist is that even if you do nothing, you'll still end up drifting in a good direction. It's just trying to happen through you. And so if we get a few things out of the way, that's our big task.

Bob: What were his methods for exploring the inner realm? He seems to be more of a geographer, reporting on what he saw rather than giving us methods for how we could best explore.

Jonathan: That's right. Most of his methodology seems to be do some repentance, be a good person. That will give you more protection and more of an idea of what you're doing there. But he does talk more tantalizingly than informatively about breath and the type of breathing that he was doing, holding his breath and reflecting. I think he had an extraordinary ability to focus his mind: he would think about a certain question and go into a very still state where his breathing was almost completely quieted. And then what I gather would happen out of that is, a desire would form in his mind, for example, "I really want to know what happens to selfish people after they die."

He uses the term meditation a fair amount. It's hard to tell whether he means exactly the same thing we mean by that. Sometimes it sounds like it just means reflection or deep thought, and yet it does have a breathing component. He would often do it first thing in the morning—what we call the hypnopompic state; it would be a transitional state where he could stay there and explore it. A lot of the narrative accounts of his spiritual experiences start that way. He has a desire, which moves him into some scenario, and he's watching what's going on. That was the vehicle that he drove, so to speak, to get here. He would wait till a desire came in and then he would follow it.

Chelsea: I don't know of anybody who's studied his methodology comprehensively, through a meta-analysis of all of his works, but to Jonathan's point, Swedenborg is focused on one thing and then that one thing is the portal that opens him up to the spiritual world (see *True Christianity* 112 for an example). From there, he goes somewhere in the spiritual world and starts having conversations. It prompts a whole sequence of events. There's some starting point that then portals him into whatever it is he's going to experience.

Jonathan: For other characters in his spiritual experiences, prayer is very important for how they move around. And yet he hardly ever says that he prayed this or that. These desires seem like a substitution for prayer in his case. He could hardly tell whether it was his desire or whether he received it by way of an inflow from the divine. He has a strange phrase, "Prayer to the Lord from the Lord," which I think is like entering a prayerful state in which you don't know whether your intention is coming from you or is coming into you.

Thought Brings Presence

Chelsea: One key principle he underscores for how things work in the spiritual world is that thought brings presence, and love creates union (*Divine Providence* 326:2; *Revelation Explained* 1099:2–3). When you think of a thing, it's present to you, but if you have love for it—which sounds like desire, longing—then there's a union going on. Even if you're in different places, there's some sort of spiritual union going on. Connecting those two in my mind just now makes me think of the principle in IFS where you can start at any trailhead in your system, and when you show up with curiosity and compassion, the Self is going to lead you, and your system is going to open up in the way that is most useful to your healing, and you can take the next step. The two line up with each other: thought brings presence, so you're focusing your thought, having curiosity, and then having some kind of love and compassion, and it becomes a portal. For Swedenborg, he would focus on thinking about something—it would become a desire—and then the imaginal realm, the spiritual world, would open up to him.

Jonathan: So much so that he says it's sort of a problem after people die—you cannot keep people separate. If they think about each other—if they desire to see someone, even if it's not a healthy person for them or whatever—there's actually no way in the spirit world to keep people apart who are desiring or thinking about each other. It is like it is magnetic.

Bob: This thought brings presence, love brings union; it parallels IFS really, really well. Self is characterized by the 8 Cs, and two of the most important are curiosity and compassion. Curiosity would be the thought, and compassion would be the love.

In IFS, curiosity is the one you cannot proceed without. If I lose curiosity for my client, I stop the session and I say, "I'm sorry, I'm hijacked by parts. Gimme a moment or two." And I get those parts to unblend. It's that important.

I've not only heard this from IFS people. When I studied gestalt, they said this too. You don't have to like a person to work with them. You don't even have to respect them, but you have to be curious about them. That's the bottom line. If you're not curious, you can't work with that person in any productive way. So that's "thought brings presence" exactly.

Chelsea: From Swedenborg's perspective, within an IFS session, that curiosity is making you spiritually proximal to each other in an effective way. If you lose that, then you're not even spiritually nearby them, so what use are you going to be?

Jonathan: Swedenborg talks in very vivid terms about how if you're paying attention to something, you're connected to that in the spirit world. If you get bored or you start thinking about something else, you disappear. To others, you'll get sort of a vague look, and then you're gone. And he says, if you reflect inwardly, you'll realize this happens to you mentally in this world too. It's certainly true. You're sitting there listening to a talk or something and you're just, like, "Oh, they lost me. I just tuned out at that point." Or you might say, "I was miles away."

Bob: I want to go one step further with this curiosity thing. And I don't know if this is IFS in general or just me, but when you pay attention to something with real curiosity in your inner world, it gets bigger. I exploit this. Somebody will say, "Oh, I sense this part as somewhere over here in my chest." I'll start asking a whole series of questions like, "How do you know it's in your chest?"

"It's a pressure."

"Oh, is it like a sharp pressure, like a pencil point, or is it a big dull thing? Is that pressure warm or cold? Does it move at all, vibrate, pulsate? Does it move around, or is it absolutely stationary? Does it have a color, and does it say anything to you?"

I just keep asking all these detailed questions and that thing they're curious about gets bigger and bigger and bigger and takes on personality and depth. After a while, I'll ask them, "How are you feeling toward that?" Because after asking all those questions, almost 100 percent of the time, they will say, "Oh, I'm curious about it." That curiosity has been seeded in there and then their inner world is very real and very vivid to them.

Chelsea: We're talking about the inner world and how the work happens in there. If we have love and wisdom—that curiosity and compassion—the next step from Swedenborg's viewpoint is for those two qualities to come down into action. That is the definition of power for Swedenborg.

So to translate that to an IFS session, there is a spiritual importance to allowing actions to take form and to roll out, to unfold in a session. The power seems to be in allowing it to come to its completion. You have a desire, like often in IFS, you'll say something like, "I'm feeling compassion for this part," then you extend compassion to the part in whatever action or form feels right and see what happens. As I've experienced it and witnessed it in others, in that moment, there is a rush of power. I think what you're seeing is that principle at play of the love and wisdom of Self coming down and being able to act.

Pathway of Transformation
Thought → curiosity → spiritual proximity
Love → compassion → connection
Action → extend compassion in an act → healing

Jonathan: The whole spiritual world, according to Swedenborg, is organized according to people's love and their understanding. Everybody is a unique love and a unique understanding, and people gravitate together on those bases. It took me a long time to realize that where you go in that world is not arbitrary. For example, when you're in a mental pit, you are in a pit because you're in a pit: that state is where you are. When you get out of there and go to heaven, it's because you are in a different state. You feel differently. You're thinking differently.

In terms of inner geography, the qualities of Self or the divine Swedenborg describes as peace, innocence, playfulness, and respecting freedom—these qualities are heavenly—you are in heaven; that state is where you are inwardly. Conversely, when you get into a state of feeling serious-as-a-heart-attack and controlling, you know that that energy is coming from somewhere else, and that's where you are in that state.

Bob: Playfulness is very interesting because in addition to the 8 Cs, IFS also has what they call the 5 Ps, which are Self characteristics especially needed by therapists, and playfulness is one of them. The five are persistence, perspective, playfulness, presence, and patience.

Chelsea: Swedenborg says how we are always in a spiritual community. Right now we are a part of not one, but many spiritual communities. He says if we had our spiritual eyes open, then we'd be able to see what those communities are that we're connected to, and we'd be able to talk with them, and would be able to decide, "Is this who I want to be associated with? Or do I want to go somewhere else?"

Bob: There's a great saying from the 12 steps: "Whenever I am in my mind, I know I'm in a dangerous neighborhood."

3
THE RELATIONSHIP BETWEEN PARTS AND SELF

In the last chapter, we covered the imaginal realm and our connection to it via our body. We discussed some principles about how to sense things in the inner realm and the way things work there; next, we delve deeper into the relationship between parts and Self, which will help us further in navigating the inner world.

Inner Multiplicity

Chelsea: We've had an introduction to Self and parts in IFS and the inner and outer self in Swedenborg. Let's explore the multiplicity within each system some more, before exploring the nature of the relationship between parts and Self.

Bob: In a previous conversation, we talked about Swedenborg's idea of the inner self. Somebody said each level, the inner and outer, has its own heart; its own will and intellect. IFS sees that we've got all these inner parts inside, and they're often in a state of civil war. The key principle is that we need to deal with them relationally and develop relationships with them, treating them as whole people. This is where I think thinkers like Martin Buber

(1878–1965) become so important, and the whole personalism school or trend in philosophy, which is unfortunately not so popular these days. For Swedenborg, are there many inner selves in each person, or is it singular? What's the nature of these layers?

Jonathan: It's often singular. But he will divide it further. But it's interesting that when he gets right down to it, when he is talking about that basic duality of inner and outer, it's singular.

One way to think about it is that, first of all, if you set the dial to two, you get inner and outer. If you set it to three, you get what is often called earthly or natural, and then spiritual, and then celestial or heavenly.

Three Possible Configurations of Swedenborg's Levels

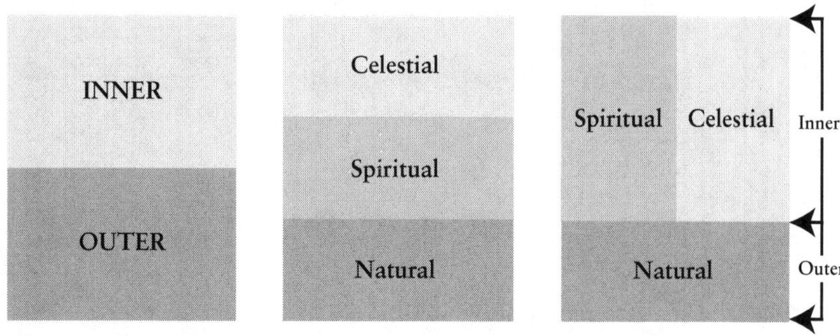

It might be helpful to point out that Latin lacks a definite article and doesn't even have an indefinite article. So you can't tell whether he's talking about *an* outer self or *the* outer self and *an* inner self or *the* inner self.

Where the multiplicity comes in for Swedenborg is in what he would call thoughts and feelings, saying that each of those is in the human form. My sense is that the inner self has many of its own thoughts and feelings, the outer self has many of its own thoughts and feelings, and they're all in the human form with their own will.

I want to reiterate that Swedenborg's view is so fractal. The divine is human and the heavens are in the human form. And if you saw all the heavens together, they're in a single human form. But if you zoomed in and looked at just one of the three heavens, you wouldn't see a part—it wouldn't be a limb; it would be an entire form. Then you'd zoom in to a group within that: the group looks like one human too. Then you zoom in on two angels who are partners, and they look like one individual. Then if you zoom in on each individual, the individual thoughts and feelings are in a complete human form.

Swedenborg was describing this beautifully fractal system before there was fractal geometry, long before anybody had come up with that way of expressing it. To me, that fundamental framework supports the idea of parts. It kind of helps to explain it. It's because of who God is that we're this way; that's why each of these little pieces can be so shockingly complete.

We are having sort of an infestation of ants right now in our kitchen. They've been crawling all over the place. I was looking at the really tiny ants and marveling at how it seems that every one of those ants feels like, "Well, I'd better pick up this piece and carry it over here." There's no difference between me and the ant—I mean, the difference is trivial. There's a beginning, a middle, and an end to the ant; that's one ant, but then you see them all together and they're working together; it's one part of a larger system. The same is true of us. Swedenborg discovered that every level of the system is in the complete human form.

Bob: I think that's super important, Jonathan. All the thoughts and feelings are in the human form. Those are IFS parts right there.

Jonathan: If you were mapping it, I think the thoughts and feelings would be a better map for parts than the whole inner self, which is more like an entire level where things are going on.

Bob: Yeah. It might be the whole inner world.

Jonathan: Right.

Chelsea: I think our ability to think about these things and put them into language kind of fails at a certain point. Because what Swedenborg says, when you get down to the tiniest level, is that our spirit is made of these pairs of love and wisdom, goodness and truth, or evil and falsity. All these little combinations. The process of our regeneration involves linking love and truth, separating out falsity and evil, and connecting love and truth through our whole mind.

So every thought and feeling is like a pairing of love and wisdom. I think of little chromosomes and their pairs of chromatids, but what Swedenborg is saying is that everything is in the human form. Each of those little pairs is its own little micro will and understanding and is going through a process of rebirth on its own regeneration path. The whole process of what Swedenborg describes as regeneration, which we'll explore more later on (see pp. 216–217), is really the Self connecting with each of those parts, reminding them of their true nature, and helping them let go of burdens (or evil and falsity in Swedenborg). When you break it down into that simplest level, you can see an amazing parallel between Swedenborg and IFS. There's a certain both/and quality at play in Swedenborg's cosmology: there are multiple levels in our minds, but also sideways or horizontal multiplicity.

Inner Relationships

Jonathan: Going back to the image of a house for the mind that we described earlier, Swedenborg has another description that takes it beyond just a matter of having three levels in a house. He describes an entire household at work inside—he even calls it a family! And this is in 1751 or thereabouts, almost 275 years ago.

> Our earthly self as it relates to our reasoning self (or our outward self as it relates to our inward), resembles the manager of a household . . . . Everything in us works the way a single household does, or in other words, the way a single family does. There is the part that functions as the head of the household and the parts that

> function as servants. The rational mind itself is what oversees everything as the head of the household and organizes the earthly mind by exerting an influence on it. The earthly mind is what carries out and administers orders. (*Secrets of Heaven* 3020)

Then it talks about autonomy; that the earthly mind has its own autonomy and contains the power of imagination and so on.

Bob: How does the earthly self and the reasoning self or rational mind relate to the inner self and the outer self?

Jonathan: I believe those align with the inner self and the outer self. The inner self is the rational mind, and the outer self is the earthly mind. Swedenborg is a little fluid with his terminology. People often want to diagram it and nail it down, but his language evades that sort of concretization. The rational is definitely farther within; it's inner, relative to the earthly mind or self. And the earthly self is definitely the same as the outer self. So I think they map well, those two.

Chelsea: It's interesting that he is saying that "our earthly self, as it relates to our reasoning self," so he's comparing the earthly self to the reasoning self, and it's the earthly self that "resembles the manager of the household." So the manager and the parts are all on the earthly level, and the whole earthly mind is distinct from the reasoning mind or rational mind and "occupies a lower level but also acts with some autonomy" (3020).

This is saying that there's a managerial function which the earthly mind has and the reasoning self is on an even higher or deeper (more inward) level, which is the Self in us that can observe what all the managers and parts are doing.

Even though he's using the terms "reasoning" and "rational," which sound so intellectual, what he means is the part of us that can be connected to love and know what's spiritually true, and that can act on behalf of goodness. So "reasoning" and "rational" doesn't mean just "really good at thinking about things," but rather that it can be opened up to heaven.

Bob: So the "reasoning self" is the same as the inner self?

Jonathan: That's right.

Bob: That makes the alignment between IFS and Swedenborg very, very close. I mean, astoundingly close.

Potential Alignment between Self and Parts and the Inner and Outer Self

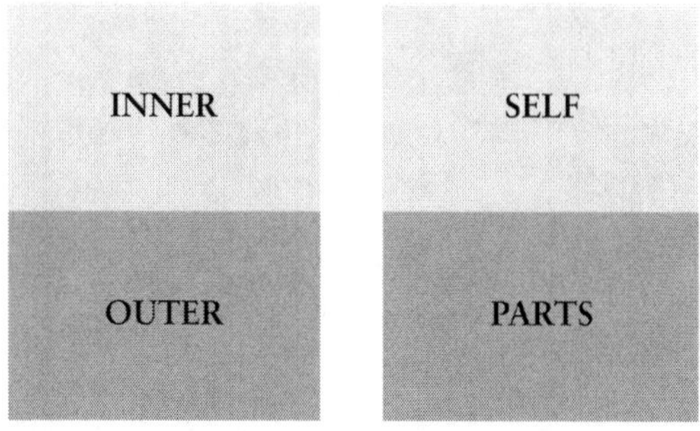

Jonathan: Yes, to underline what Chelsea was just saying, the rational self is heavenly; it's a part that we may not even be aware of. It's not like our cognition or our cerebral activity. Swedenborg uses the term "rational" somewhat differently than other people do. To him, the most rational thing is to be loving. He knew lots of supposedly rational people in his time who he said were not rational at all because they were nasty or self-centered, or whatever.

The Latin here can help us again. The word in Latin he is using is *ratio*. It has many, many different meanings in Latin, but one of the ways that we translated it is that a *ratio* is a relationship; for example, in English, a ratio is a relationship between two numbers. You can think of the rational mind, when used as a term for the inner self, as the relational self or the bridge that reaches both the outer self and the divine inflow. It's the relationship mind. It's the part of us that has this relationship with heaven and with the earthly level. So he's not just talking about "Oh, I'm a cerebral person," or "I'm a thinker."

Chelsea: Going back to the quote, *Secrets of Heaven* 3020, I feel like we need to read the third subsection because he describes the reasoning mind as the rational mind, and equates it with the inner self.

> The rational mind is deeper, though. The knowledge it holds—specifically, the entire contents of the inner memory—does not lie open to us but rather is imperceptible as long as we are living in our bodies. Every thought that harbors a perception of what is fair and just or of what is true and good also belongs to the rational mind. So do all spiritual desires, which are the truly human ones that distinguish us from brute animals. The rational mind exerts the influence of such knowledge, thoughts, and desires on the earthly mind, stirs up what it finds there, casts a critical eye on it, and in this way judges and decides. (3020)

The Rational Mind as the Relational Self

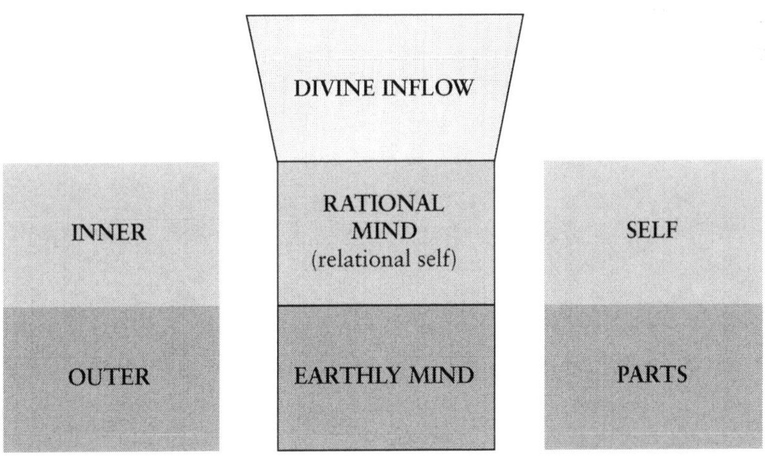

That feels like Self-leadership! It continues, "Clear evidence that these two levels of the mind are different is this: In many people, the earthly mind controls the rational mind or, to put it another way, the outer self controls the inner self" (3020).

So he's making that equation right there.

Jonathan: Yes. He absolutely makes that equation right there, doesn't he?

Chelsea: He finishes by saying, "The only people in whom it does not dominate but serves are those who devote themselves to goodness inspired by neighborly love—that is, who allow the Lord to lead them."

Jonathan: That last little bit about the Lord is what equates in my mind to Self with a capital S. When that's leading, when that has a relationship with those other parts, that's when all is well in your kingdom. Otherwise you have all these parts, but there's a degree of chaos in there.

Bob: The human condition.

Chelsea: Yeah, a nuance Swedenborg brings to the concept of Self is that your inner self can be opened or closed to the inflow of the divine, which is love and wisdom. So the inner self, the relationship self, is the "go-between" between our outer self and the inflow. But the fact that we have an inner self is what makes it possible for us to feel like the inflow of love and wisdom is us. That's what makes it a *self*, our identity.

Swedenborg describes this bridge function in *Secrets of Heaven* 4963:

> Every person born has an outer and an inner self. Our outer self is the one visible to the eye, the one that enables us to interact with other people and to carry out the business of the earthly world. Our inner self is the one not visible to the eye, the one that enables us to interact with spirits and angels and to carry out the business of the spiritual world.

That's how we were created to be. He says, "Heaven flows into our outer self through our inner" (4963).

The business of the spiritual world is everything we're talking about: healing, the releasing of burdens, and waking up to reality, waking up to love and wisdom. To me, IFS gives us a model, a protocol for how to carry out the business of the spiritual world right now through our inner self, through that interaction.

This dynamic is spelled out so well in another passage, *Secrets of Heaven* 5427:3, where he introduces the concept of the middle ground:

> The situation also resembles that of the inner self, or the human spirit, which is also called the soul. The inner self can see each and every thing that exists and happens in the outer self, but the reverse is not possible unless there is a correspondence and middle ground [between the outer and inner selves]. To an outer self that lacks correspondence, then, the inner self has no reality. In fact, when mention is made of the inner self, it seems so obscure that the outer self does not even want to turn its gaze in that direction. Either that, or the outer self sees the inner as a nonentity and nothing to believe in. When the outer self does have correspondence, though, then by means of the middle ground it sees what is going on in the inner self. The light belonging to the inner self flows through the middle ground into the light of the outer self—heavenly light flows into earthly light—and illuminates it, and the illumination makes the contents of the inner self visible. This yields understanding and wisdom in the outer, earthly self. However, if there is no middle ground, and especially if there is no correspondence, the inner self sees and perceives what is going on in the outer and to some extent even directs it, but not the reverse.
>
> If the outer self is opposed enough to completely pervert or stamp out the inflow from the inner self, the inner self is deprived of the light it receives from heaven. Heaven is closed off to it, but contact with hell opens up to the outer self.

So there's this dynamic between the inner and outer self and how you need this middle ground, and then when the light of the inner self can flow into the outer self, you can then see and perceive and direct it. That's what seems to happen when Self shows up in an IFS session—suddenly you're able to do all this work.

Bob: I think this idea of a middle ground is very much the IFS idea of a relationship between the Self and the part.

If you build a good, strong relationship between the Self and the part, healing happens.

I've even heard people say that there are three fundamental things in IFS: the Self, the part, and the relationship. So that sounds like it would fit with the "middle ground."

Chelsea: That's where Swedenborg brings in the word "correspondence." When there is a correspondence and middle ground, that's where you start having this relationship. When he says "to an outer self that lacks correspondence, then the inner self has no reality. In fact, when mention is made of the inner self, it seems so obscure that the outer self does not even want to turn its gaze in that direction" (5427:3). That's something that literally happens to parts in IFS. They are like, why would I even look in the direction of this imaginary thing you're telling me about? So the process is building that correspondence—that connection—through that middle ground to start to facilitate healing.

Bob: I had a client who called his Self "that useless old hippie."

Jonathan: A lot of what I've been editing lately is Swedenborg's explanation of the whole story in Genesis of Joseph reencountering his brothers in Egypt (Genesis 42–47), which I mentioned earlier (see pp. 29–30). It's amazing how much the story seems to bear out what Swedenborg says. If you look very closely, Joseph's brothers absolutely do not recognize Joseph. Joseph recognizes them, but he seems very harsh and tough on them.

He keeps pressing for Benjamin to be there. And Swedenborg keeps saying, Benjamin is the middle ground. Joseph insists that Benjamin needs to come down to him in Egypt, but everybody's resistant. Nobody wants Benjamin to go; the father doesn't want to lose him. But finally, when he comes down, that's the first time the whole group is taken to Joseph's house. Joseph is now able to connect with them in a different way. He seats them all in the right order at the table. So some kind of organizing goes on.

Joseph means this inner dimension, and the brothers are the outer dimension. And only once Benjamin is there, who is the middle ground, do they start talking to each other. Joseph has been talking to the other brothers, but they don't get it; they think he's somebody completely different than he is. They think Joseph is this austere Egyptian demigod. But with Benjamin present, then they recognize him.

The story weaves over chapters and chapters of finally getting Benjamin there. And then Joseph can reunite with his father. Everything happens when you get that middle ground meant by Benjamin. It's really interesting to think about that from the standpoint of IFS and inner work: the Self, the parts, and the relationship. It does seem like healing.

Chelsea: Isn't it true in the case of Benjamin and Joseph that they have a connection that isn't quite the same as with the other brothers?

Jonathan: They are the two sons of Rachel, whom Swedenborg says means a desire for inner truth.

The story speaks to that sense of disconnection. All these brothers don't understand the Egyptian leader at all. They think he's angry with them. He tries to do them a kindness and leaves their silver cup in their bag; he returns their money. This scares the hell out of them. They're terrified, thinking, "He's going to kill us. He's going to throw us in prison forever." They don't understand anything about what Joseph is doing until Benjamin's there and all of a sudden they can see, "Oh, you're loving; you're our own flesh and blood."

Chelsea: That sounds like building trust. In an IFS session, the Self offers love or curiosity to the part in a very gradual way depending on the receptivity of the part. Some parts just can't take it. Pushing too much works against the intention of connection, so Self just needs to be present until the part feels safe enough to turn and realize there's a presence there that can help them, that loves them, that has genuine good will for them and isn't manipulative. I feel like that moment of a shift is when you could say, "Benjamin has arrived." The quality of connection is such that the relationship can now develop and deepen.

The goal is having those two levels have a relationship with each other such that the inner self, with its inflow from heaven of love and wisdom, influences and leads the outer self. The regenerated state, as Swedenborg defines it, is to have a correspondence between the inner self and the outer self.

Our Sense of Identity

Bob: Dick says, from an IFS point of view, the definition of enlightenment is shifting your sense of identity from the parts and managers to Self.

Chelsea: Yes. That is in effect what Swedenborg says. If we just go with the flow of the spiritual influences in our mind, we get pushed by the currents of other people's thoughts. But when we put our identity in that highest *something* in us, then we have authenticity, and that's where our real self-identity comes from, because it's the unique nature of the vessel of love and wisdom that we are: our will and intellect with the divine inflow happening.

Jonathan: Yes, Swedenborg's definition of enlightenment is quite the opposite to religious philosophies that say you merge with a divine and you're not you anymore; you've merged with something, and you lose identity.

This is *Divine Providence* 43:

> Union with the Lord makes us feel that we have freedom and therefore identity and the closer our union with the Lord, the greater our freedom and our identity. The reason our identity seems clearer is that divine love by its very nature wants to give what it has to others.

Doesn't the "nature of divine love" sound like Self?

> Further, the Lord never forces anyone because anything we are forced to do does not seem to be ours. And anything that does not seem to be ours cannot become part of our love and so be accepted as our own. (43)

And then he goes on to say that "the more closely we are united to the Lord the wiser we become" (44). That is one of a list of characteristics that the angels experience in this relationship. They know that,

> The Lord does not flow directly into the things that their wisdom enables them to sense and think but into the desires of their love for what is good, and through these desires into the effects of their wisdom. They sense the flow into the desire that prompts their wisdom. Then everything they think because of their wisdom feels as though it is coming from themselves and is therefore their own. This is what makes the union mutual. (44)

It was very striking to me that you feel more and more your true self as you get closer to that divine inflow within. You feel like, "This is who I really am."

Bob: In IFS terms, when you shift your sense of identity from the parts to Self, your parts don't lose their identity either. I think this is important, because it's all about personhood to me. We stay people; we stay persons at each level.

Chelsea: In terms of staying people, Swedenborg makes this interesting case that the divine is the only person, the only human. He references ancient peoples that he had connection with through the spiritual world who, he writes, acknowledged that nobody is human; only the divine is human. So our whole journey is to become human through our relationship with that divine *something* that's flowing into us, that connection point.

This connects with what you said Pia Mellody wrote about—that our parts are wounded children and adult-adapted wounded children. My own experience with IFS is that my parts walk around thinking they're adults when they're not; and then the exiles are traumatized because their only experience of adults are these adult-adapted wounded children. So it takes a while to develop trust with the only actual adult in the room—my Self, the divine-connected part of me. But that's a new experience for our parts. Has anybody actually met an adult? We've only met adult-adapted wounded children. I see that connection with Swedenborg's claim that the ancients had some kind of acknowledgment of this—we're not human; only God is human, in the same way that Self is the resource of compassion and wisdom for our parts.

Bob: Is God as the only real human the entire Trinity or a member of the Trinity?

Jonathan: Swedenborg believes that in the sense that we are created in the image of God, we have a spirit, or soul; we have a body; and then we have what goes out from us that has our fingerprint on it, so to speak: our emails, our books, the things that we've created that go out into the world. He says the Trinity is truly like that. It's one person with three aspects. That's the sense in which the "threeness" shows up in us. There was always the soul part (the Father), then Jesus was the body, and then the Holy Spirit is the presence of Jesus everywhere after his resurrection.

As he says, the earliest people on this planet wouldn't even use the term human to describe themselves. It was just a quality of God. That seems similar to the idea that maybe there is only one Self. You're really tapping into something that's universal when you connect to Self, and we partake of that. Swedenborg would say that we're vessels for that divine life, but there's only one life.

Chelsea: And I might tack onto that framing of the Trinity even more essential terms that Swedenborg talks about. He describes divine love as the soul or Father, wisdom or divine truth (which is the form of love) as the body or Son, and then together their influence—usefulness, action, emanation—in the world is what Swedenborg calls the "divine proceeding," and that's the Holy Spirit. So that's another way to frame the three aspects. Love, wisdom, and action.

Swedenborg talks about the divine appearing like a sun in the spiritual world, so that's this love and wisdom, and he says that heaven, as a whole, is the body of the divine—it is this vessel that receives that inflow. The emanation is what creates this single body out of the multiplicity of heaven.

Introducing the Proprium

Swedenborg uses the term "proprium" for our sense of self, which is not capital S self in IFS. It's this thing that makes me think it's me. It is key to our spiritual life because it's what differentiates us; it allows us to have that distinguishably one relationship with Self. We need to have this separateness, but that comes with risk. I think of the way kids experience it: something bad happens and a kid says, "It's all my fault." Shame is just written into the way our nature responds. We think it's all our fault and yet that's really just an appearance. It's only through Self, the inflow, and this wider perspective, that you can let go of believing the false appearance.

In terms of the levels of our minds, the inner level can start to understand spiritual truth, but he says that the outer self just isn't wired that way. It can kind of get on board, but it really just thinks in terms of appearances.

Jonathan: Right. In Swedenborg's worldview, the outer stuff is closer to the body and the physical senses. And so he talks quite a lot about the fallacies of the senses, even quite literally to the point where to your own eye you look huge, and everybody else looks small. That's a fallacy of the senses, but that's the way that the outer self sees things. You have to get up to a higher level to say, "Oh no, I'm just one of many here."

Chelsea: The nature of the outer self is an asset because it helps us navigate this material world, but it becomes a stumbling block to the deeper spiritual realities. Swedenborg's point is that we're not here to change the nature of the outer self from being the way that it is; it just has to start living and acting in partnership with the inner self.

It's always going to be the outer self, even if it's an outer self that is receiving inflow from the inner self. There's still a certain quality and nature to it. And I think there's something there about parts and managers. It's not about trying to make them something that they're not, but it's working with who they are and their nature—which is inherently beneficial—and having a relationship.

Swedenborg describes the inflow in this way:

> The Lord works from what is peaceful within to control what is messy and uncontrolled on the outside. Through this core of peace he reduces the chaos on the outer bounds to order, rescuing each part from the error of its own nature. (*Secrets of Heaven* 5396a)

Bob: From an IFS perspective, the error of our own nature would be the burdens. It wouldn't be who those parts really are.

What the error of our own nature might be is our proclivity to take on burdens. And in that sense, proprium might also be burdens themselves, different than what IFS would call the core Self. Because I think in some places Swedenborg says the proprium is evil, right?

Chelsea: "It's nothing but evil" is a way he puts it in several places.

Jonathan: Certainly to begin with. Swedenborg identifies it with our sense that we are just independent autonomous life forms. We are only one thing. We know everything about ourselves, and that sense, as you say, of the ego or whatever it is: "That's me," or "I did that." This false sense of autonomy. Then he says that there is a good version of that that you can get to where everything is transformed. It's softened and doesn't take itself so seriously.

Chelsea: In the same way that he says the Lord is the one human, he talks about the divine proprium. You could say that is Self. The Self is the divine proprium. When we get our self reborn—a new self—we've sort of hooked up to that.

Bob: This lower self or this lower proprium seems to correlate to me to our taking on these burdens, taking on these false beliefs.

I think in terms of unattached burdens and possession and all of that. In Yiddish, the word for a negative spirit that possesses someone is *dibbuk*, which comes from the same root as the Yiddish word for glue.

And that's what this proprium seems to be like. It's sticky. It goes around all this yuck and that yuck almost becomes who the person is, covered in yuck.

Chelsea: I think that makes perfect sense and lines up well. He'll often say that pride in our own sense of self-importance, or pride in our own sense of self intelligence is the core thing that blocks the inflow (see *Divine Providence* 215).

Jonathan: It's really placing yourself in the place of God. And yet we must have this folder of "self" to have the whole magic happen. So it's a risk in the whole system that to be somebody, you run the risk of mistaking yourself for more than you actually are. So a lot of the journey of life is learning how things really are.

Bob: I've come to believe, especially doing this work with unattached burdens and spirits, that pride is the most dangerous—the most destructive. It is so seductive because it's sugarcoated.

Jonathan: The change that needs to happen in the outer self is depicted in Swedenborg's view of the creation story in Genesis. In the beginning, with the heavens and the earth, that's the inner self and the outer self. The only thing that gets created on the inner level is the sun, moon, and stars. Everything else is about what happens on the lower level. In other words, the healing is all about the lower level. It's very valuable to have the sun, the moon, and the stars, which represent love, wisdom, and spiritual knowledge. But most of what needs to happen is all this growth and development on that outer level.

The lowercase self has a certain nature, and it's meant to be that way. It helps you function. But getting the inner and outer together is important. When they eventually get on the same page, that's the correspondence we've been talking about. But it's a long process; it's not a quick fix. There's an iterative nature to this.

I used to watch Cesar Millan, the dog whisperer, and he had an American pit bull terrier named Daddy that he had been working with. The dog used to be insecure and aggressive, but became so mature and calm and reliable. That's how I picture the lower self after a lot of this work, once it's on board. It helps out with all these other less mature dogs that are going crazy all around it. It's still a pit bull, but it's the most peaceful, loving pit bull.

Chelsea: In the first volume of *Secrets of Heaven*, Swedenborg talks about our new self that gets created. The old self is us identifying with all the lower-level stuff. It takes a while to shift your sense of identity from down here to up there. But that new self is you connected to the divine. Swedenborg defines the new self as a "self that has been brought to life by the Lord."

Jonathan: Yes, the "self" there is the word *proprium* translated from the Latin. It's being brought to life. Vivified.

Chelsea: Being brought to life is the shifting of our identity. That's spiritual healing, and it takes time. Every new relationship with every part of yourself that you meet. One more little part knows not to identify with its burden, but to identify with the inner self instead. "Proprium" might just be the act of identifying itself. What are you identifying with?

Bob: That is exactly the definition of Self-leadership in IFS, where Self is leading the system and the parts are unburdened.

Self-Leadership

Bob: In all we've been talking about, how do we develop Self-leadership from Swedenborg's perspective? How do we shift our sense of identity? How do we develop that middle ground, the correspondence? What are important factors to consider?

Jonathan: There are a few factors that Swedenborg describes, which I think play a role in us developing the parallel of Self-leadership in IFS. Namely, what he writes about the remnant, freedom and choice, and times of crisis.

The Remnant

What Swedenborg calls "the remnant" is something everybody has, so it's not something you have to acquire. He uses different terms for it, but it's a capacity for spiritual experience, a capacity for knowing God that develops in all of us in childhood that forms a basis for allowing some of these things to happen. Everybody ends up with a remnant, but it is nevertheless possible for your parents and others to mess with yours; in other words, not everyone has the same size or amount so to speak, but everyone's got it. You couldn't live or function without it.

Bob: That aligns with how this inner core cannot be damaged. That is absolutely revolutionary, and it's still not accepted in Western psychotherapy. There are all these people with more degrees than a thermometer who believe in these foolish diagnoses. And they're basically telling people, your brain is broken. There is no hope for you, and the most intense and emotional experiences of your life are absolutely meaningless.

That's horrible. That's poison. There's an article by an anthropologist that says modern Western psychiatric diagnosis is morphologically the same thing as a curse by an African witch doctor.[51]

You could not give a person a more poisonous message: the most powerful, emotional, spiritual experiences of your life are absolutely meaningless. This is so devastatingly poisonous, because finding meaning is the only way to survive something like that.

They're receiving the medical ruling that any meaning they find, it's just their broken brain.

We used to honor visionaries. Our culture, I think, is absolutely the worst in terms of dishonoring visionaries. If Swedenborg were alive today, he probably would've been locked up.

---

51 Martin Deahl and Michael Andreassen, "Psychiatric Colonialism, PTSD and the Western Psychiatric Diagnostic Tradition . . . Is One Man's Food Another Man's Poison?" in *International Journal of Social Psychiatry* 70, no. 1 (2024): 36–39.

Can you say something about why he calls that the remnant? Or does he have a special meaning there?

Jonathan: It's based on a Biblical concept. It is really a twofold idea. In the story of the children of Israel, the people were finally living in the promised land; then many were taken off into exile, but a few were left to work the land. Those few were a remnant. Prophecy said that others would later come back, again just a small subset of the original group, which again is called a remnant. Swedenborg says that we all have a remnant of spirituality. Basically, in our childhood, we don't have enough of an organized lower mind to prevent ourselves from having spiritual experiences.

And so we've all had a taste of these things. I'm thinking of the scripture in the book of Revelation where it says, "Remember from where you have fallen." We've all been somewhere good. Swedenborg talks about this remnant as absolutely vital to our spiritual lives. We've already got the library card for heaven, the ID; everybody has that.

I was very struck after our previous conversation with a sense of the goodness in the parts. I was so stunned by what you said about addiction and even suicide as a kind of selfless act on the part of these parts. They're willing to be that extreme for the good of the whole—however they perceive it in that system—with what the person's facing in the situation. That sense of goodness in it is remarkable. There are so many darker perspectives out there about who people are and what they're doing and so on. And obviously, when you're doing therapy, I imagine you're pretty much all day dealing with problematic parts of people or horrendous things they've been through. But to have such a beautiful view of it.

I was thinking the remnant might relate to this layer of goodness that's underneath any part's extreme behavior. So there are burdens, but there's something behind that. That's goodness. Even though we have hereditary evil from ancestors, and most recently from our parents, which tends to grow over time unless people are getting things turned around, nevertheless, what offsets that is this remnant; in effect, God got in there first and put this goodness in there and that enables us to have spiritual experiences. He says it's what enables us to go to heaven, and to become angels.

Bob: That fits perfectly, I think. In IFS language, it would be that whatever part it is still has Self. The IFS version is that parts are made just like we are. Parts have parts and Self. So each part has protectors, firefighters, managers, and exiles inside it. And each also has its own encapsulated Self. It's a system of holons. And we are part of larger parts like that. I think "the remnant" would be the Self who exists even in the most destructive parts of us. Like the part of us who's been drinking for forty years, or the part of us who molested our children, or the part of us who was a serial killer. There's still a remnant, and it can't be killed. I think that's the idea of how the Self is indestructible.

Jonathan: It enables anyone at any time to turn things around. It doesn't matter how long the trajectory has gone one way; it's counterbalanced, and we're kept in a spiritual equilibrium (see *Heaven and Hell* 589–596). We can turn the other way. That choice is there.

Freedom and Choice

Another factor for people in developing Self-leadership is being of adult age, which I might also equate with having freedom and rationality. In other words, Swedenborg talks about the fact that people are not spiritually tested until they're of adult age, because you need to have certain truth—certain concepts under your belt—or it would just be all over.

At that stage, we have certain concepts or truth or something that's close enough to true that it can be used as truth; the more genuine that is, the better. You're not going to be tested about whether God loves you unless you have some concept of God and some concept of love. Somebody put that idea in your head, and angels use the contents of our memory to fight back against the influence of evil and falsity. They must use whatever we have on hand (*Secrets of Heaven* 1661). So it's helpful to have certain concepts.

Swedenborg is not a determinist; we all have freedom. There are different kinds of freedom. He sees the freedom to do evil as different from the freedom not to do it. There's a kind of compulsion or slavery in the freedom to do evil. True freedom is the freedom not to do it. To a lot of people, freedom is just, "Let me do what I want to do. Get outta my way." But he sees that as actually a kind of slavery.

Bob: I had a client this morning, and we had this UB almost out, but there was one final part who wouldn't let go of it. That one was sort of this martyr-like, very "Christian" part who believed she was bad and needed to suffer, and that was what the negative energy was able to hook into. It was really hard to help that part separate out from that.

One of the super important things about IFS is that it's all relational. We don't throw out any parts. We don't try to jail any parts. Cognitive behavioral therapy is trying to jail parts; it's putting up more bars and better soundproofing. IFS doesn't do that. A lot of clients only want to go so far, though. They want to be able to get rid of their symptoms enough to get back to doing what they were doing. They'll often fall apart again in the future. I remember a meditation teacher complaining to me, "Most of the people who come to me now just want to learn meditation so that they can tolerate a totally unspiritual life."

Jonathan: It's just the human condition though, isn't it? Like I want my bright shiny penny. I'm really attached to this thing that's ruining my life. Can you help me feel better as long as I don't have to give up the penny?

Chelsea: Swedenborg has this phrase for how the nested systems work. Each part acts on its own initiative on behalf of whatever is higher or deeper. You can think of it like the parts of our body: every part is acting on its own initiative on behalf of the whole. A part acting on its own initiative is critical, according to Swedenborg. The most spiritually powerful thing we can do is engage our free choice. What he calls real, true freedom is acting on behalf of divine love—the divine will.

I think one of the most phenomenal things about the IFS model is that it respects parts as these fully autonomous beings—that we're not just sort of bypassing them; we actually have to respect them. And the work becomes more powerful when the parts are engaged from their own free choice.

Bob: I think this issue of personalism that you're bringing up is central. Dick has progressed on this. Years ago, when I started with him, he said, "Well, it's best if we treat the parts as though they're independent, but who knows what they really are." Now he just says, "No, they're independent, fully formed subpersonalities." I think this is the key to why IFS is better than other parts-work methods, because it is respectful. The respect gives it the potency. That's very counterintuitive for modern Americans because they think you're potent when you don't respect anyone, and you just go barging in. So that's exactly backward, almost exactly backward. And I think this is the biggest issue in dealing with unattached burdens. It goes better if we treat them as fully formed people, and that much I think is demonstrable. I also have come to believe they *are* fully formed independent beings, but that's not provable.

Jonathan: When Swedenborg talks about an inner and an outer self, he talks about them often being in not just battles, but a long war. There's a long-standing tension between these two. But it's as if you are a choice watching this; it's almost like you're a spectator watching the battle, and he encourages you to take one side or the other, whichever you choose. Your consciousness is watching and experiencing this battle. And he says the whole thing is tied to angels and evil spirits. It's sort of a proxy war in a way, but it's happening in your own mental and emotional space. It's interesting that you just sort of fight on whichever side you want to win, understanding that your force will do nothing, but it'll still carry the day, because in his view, the divine is attentive to what your choices are or how you feel about this battle that's going on.

Bob: That's IFS. Along these lines, I was struck by *Secrets of Heaven* 5036:2 where he talks about the spiritual inflow. He says, "We sense scarcely a thousandth of the issues over which the evil spirits and angels are fighting." We're astoundingly ignorant.

Jonathan: It's happening in our own headspace, but we have no idea what's going on.

Bob: Yes, and parts ultimately have a choice too. I like the emphasis on the word *choice*. They get to choose. We can't coerce that. And if we do, it always backfires. Self-leadership isn't coercive in any way.

Willingness and consent

Chelsea: Another factor, which is sort of a nuance of freedom and choice, is what I would call willingness or openness, or consent. When parts are blended, we can ask parts to unblend in IFS, and very often they are willing to. Then once the part has unblended, you then get to know the part, and you connect the part to Self and the Self to the part. There's a detail in that process that I've found to be true in my experience of IFS that Swedenborg puts his finger on. He says it's about turning. This is *True Christianity* 491:2.

> The Lord flows into every one of us with spiritual heat, which is essentially the goodness of love, and spiritual light, which is essentially the truth of wisdom. How open we are to these qualities depends on which way we are turned, either toward God or toward ourselves.

When I'm getting to know parts, it very often is a matter of whether they are willing to turn toward the Self or not. Are they willing to turn toward me? For the ones that aren't willing, you just have to be there with them for a long time before they're willing to turn. But so often the relationship really gets started and begins to bloom when the part, of its own free will, decides to turn toward the Self. So that's a useful technique in IFS, to ask a part to turn toward the Self and look and see, which Swedenborg spells out here in spiritual terms. Someone reading Swedenborg may think he's being abstract, but there's a spiritual reality to it when you do inner work with IFS.

Bob: Also, when a part won't unblend, the classical thing to do as an IFS therapist is to do direct access with it.

Chelsea: Right.

Bob: You would say, "Okay. You don't want to separate out. Would you talk to me directly?" You're basically loaning your therapist Self to that person's system. It's still relational, but you're offering a kind of bridge relationship.

Chelsea: Then you're having that part learn to trust or turn toward that therapist Self to realize, "Oh, maybe there's something good for me in here, or some help being offered." That's a way to get them on board.

The Role of Crisis in Our Spiritual Journey

Jonathan: Another contributing factor for developing Self-leadership can be a crisis. Going through a crisis can help break up the hegemony of the lower self and its false beliefs.

Bob: That's a great phrase. It breaks up the hegemony of the lower self. A lot of the Native Americans talk about Western psychotherapy as colonizing the mind.[52] I think you're onto exactly the same thing.

Jonathan: In a crisis, things get shaken up and start to break apart. He says that you can go through an earthly crisis without a spiritual crisis, but there's a phrase I've heard, "An earthly crisis is a shame to waste."

Chelsea: Having something like a crisis break things up works because there is this motivation, this intention from the divine, that's always willing to take advantage of the opportunity that's there.

Divine energy never acts against our own will, so that's why consent—some willingness—is so important.

Bob: I want to come back to the hegemony of the lower self. I think that's a super important concept. One of the major theories of how psychedelics work is that they downregulate the default mode network. The default mode network is the part of your brain that generates your regular patterns of perception. Who you are and what goes on in there when you're not focused on anything else: that would be the hegemony of the lower self.

Research is being done by the Center for the Neuroscience of Psychedelics, overseen by director Jerrold F. Rosenbaum, into how this may work through interrupting the patterns of rumination, because rumination is a common feature of depression and anxiety.[53] Rumination basically means stuck, looping thought patterns. That's the hegemony of the lower self.

He says this is probably housed in the default mode network and psychedelics work by downregulating this, by turning it

---

52 Hodge, Limb, and Cross, "Moving from Colonization toward Balance and Harmony," *Social Work* 54, no. 3 (2009): 211–219.

53 Io Y. Gilman and Kendall I. Shields, "At Harvard, Psychedelic Drugs' Tentative Renaissance," *The Harvard Crimson*, February 19, 2022, https://www.thecrimson.com/article/2022/2/19/psychedelics-tentative-renaissance/.

off.[54] Psychedelics do not turn the brain on. They turn it down, way down, in almost all areas. This is super important because it contributes to the filter theory of mind, that we're opening up the filter so that all the divine stuff can flow in.

Jonathan: What an interesting example of changing the state of your outer self just through a psychedelic. All of a sudden, you see yourself in a different light, and you see reality in a different light, and it disrupts that rumination. I really like that.

Bob: There is tons of evidence on this, and more and more continues to come out. Neuroplasticity persists into adulthood, even for us seniors.[55] Our brains can change and grow. The Western intellectual tradition used to think that by the time we were twenty, it was all set in concrete. Totally wrong.

The Self's Perspective

Chelsea: Even with all the burdens the outer self and all its parts may take on, Mike Elkin, the IFS lead trainer for my Level 1 IFS training, is so clear about this quality of Self: that Self sees Self. There is no judgment. When Self looks at a part, it just sees curiosity and compassion. It sees Self in the part. It was cool to hear him say that so distinctly. Swedenborg says something very similar. The divine sees us "not how we are but how he wills us to be" (see *Secrets of Heaven* 1871), which I take to mean our fullest, most beautiful potential, no matter what our current circumstances are. It's not blind, but it just sees the beauty of our wholeness.

---

54 Allison Eck, "Altering Perceptions on Psychedelics," *Harvard Medicine*, Spring 2022, https://magazine.hms.harvard.edu/articles/altering-perceptions-psychedelics.

55 Eberhard Fuchs and Gabriele Flügge, "Adult Neuroplasticity: More than 40 Years of Research," *Neural Plasticity* 2014, no. 1 (2014): 541870.

Swedenborg says that's also how angels see us; they have the power and ability to see us that way because they're so open to the divine inflow. They've opened themselves up to that Self-energy so completely that it's the Self in them that is seeing Self in other people. That's something you must remember whenever Swedenborg is mentioning angels and their power and what they're like—it's because that's what the divine is like.

Another thing Swedenborg says about angels is that they do not look at our faults, which you could sub in as burdens in IFS terms. If they see anything of evil or falsity, they put a good interpretation on it (*Secrets of Heaven* 1079, 1088). It's like seeing the good intention of a part.

Jonathan: Swedenborg says beautiful things about how angels forgive, excuse, overlook, and put a good interpretation on our faults, as you were saying, and just kind of ignore them.

An interesting statement that Swedenborg makes is that the Lord is constantly trying to rescue the evil spirits in hell from hell. Like he sees hell as separate from them, not identifying even people who are very solidly in hell—not identifying them with that hell. That's separate. He's saying, "You're something else; you're better than that. You've got more layers to yourself than that."

Bob: This quality becomes practical in IFS. Self is always the witness; it's always the eyes. It's whoever is looking, and that's why you can't ever see your own Self. You might see some arms holding a young part, but you don't see your Self cradling other parts. If you see that, that means it's a Self-like part trying to step in and take over for you. Self is always the witness. Meister Eckhart says, "The eye with which I see God is the same eye with which God sees me: my eye and God's eye are one eye, one seeing, one knowing, and one love."[56] There's only one witness.

---

56 Meister Eckhart, "Sermon Fifty-Seven" in *The Complete Mystical Works of Meister Eckhart*, trans. Maurice O'C. Walshe (New York: The

Chelsea: It makes me think that in IFS, in Swedenborg's terms, you are getting to see things and act from your inner self. The inner self is the one doing the cradling.

Jonathan: Swedenborg has a great passage about this in *Secrets of Heaven* 1954. It comes up where Hagar, in the Bible, says, "You are a God who sees me" (Genesis 16:13). He's got this great riff about how our eyes don't actually see. Our mind sees through our eyes, but it's not our mind that sees; it's our spirit that sees through our mind, but it's not that. And eventually the focus goes all the way up.

He says,

> *You are a God who sees me* symbolizes an inflow . . . . Insight from our higher self into our lower, or to say the same thing another way, from our deeper self into our shallower, is called an inflow, because that's how it operates. Take a person's deeper power of sight, for example. If our deeper power of sight did not constantly act on our outward eyesight, our eyes would never be able to seize on any object and make it out. It's more our inward power of sight that uses the eye to take in what the eye sees. It's never our eyes that do this, although they seem to.

He uses the example right here of the fact that we dream and we see things when our eyes are closed.

> It is our spirit that sees things, not our eyes, although it sees them *through* our eyes. Dreams illustrate the same point, since in them we sometimes see as clear as day. Even so, this deeper sight of our spirit functions in the same way. Our more inward eye does not see anything on its own but only from the still deeper sight of our rational mind. In fact, neither does this power see anything on its own; there has to be an even deeper power, which is that of our inner self . . . . Even then, it is not the inner self that sees but the

---

Crossroad Publishing Company, 2009), 298.

> Lord working through our inner self. He alone sees, because he alone lives and gives us the power to see—and to feel as though we see things on our own. (1954)

It traces it all the way up to where this divine consciousness is really what you're tapping into when you see. That's a gift that comes from above.

Bob: There may only be one Self; there may only be one witness, which sounds exactly like what Swedenborg is saying in that passage.

Chelsea: In the IFS model, Self-leadership is what ends up creating healing and wholeness within a person. And as we said, Swedenborg describes the divine as the ultimate Self; that divine Self is the divine that is ordering all things. So just how in an individual system you start to trust the Self and the Self has this intuition about how best to organize the system, to work with the parts, respecting the different parts and understanding them, *that* is what the divine is doing in a universal way with all beings for all time. It is this Self-leadership of a divine Self who is guiding everything, and the term Swedenborg gives to that is "divine providence." The workings of divine providence are always taking care of us, so that even in the most minute personal moment, when somebody is having a negative thought arise, or an inclination of some kind, and experiences some kind of a moment of choice, there's a wisdom and understanding that is present in all of those moments for everybody, which is a crazy grand concept.

Bob: Chelsea, let me just make sure I get this. You're equating Swedenborg's term "divine providence" with "Self-leadership."

Chelsea: That's right. They have the same activity, as I understand it from both perspectives.

Sensing the Inflow of Self

Chelsea: So the goal in Swedenborg's terms is to align your lower self with the divine inflow, to develop that correspondence. He spends a lot of time clarifying what the differences are between the inflow from hell versus an inflow from the divine. Part of our process is learning how to recognize what the quality of the divine inflow is, and then aligning ourselves with that more. As we do that, we start to change in how we're relating to all of our parts and all the people we interact with.

A big shift for me was bringing this down to a somatic level. I studied Swedenborg for many years. It was my primary lens for spiritual life, even though I've mixed in a lot of yoga and other perspectives. I did a lot of meditation, and after years of meditating, I had this breakthrough. I came to understand, through metta—compassion meditations—that self-compassion is a real, somatic feeling. The sensation is real. You can feel it in your body. You can conjure that feeling in meditation and get to know what it feels like. You can build up a somatic imprint through the practice of imagining giving and receiving loving kindness.

But then, connecting that to Swedenborg: if you're feeling compassion, you are feeling the inflow of love and wisdom from the divine. It is not different from the feeling you get in your body when you're feeling that quality of compassion. The energy and sensation is a spiritual thing, even if it's what you're sensing in your body. It is manifesting in your physical body through its sensations; it's lighting up neurons and neurochemicals are flushing through. All kinds of stuff is going on. How that happens, Swedenborg says, is through correspondences. So when we talk about the Self and we talk about parts in your body, you can get to know what Self feels like and what parts feel like. Swedenborg is all about getting familiar with that, encouraging folks to pay attention to noticing what the divine feels like; and then once you know, you can tune in to it more. And on the flip side, you notice what is not Self; what it feels like to be clouded from the inflow of the divine.

When you're in that state, when you notice the inflow has been clouded over, it's just a matter of reopening to the inflow of the divine that's always there. You start to recognize, "Oh! This isn't me. I'm stuck in this weather system," which is how you might describe it in Swedenborg's terms. I love that IFS brings it down to understanding that within each of those clouded states is a part who you can get to know. You can talk to it about its history; there's so much more to work with.

Jonathan: I did a study a while ago of what Swedenborg said about the presence of the Lord. He uses this phrase, and he says that often people can't tell when they're feeling it. Like they're feeling it, but they can't tell because—I'm putting my words to it—they haven't acquired that taste or that recognition of the hallmarks. I was very interested that there can be a distinction between feeling it and recognizing that you're feeling it (see *Secrets of Heaven* 1616:2, 5962:2, 5963, 6469, 7056:3; *Revelation Explained* 815:8).

I think the presence of the Lord is the same as Self—the compassion and all of the 8 Cs; after a while, you develop a taste for it.

Bob: That's totally congruent with IFS. I've trained way over a thousand people in IFS. One of the things I teach them is how to somatically know when you're in Self, and it's different for everybody. It's crucial that people know when they have a critical mass of Self on board. You can't say you're going to feel a little tingle in your left elbow. Wouldn't it be nice if we could say, "You'll feel a twitching in your left bicep"? But there is no common denominator for that. None. Zero. Everyone experiences Self differently in their bodies.

For me, it's primarily in my visual field. I get almost tunnel vision, but it's a very pleasant tunnel vision; the colors are more pastel in the periphery, and the focus is really warm and centered. It's a very pleasant, euphoric tunnel vision. Everything gets very vague except the person I'm focused on, and they fill my universe, and it's sweet. Very often for me, tears start running down my face. Dick has said for him that it's a resonance in his voice. It's all auditory resonance and a tingling in the front of his body.

I've tracked it with many people now. Other people have had all these radically different things. This one woman who was a runner, she said her thigh muscles would start moving, which were her big running muscles. The weirdest one—I never in a million years would've guessed this one—a woman said, "Oh, when I'm in Self, I smell chlorine." And I went, "Chlorine? That's poison! Are you sure you understand the question?" And she said, "Oh yeah, I understand the question. When I was a kid, my family was horrible. The only safe place was the community swimming pool down the road. It smelled strongly of chlorine. That's Self; that's safety for me."

Jonathan: Wow. The safety. Yeah.

Chelsea: Yeah, wow.

Bob: Yeah. That's Self. Everybody has to track their own, but everybody has some kind of sensation. There are some commonalities, but it's really unique, and the unique stuff is the most information laden. I call it a physiological early warning system.

Chelsea: I love that.

Bob: I work with people when I'm training them to develop that, so you know when you're in Self, and you can tell; then if you have that, you'll also be able to tell when you're losing Self. It gives you something very concrete to work with.

Jonathan: That's awesome. I can't tell you how much I love that. For people to be able to identify, just to sort of know, and then notice when you feel it, because that's exactly the way

Swedenborg describes it. When it comes back again, then it's like, "Oh, last time I was in this state, good things happened."

Chelsea: I think what I love about that is that the journey of getting to know Self is so personally customized. It's so important for you to connect with Self in yourself. Swedenborg emphasizes our personal relationship with the divine. That's the all-in-all, to have us in the Lord and the Lord in us. That's the relationship. Nobody else can do it for you. He recalls the Bible story of how everyone needs the oil in their own lamp (Matthew 25:1–13; *Secrets of Heaven* 4635–4638). You can't get into the wedding by borrowing somebody else's oil. You can't just say, "Oh, they feel Self like that? I'll just start to try to feel Self like that, too." The system demands that you do it yourself, but that's because you matter—because how *you* experience it matters. That is so important.

Jonathan: This is a little tangential to what you're saying, but I think it's connected: Swedenborg talks about—and I've certainly experienced this—that your breathing changes when your state changes. If you go into a part, or a part blends with you, you're breathing differently. I imagine from the descriptions that you have in your book, Bob, that it's very important when you're doing a session to feel when you're sliding out, like if fear starts to engage; you realize you need to get back to the right state. The nature of the breath is something that Swedenborg talks a lot about as a kind of an index. It's another tool to be able to tell what state we are in.

Chelsea: That might be useful for people. Your breathing can be a refuge—if it feels safe for you. For some people, it's totally not; just having to think about their breathing can bring on an anxiety attack. It's a paradox that we're all in the same form—we all have this human form—and yet we're all completely different, down to the level of our fingerprints. There must be such an amazing interplay between commonality and entirely unique ways that each of us experience Self-energy. It'd be so interesting to get a whole long list of all the different ways people experience Self-energy.

Jonathan: Some people find Swedenborg kind of abstract, but he says, "I'm deliberately being somewhat abstract about this." And I would say for exactly this reason, that it's not one-size-fits-all. So if he said, "Your elbow," or something, somebody's thinking, "Well, it's chlorine for me. Maybe I'm not doing it right." He wants to avoid that happening.

Bob: "Maybe I'm crazy."

Jonathan: Yeah.

Chelsea: And that's one of the hallmarks of evil spirits: they will say, "Oh yeah, it's just this one thing," or, "You have to do it this one way," so that's a tip-off in the other direction, if you notice yourself getting caught up in thoughts that there is only one way.

Bob: There's warmth and a bunch of other things. People see shimmering, this fine tremor.

Jonathan: I haven't studied this the way you have, but colors become very vivid for me, like there's a beauty that shines out of things that I'm used to looking at all the time but not seeing in that way.

Swedenborg says, as I mentioned before, that a lot of people, unless they've learned how, can't tell when they're in what he calls the presence of the Lord. He talked about one time that he was in London, and he was walking along the street, and then this presence that he felt was so powerful (*Spiritual Experiences* [144a], [145a]). Again, he doesn't specify; he doesn't say it'll be this or that. But he talks about the fact that until you become kind of a connoisseur of it, you don't realize that's what you're experiencing, but that is what you're experiencing.

Bob: I think that's a super important point, Jonathan.

Example Session

Chelsea: We've covered so much ground. I thought it might be useful to give people an example of how all of this might play out in a session. I had a classic IFS inner experience recently doing a brief IFS session with someone in which I was the client. Here's a synopsis. It showcases many of the elements we've explored so far.

I was connecting to a part.

First it started somatically for me, which often is the case. I noticed a strong sensation in my abdomen.

And then we asked questions about what its job is and what it is afraid of, and how old it is. It said it was five years old, that it was scared, and that it was afraid of getting hurt.

I started to see this five-year-old figure, and I could see what it was experiencing, what the memories were that it was holding. The five-year-old was showing me visions of our family room in my childhood. I was just bringing curiosity to it, extending the energy of my interested, compassionate curiosity. And for whatever reason I began to notice, "Oh, the figure is just all white."

It looked like a flat white shape of a human. I shared, "I'm also getting that this figure is two-dimensional; it doesn't even look three-dimensional." That's what I was seeing in my mind's eye: this flat white thing.

I also noticed that I was really far away from it. As I tried to move closer, it kept moving farther away. I had this "huh" that I shared with the person who was facilitating me. "This part keeps moving far away every time I try to go closer." She said, "Well, let's ask, why does it need to keep being far away?" which is bringing that element of curiosity again. When I posed the question to it, it opened up this immediate knowing, which feels like the description of the rational mind—how it harbors perception.

Jonathan: And perception is a very deep word for Swedenborg. The highest angels have this kind of perception.

Chelsea: So in that moment, I just knew what was going on for the part. I perceived that its moving away was letting me know that it feels like it has to; that it has to do things on its own. It doesn't feel safe, but it also feels like it has to figure out a way to be safe on its own.

I just sat with that and accepted it, and just kept bringing curiosity. I'm just noticing it's white. I'm noticing it's two-dimensional. I felt connected to Self, like I had a lot of Self-energy I was offering it. I wasn't trying to figure it out. Then it opened up to me this realization that those qualities are how it's doing its job. The whiteness and the flatness was how it keeps itself safe. This part could be safe as long as it's nothing but white—nobody can find any fault with it—and it's not taking up space. It's not a problem for anybody as long as it's not three-dimensional and it doesn't have any color or defining attributes. I reflected that insight to the part and said, "Oh, I see you; I see that this is what you're doing, that you figured out this way to do it." Then I brought a possibility to the part by asking, "What if you could feel safe with me? Here I am. I'm here. What if you didn't have to do this job?"

And with that question, I think there was just a critical amount of Self present because just in bringing that possibility, suddenly the figure had latches on the side of it and the latches opened up. It opened up like a pizza box on its side and this three-dimensional person came out. She had long hair and a three-dimensional body. She was shaking her hair out, like she loved to be moving, not stuck in a white flat box anymore. Then we went through a process of inviting her where she wanted to be, which was in my heart, in my body.

The facilitator asked, "Is there anything else that this part needs to happen to feel complete?" The part said, "Let's torch the box." So we burned the white cardboard box, then we dispersed the ashes into the air, into the wind.

Somatically, I felt a difference of not feeling a certain nervousness that I had been feeling around an interaction that I was anticipating, just by being present with her.

So that's a little summary of the power of that perception, the curiosity, and what blooms in our minds when we open ourselves to Self.

4
THE NATURE OF BURDENS

We have deepened our journey, having explored inner relationships and how we can perceive Self within us right now and the nature of Self-leadership and how to align our inner and outer self. We closed the last chapter by getting a taste of how a session might go and got a glimpse of what the process is like for a part to let go of a burden. Now, we look at burdens themselves and unpack the often-triggering words evil *and* sin.

Unburdening the Proprium

Chelsea: On the subject of burdens and how parts have burdens, in my example, the white box was a representation of the burden of that part, and the experience of the burden was the sense the part had that she needed to do things on her own, that she wasn't safe, and she needed to make herself safe; the life of that burden for her became how she existed in the flat white box.

So I'm curious for our conversation now to discuss how sin and hereditary evil—terms Swedenborg uses—line up with burdens in an IFS sense.

In IFS, a burden broadly lines up with what Swedenborg would call evil, but in Swedenborg's framework, evil isn't inherently condemnatory for us. There's falsity and evil—the two core qualities of hell—just as the two main qualities in heaven are love and wisdom. Evil is what is not loving, and falsity is what is not true. That's what burdens seem to be: getting caught up in believing things that aren't true and feeling ways that aren't loving. But that's not the same as sin.

Jonathan, maybe you could talk about how Swedenborg holds the concept of sin.

Bob: One of the roadblocks is the word "sin." How can we translate that into other terms where the value of that is clear? One thing that was immensely helpful for me, and I don't know if Swedenborg would agree with it, was the idea that the Greek word meant missing the target.

Jonathan: I'm trying to remember if Swedenborg gets into the etymology of the word or not.

This is just a small point, but Swedenborg much prefers to talk about evil. As Chelsea was saying, to him, you're not necessarily culpable for it. It could be something you inherited, as we talked about with legacy burdens.

Left to his own devices, he talks a lot more in terms of evil. When he's in a particularly Christian context or when he's quoting the Bible or something, sin will come into it, but it's not his favorite word.

He describes sin as a stumbling block; something you trip over.

Bob: I think that would be totally acceptable in the modern therapeutic world. And I have a quote for that too: "The only difference between a stumbling block and a stepping stone is your attitude toward it."

Chelsea: Swedenborg's next-level concept of sin is everything we've covered so far about the importance of identity. He says the distinction between evil and sin is that it's a sin when it becomes something that you do with your whole intention. It's something that you've made *your own* (Latin: *proprium*). You've identified with it. That's when evil becomes sin. Sin is evil that you've made your own. This definition is useful in the spiritual physics of our psyche. Because then it's like, "Oh, guess what? What do you have to do to get rid of sin? Stop identifying with it." Create that separation, and then it just floats away.

Bob: That's unburdening.

Chelsea: Yeah! There's no actual stickiness to it. It's a matter of choosing what you identify with. But in the Christian world, sin is so often paralleled with condemnation, which is not the framework Swedenborg is operating in. He is using Christian terms but in a spiritual physics kind of way.

Jonathan: The remission of sins literally means sending them away—letting them go. Both in the Greek and the Latin: ἀφίημι (Greek, aphiémi) and remittere (Latin). It's cognate with our word remission.

Bob: Unblend, detach—all of that.

Jonathan: "Remission of sins" on the surface just sounds like a Latinate phrase that may not mean much, but it's sending away, and it's the same word as forgiving, meaning forget about it. Don't worry about it. That gives a very different sense.

Bob: Proprium then would be the whole key, wouldn't it? Proprium means being blended and hijacked by a part. Proprium is the whole way our psyche identifies with our burdens. A "reborn proprium" is an unburdened part.

Chelsea: Yes!

Bob: So of course then that would be a key to how and why we behave so badly all the time. It seems so important to Swedenborg, and it's so crucial to IFS. And it actually is the idea of spirit possession. Craig Stephenson wrote an entire book saying that possession is the key metaphor to all of Jung's work.[57] Because we get possessed, we get hijacked; we bring things into our proprium.

Chelsea: That's the key about identity. Where do you identify yourself? What do you make your own? You could draw a picture of these levels of the mind and their interconnection with the Self, love and wisdom, the earthly mind with the managers and the household, and the rational mind of the inner self, with a sign, "Where are you?" like on a map. "You are here." You get to control where you decide you are. Go ahead and stick the dot way up at the top, in Self. You get to be the observer of everything else in here. When you make that choice, because you're using your freedom, which is the key—that agency—that's what is powerful. Then the things, the burdens, the evil—what was once "sin" because we were identifying with it—are just blown away, sent away. They leave.

Jonathan: I'm paraphrasing, but Swedenborg writes that if you look back on your youth with regret, there's hope for you.

Bob: I'm going to write that down and put it in my book.

Chelsea: And I think Swedenborg was talking about himself there, from personal experience.

Jonathan: In his words,

> If we resort to evil (which most people do as young adults) and feel somewhat uneasy in reflecting on the evil we have done, it is a sign that we will still accept the influence of angels from heaven in the future. It is also a sign that we will allow ourselves to be

---

57 Craig E. Stephenson, *Possession: Jung's Comparative Anatomy of the Psyche* (New York: Routledge, 2016).

> reformed. However, if we do not feel at all uneasy in reflecting on the evil we have done, it is a sign that we no longer want to accept the influence of angels from heaven. It is also a sign that we will not allow ourselves to be reformed from then on. (*Secrets of Heaven* 5470:2)

What we're saying about identity matters because I think it makes a little gap. It's not so much, "Did you do this, or did you do that?" That's important too, though. There's an irony in what he says, because you're supposed to acknowledge sin; you're supposed to really look at it. And yet if you feel regret, there's a part of you that's not that thing, that feels like, "Oh, I was a fool."

Bob: This idea of the proprium and the hierarchy of eyes—well, it's not my eyes, it's my mind; it's not my mind, it's my spirit—just getting up to that great big witness, where you can choose to place your identity, is really key. It's exciting.

Jonathan: Swedenborg is clear that nobody's ever condemned for evil that they inherit. It's only what evil you actively do. If I had to describe the nature of evil according to Swedenborg in a nutshell, I'd say evil is how you hold it. If you think that's you, that's what evil is. If you think "That's not me,"—no matter what it is, how dark or how good—if you really understand that you're a choice, then you wouldn't take credit for the good, and you wouldn't blame yourself for the evil (*Heaven and Hell* 302; *Divine Providence* 320; *Revelation Unveiled* 224:10). You're not that thing; that was input, something coming in. So you're not this goodness either, which comes from God. It's a new way of understanding what evil is. It's kind of a meta definition of evil.

Chelsea: What you're saying reminds me of how it is for burdened parts in a person's system. So often, once Self is present, it's not like, "Oh no, get rid of all this burden in here!" It's more like you can be with it because it's no longer a threat; there's no threat involved. So even if it's actually in the system, it has no attachment. And that's what enables it to just be released. So even if it's there, it's not a problem. There's no, what Swedenborg would call, appropriation going on. Once you really see, "Oh, this isn't me," or if a part understands that they're not the burden and they're being witnessed by the Self, so their true nature is being brought to their awareness in the presence of the Self, then that evil just gets let go and they can receive all this goodness in its place.

One other comment I want to make on the interconnection between goodness and evil is how Swedenborg says that love, divine love, is the thing that comes in and orders everything on these different levels. It's love's intuition that does the reordering. When parts of us are willing to soften enough to let love in, it allows the work to happen. The parts of us that close themselves off to love are these hardened, calcified things that don't want to let it in.

Rather than fighting head-to-head, even though there can be a lot of that energy, it's ultimately that love is just this relentless softening power. It's the evil, or "not-love," that just can't help itself but attack goodness. So the fighting, conflicting energy is coming from that desire to attack goodness, whereas goodness or love knows how to rearrange everything and make change happen.

Bob: It's a remarkable thing you're saying—that divine love and intention can reorder the whole system if we soften enough to let it in. This is, to me, a different language for how the Self-to-part connection heals. If we can open enough to that. That seems to be a very accurate translation from one language to another.

You've mentioned, Chelsea, how our vessels are turned away from the inflow of love and wisdom, and that healing is our turning toward this. That's a perfect description in another language of creating the Self-to-part connection. The healing for a part is turning toward Self, opening to that inflow of Self-energy.

I think that's a near perfect parallel. Swedenborg adds a new, deeper dimension to this.

Jonathan: Swedenborg talks a lot about that. The language of the old translations was "suffering ourselves to be led by the Lord." It's a kind of letting go. I think it's some of these sorts of thoughts that have made his work attractive to certain segments of Buddhism. Similar to the concept of kenosis, he's got a philosophy about our nothingness as an important concept, that humility.

Chelsea: This might be a good reference point for the softening idea. *Secrets of Heaven* 3318 says:

> A human being is nothing else but an organ or vessel that receives life from the Lord; we do not live on our own . . . . That life that flows into us from the Lord comes from his divine love. This love, or the life that radiates from it, flows in and bestows itself on the vessels in our rational and earthly minds.
>
> Such vessels in us face away from the life force because of the evil we inherit by birth and the evil we ourselves acquire by committing it. However, so far as it can do so, the inflowing life repositions the vessels to receive itself. The vessels in our rational and earthly selves are what are called truths. In itself, truth is nothing but a perception of the way these vessels change shape and of the alterations of state under which the various changes occur, taking place as they do in indescribable ways in the most refined substances. Goodness itself—which possesses life from the Lord, or *is* life—is what flows in and realigns the vessels.
>
> These vessels, whose shape is ever changing, face backward and upside down, away from life, as just mentioned. Clearly, they need to be brought into alignment with life, or subordination to it. This can in no way be done as long as we remain in the state we were born in and reduce ourselves to, because our vessels are not subordinate to life.

> They stubbornly resist life and oppose the heavenly paradigm by which life acts, hardening themselves against it. The good that moves them—the good they obey—is the good sought by love for oneself and one's worldly advantage. The crude heat burning within this love gives such vessels their character. Before they can become submissive, then, and fitted for accepting any of the life belonging to the Lord's love, they have to soften, and the only way they can be softened is through times of trial. Tribulation takes away elements of self-love, contempt for others, and therefore vain pride, and elements of a consequent hatred and vengefulness as well. So when these evils are somewhat lessened and conquered by our trials, the vessels start to become yielding and obedient to the life of the Lord's love, which is constantly flowing into us.
>
> The result is that goodness in our rational self, first, and in our earthly self, second, starts to unite with the truth there.

Then he says, "Truth, as noted, is nothing but a perception of changes in shape that conform with constantly altering states, and perception is a function of the inflowing life force. That is why our trials (our spiritual struggles) regenerate us, or in other words, remake us and give us a different character ever after. We become gentle, humble, sincere, and chastened at heart" (3318).

Jonathan: I'm really interested to have the thought—I'd have to think about it more—about the vessels being parts. What he's describing is a very multiple thing of these vessels, and they are hardened or they are softened. It seems to mean these relatively autonomous parts who then turn around and get softer and start to receive what is flowing in. That's really interesting.

Opening to Love

Bob: Swedenborg talks about love all the time. Is there enough material in what Swedenborg says about love to sort of operationalize his idea of love? Truth without love isn't true. So how do we know we're being loving, or how do we know we're not deluding ourselves?

Jonathan: It's true that people may mistake it for other things.

Swedenborg has a great account of a spiritual experience where two angels meet, and they're discussing which is more important—love or wisdom. One angel asks the other, "What is love?" (*True Christianity* 386:1–2). I love the fact that some angel is still asking that question. So mainly I want to honor the question, but I like the idea, and I've never thought of it this way before, of operationalizing it, like breaking it down to elements like those 8 Cs.

Chelsea: One way Swedenborg operationalizes love is when he talks about how to love the neighbor. He uses the Bible story where Jesus is talking about "I was sick, I was hungry, or I was in prison" (Matthew 25: 31–46). Swedenborg says that it was the science of the ancient peoples to know how to love your neighbor well. And it's not a superficial thing. It's about knowing the state of your neighbor and then knowing what is going to help them in that moment. Not just a blanket do this or do that. You don't treat two people the same. It's all about getting a perception of what the state of the neighbor is, and then giving something to them that is appropriate to their state. So every state mentioned in Matthew 25 has a correspondence to a spiritual state (*Secrets of Heaven* 4958).

Sick is being caught up in evil; being in prison is being locked in falsity; being hungry is not feeling a connection to love; and being thirsty is a desire for knowing the truth.

But Swedenborg doesn't spell out how to actually know the state of your neighbor. He just says these most ancient peoples, the wise ones of old, this is what they spent their time trying to figure out. It was their greatest science.

Jonathan: He says that this ancient practice was to try to figure out pretty quickly what would be useful to this person. It was so much about the question, "How can I move you forward in your life?" There are six labels in that parable, but there's a lot more of them—maimed, and the lame, and the blind, widows, and orphans, and on and on and on. These were their categories of trying to figure out, "Oh, I think this person is spiritually widowed. Here's what you give a widow." But mostly all he tells you is they really knew that. They were really good at that.

Bob: That's teasing.

Chelsea: Yeah!

Jonathan: It's teasing; it's true. The other thing that occurs to me, that he says in his book titled *Life*—sort of a brief book about how to put the Ten Commandments to work in your life—is basically the main thing is to stop harming people. If you can stop yourself from harming them, love will flow in and take over. So in some ways, our most conscious work is to stop. Figure out how you're wronging others and try to stop it.

Bob: That's kenosis and constraint release.

Chelsea: It's a surrendering process. It's like it's not up to us to know how to love. When we move things out of the way that we assess are not loving, then this higher thing that actually knows anything and is loving can come through us. Swedenborg writes, "Ceasing to do wrong is left up to our free will. We then receive an inflow of good from the Lord, which is never absent, because it is present in the very life the Lord gives us. The amount of good we receive with our life, however, depends on the amount of evil that is moved aside" (*Secrets of Heaven* 9378:2).

Jonathan: Like siphoning. The more you get rid of that, the more you become this opposite way.

Bob: You left me hanging, Jonathan, with your first comment. The one angel asked another, "What is love?" What did the other angel say?

Jonathan:

> The other angel replied,
>
> The love that originates from the Lord as a sun is the vital heat that angels and people have—it is the underlying reality of their lives. The derivatives of love are called feelings. Feelings produce perceptions and therefore thoughts. It flows from this that wisdom starts out as love, and therefore thought starts out as the feeling related to that love. (*True Christianity* 386:2)

Bob: I have three definitions of love. I want to bounce them off you and see if any of them resonate with Swedenborg. One is putting another person's spiritual development ahead of your personal connection to them. Another one is holding a person in a warm personal regard, whether or not they're treating you well. And the third one—which I think is an example of great love, but it's really painful—is best defined via a story: This woman from Al-Anon had a daughter who was a drug addict and an alcoholic. On a cold, rainy night in Santa Cruz, the daughter shows up at her mom's front door and says, "Mom, just let me in. I need a dry place to sleep." And Mom says, "Are you still drinking? And drugging?" The daughter says yes. Mom says, "No, you cannot come in here. I'll send you to rehab if you want to go," and then shuts the door, cries, and calls her Al-Anon friends.

Chelsea: I think all three of those do line up with things Swedenborg has said about love. It brings to mind a quote of his, that "feeling the joy of someone else as joy within ourselves—that is loving" (*Divine Love and Wisdom* 47).

Another is to non-personalize things for everybody, for anybody you meet; not attach them to whatever it is they're doing.

Swedenborg writes, "When angels think and speak about the hells, then, they think and speak about falsity and evil in the abstract, separate from hell's inhabitants. Angels always set aside any thought of the person, staying with the thought of the thing itself" (*Secrets of Heaven* 8343).

So to love people is to not personalize their burdens.

Jonathan: Another way Swedenborg puts it is loving what is good in that other person. He writes that "the nature of each person's goodness determines both the level at which and the way in which that individual is 'a neighbor'" (*New Jerusalem* 87).

Not just loving them regardless, but what's the healthiest or best part of this person? How can I support that?

Bob: Can I make this question even more pointed? What does it mean to love Jesus?

Chelsea: Swedenborg definitely has things to say about that. What's coming to my mind is that loving what God/Jesus loves is how you love God. Swedenborg would also just say usefulness: "Being useful is the main way to worship the Lord" (*Secrets of Heaven* 7038:3).

Jonathan: Usefulness was the word that I wrote down too. That's one I've been working on for decades, and I don't feel that I really know the answer. Swedenborg talks a lot about how you treat other people. I mean, that very parable, in the New Testament, that we started with is "as you did it for one of these people you did it to me." Swedenborg says in a wonderfully refreshing way, hey, there are things God can't do directly in people's lives; he needs boots on the ground, you know? Well, that's a paraphrase. What he writes is:

> Goodwill makes the connection, because God loves every one of us but cannot directly benefit us; he can only benefit us indirectly through each other. For this reason he inspires us with his love. (*True Christianity* 457:3)

One takeaway from that for me is to not wait around for some divine intervention. We're here to help each other.

Chelsea: Jesus says, "If you love me, keep my commandments." And that's the whole idea of not doing harmful things. Just try with your sense of self, go through the motions of trying not to do evil in your life, and then don't worry; it's going to be okay.

Bob: Kenosis, total constraint release. There it is again.

Jonathan: That really is key to his system, as is usefulness. He writes that "the Lord disposes us to be useful and oversees the useful activity itself" (*Secrets of Heaven* 5949:2). It's very present. Anytime something useful is being done for someone else, there's a presence there of the divine.

Chelsea: Part of why I think the idea of Self and Self-energy resonates so much with me is because it lines up with what Swedenborg says about God. Yes, you can relate to God as a person; there's this relationship that you're having. And yet Swedenborg talks about the Lord overseeing useful activity, and being love itself—like the "divine" is actually everything. All the energy, all the goodness that is being exchanged, all that love is the divine presence with us. It brings to mind the core idea that Swedenborg expands on, about how the Lord is in us, and we are in the Lord. Partnership is the goal. Reciprocal partnership. And however we can open ourselves up to that partnership is good with God.

Jonathan: There's a great line Swedenborg says: "The Lord never teaches us the truth openly, but uses goodness to lead us to wonder what is true" (*Secrets of Heaven* 5952).

Chelsea: That's curiosity right there!

Jonathan: Now how great is that? What a great teaching method to get you to just wonder.

Chelsea: On the question of operationalizing love, one of the things that came to my mind in thinking about that, which was a real shift for me in my own life, was to make it very tangible. So less of an exchange of what am I doing? How am I treating another person? But more of what does love actually feel like? It was so transformative for me to really allow myself to feel love, as I mentioned before (see p. 106). That may sound strange, or so simple, but it actually was a game changer for me. In metta meditations, you imagine a being before you who is loving you, and they are just loving you with all the love you can imagine. You imagine that experience however it feels most potent for you. It might be someone beaming at you with their arms wide open, so overjoyed at seeing you.

You let yourself imagine whatever that is, and then you let yourself really feel it, and you reflect on, what does it feel like to feel that love? So you start getting this sensory map of it in yourself. It was remarkable to notice how there was a whole lot in me that resisted feeling love like that. Over time, I was able to become more open.

Once you know it as a sensation in your body, you can't forget it. Then you have a kind of touchstone.

Jonathan: Swedenborg has beautiful things to say about this particularly in the spiritual world, where you can actually feel it. He was feeling a lot of joy, then he would wish it on someone else, and it would deepen and increase (*Heaven and Hell* 413). So he could viscerally feel that the joy increased when he wished it on someone else.

Another point of his teaching is that the act precedes and willing follows (*Secrets of Heaven* 4353:3). I have experienced this sometimes. One time when I was out to dinner with a whole group of people, someone wanted something that I had on my plate, and I gave it to that person. And *after* giving it to the person, I felt this rush of love.

And really, I think it works both ways, that there are times that I'll lash out at somebody and then the anger doubles; I suddenly feel twice as much feeling as I actually had at the time that the person said a little snippy thing. It increases when you act on it.

Bob: You brought up metta. I think in Buddhism, you could consider the four immeasurables to be a way to operationalize love. There's loving kindness, compassion, appreciative joy, and equanimity. But I think that's what I was sort of hoping for in Swedenborg, that he would have four immeasurables or twelve somethings, something like that.

Jonathan: Let me think on it. There might be. He loves lists. So there might be something that'll pop to mind.[58]

Bob: Going back to the subject of evil, is there some other concept in Swedenborg other than, or in addition to sin, which is parallel to the IFS concept of burdens?

Jonathan: The first thing that comes to mind that I'll need to get out of my mind before anything else can come in is that Swedenborg says that evil is heavy. I like the word burden. He says evil is heavy and falls of its own accord into hell (*Secrets of Heaven* 8279, 8298). So it's kind of like the ancient Egyptian

---

58 Added after the conversation by Jonathan: A simple way to operationalize love is to (1) know, (2) understand, (3) practice, and (4) love. Another is that if you want to have a certain kind of love, pray for it and take prayerful steps to learn what its opposite is, find it in yourself, and remove that from your actions and attitudes. Another would be to consider what particular goodness our neighbor has and how specifically to support that goodness, which may involve putting ourselves as much as we can in the other person's shoes. Another would be to ponder what we could do for others that would benefit the greatest number of people in the deepest way over the longest period of time and in the way that would best use our own unique passions and abilities to meet needs not otherwise being met.

belief about the weight of the soul—how it should be as light as a feather. He specifically says that evil has weight. So it's interesting to think about these parts being weighed down compared to their natural state, where they would be more free.

Chelsea: Another concept from Swedenborg that we touched on before is that we are vessels, and we receive love and wisdom from the divine. What's going on in our spirit in the case of evil is just turning away from the love and wisdom that's flowing in. So love and wisdom is flowing back here, but it's not getting in because we're focused over here. The whole process of healing is turning toward love and wisdom, opening ourselves up to it, like releasing the constraints that keep us from letting that in, as we've discussed.

Jonathan: It's really striking, in terms of the IFS work, that Swedenborg says that evil and falsity have no real power. So an analogy would be how hard the shadow can fight back against the light when the closet door is open. It puts up no struggle whatsoever. It's absolutely powerless in the face of light. It does have power over itself or what is of itself, so Swedenborg takes very seriously the hold that it has on people, but in the face of heaven, it's not a contest. The balance between heaven and hell is only a balance because heaven allows it to be. Heaven holds all the power. Hell has none.

Parts Are Not Their Burdens

Jonathan: The other concept I wanted to share that came to mind in connection with these burdens was Swedenborg's teachings about the pit, or lower earth or realm; language like that. The Bible speaks about the pit. Swedenborg has a lot to say about this pit. At first when I heard these descriptions, I thought, "That's so weird what he's talking about." Then as I spent more time with it, I realized, "Oh, you mean where I've spent most of my life and my initials are carved into the wall right next to the Roman numerals I carved for how many days I've been down here?"

The pit is where you believe something that's false to be true. That's basically the definition of it. One of the crucial false things, one core false thing would be, "I am this habit of mine" or, "I am this addiction of mine," or whatever it is. He says that the pit is not entirely a terrible place because it's open above; there's a heavenly kind of input that flows in from above, and yet it's surrounded by hell. It's very close to hell, but it's not in hell. The nature of it is that you are believing things that are not true. One example he gives of a false idea is that you can earn your way to heaven. It's what I would call, "Oh, what a good boy am I!"

So people are processed while there, he says. Their false ideas are eventually broken up by being in this pit. And when they rise up out of there, they experience great relief. Psalm 40 describes being stuck in the miry clay and praying to be lifted out of the pit and have your feet set on the rock so that you can be free. Rock corresponds to truth.

If I think, *I'm fundamentally no good. I don't deserve any better than this thing that's going on*, from Swedenborg's standpoint that's a falsity. And you can live there. You're in that pit. And when you come to see the real truth, it lifts you out of that pit and you get to the rock; you start to get traction where you can go somewhere. You're not stuck anymore. It's quite different imagery than the imagery of burdens, but that's what came to mind. I think it's connected in some way, because in IFS, the burden is not the part; I don't know who figured that out, but that's a great piece of insight.

Bob: I think it lines up perfectly. The pit is a part believing that it is its burdens. The pit could be another image of the isolation of the part, separated from Self and from being a good part of the system, from taking its deserved role. That's a very resonant image. You said, "I'm not my habit." Well, I think you could say a part believing "I am my burdens" keeps it stuck in that pit, and it can't get out.

First of all, you have to recognize you've been hijacked, and then you have to have a way to get unhooked from the small part.

Chelsea: So it's maybe worth just pausing for a moment here and talking about that. One of the amazing things that connects with the concept of divine providence that Swedenborg describes is that we're all going through cycles of states. Our whole life is a sequence of states—states of mind. Our changes of state are what our experience of life is made out of. The natural cycles we go through (day and night; seasons) are a picture of the cycles of changes of state that are necessary for healing.

Swedenborg makes the claim that all the changes of state are directed by the divine itself (see *Secrets of Heaven* 2796). What a mind-blowing statement. But when you think about that in your day-to-day life, it is amazing to ponder what our changes of state are. One of the functions of our continuous changes in state is to allow us to increase our knowledge of love and wisdom, and our ability to embody that. It's a spiral. So we're always cycling, going through these cycles of states, and yet we are getting the experience of being the one making choices, noticing that we're in a particular state and wondering, what are we going to do about it? What might we do differently? But at the same time, that state is going to change. Like how day follows night, night follows day. We're going to continue to go through these cycles of changes of state. And this whole process is being guided by divine providence.

Bob: I don't think I ever heard this phrase in Swedenborg before today: changes of state. That sounds very much like being hijacked by different parts. Or getting blended with different parts. Is it that the idea of state might be being hijacked or blended with a part?

Chelsea: I think it really is, which is fun to think about. Because your state has to do with your love and wisdom. Swedenborg writes that,

> Angels are not constantly in the same state as to love, and consequently they are not in the same state as to wisdom, for all the wisdom they have is from their love and in proportion to it. Sometimes they are in a state of intense love, sometimes in a state of love that is not intense. It decreases gradually from its most to its least intense. When they are at the highest level of love, they are in the light and warmth of their lives, or in their greatest clarity and delight. Conversely, when they are at the lowest level, they are in shadow and coolness, or in what is dim and unpleasant. From this latter state they return to the first, and so on. The phases follow each other with constant variety. (*Heaven and Hell* 155)

So angels go through changes of state, too. Swedenborg uses the term "sense of self" in this next passage, but it really sounds like blended parts, and how, when parts blend, they create the changes of state.

> I have been told from heaven why changes of state like this occur. Angels have said that there are many reasons. First, the delight of life and of heaven that angels enjoy because of the love and wisdom given them by the Lord would gradually pall if they were constantly engaged in it, the way it happens for people who are involved in pleasures and enjoyments without variety. A second reason is that angels have a sense of self or self-image just as we do, and this involves loving themselves. All the people in heaven are kept free of their sense of self, and to the extent that the Lord does keep them free, they enjoy love and wisdom. To the extent that they are not kept free, however, they are caught up in love for themselves; and since all of them do love that sense of self and carry it with them, these changes of state or successive alternations do occur. A third reason is that they are made more perfect

> in this way, since they become accustomed to being kept in love for the Lord and kept free from love for themselves. Further, by these alternations of delight and discomfort, their perception of and sensitivity to what is good become more and more delicate.
>
> They have gone on to say that the Lord does not produce these changes of their states, since the Lord as the sun is always flowing in with warmth and light, that is, with love and wisdom. Rather, they themselves are the cause, since they love their sense of self, and this is constantly misleading them. (*Heaven and Hell* 158)

In this world, we live in time and space: where you are in space and when you are in a sequence of time. Swedenborg makes the point that the spiritual world has the appearance of time and the appearance of space. The appearance of space has to do with love and wisdom in relationship to each other. The appearance of time has to do with the sequence of spiritual states, which corresponds to the changes of day and night, and the seasons. When working with parts, you could consider what state the part is in. Is it shining where they are? Is it kind of cloudy? Is it in a dark space? Is it a pit? It's just interesting to consider that line of inquiry about the state that a part finds itself in.

Jonathan: A cornerstone principle that Swedenborg keeps coming back to is stated succinctly in *Divine Providence* 320:

> If we believed that—as is truly the case—everything good and true comes from the Lord and everything evil and false comes from hell, then we would not claim the goodness as our own and make it self-serving or claim the evil as our own and make ourselves guilty of it.

That seems related to the concept of unblending. We're falsely blended with whatever. It's whether we're proud of ourselves excessively for something that really just flowed into us, or we blame ourselves. Swedenborg talks about contrition, which is really a Latin word, *contritio*. The root is *ter*, which means to grind down, and *con* is an intensifier, making it mean to crush.

So it means what we would call beating yourself up. It's literally an intensive beating. And Swedenborg says contrition is not repentance (*True Christianity* 512–515); beating yourself up is not repentance—that doesn't lead to change. It only strengthens the idea that you're attached to it. It needs to be looser than that, to see you're not attached to whatever the burden is; you see a distance, some daylight between yourself and that thing.

Bob: In IFS language, the fact that beating yourself up does not lead to change is the same concept as the idea that managers cannot create lasting change.

Another thing that's really a buzzword in therapy-land is agency. We've been talking all around that on this subject without actually naming it. This thing about how you're not responsible for evil if you didn't really choose it: that's all about agency and compromised agency; when do we really have agency? In IFS, one of the things we do is we give the parts agency.

Traditional talk therapy thought that the healing occurred between the client and the therapist. We therapists were supposed to have these brilliant insights that we would pontificate about, and the client would go, "Oh, you saved me, and everything's better." The agency's all in the therapist; the healing power of the agency is in the therapist.

One of the things, when I train people doing IFS, is to hand that agency back to the client as much as possible. Often there might be a part inside a client who is extremely distressed. I'll say something like, "What do you want to say to that part? And if you don't have words, I'll then offer you some." So I'm promoting them, going, "Here, you are the healer, and I'm here behind you with some extra stuff in case you need it." There's a lot of promoting the client into agency. More accurately, helping them know their inborn agency.

There's a second level to that promotion: having the client promote the part into agency. For example, when someone's getting to meet a part who has been very shy, I'll often say to them, "Why don't you tell the part that they're in control now? Ask it, 'Do you like being right at the distance you are now? Would you like to be closer or farther away?'" That's giving agency and control over the nature of that relationship to the part. There's two steps of giving agency: from the therapist to the client, from the client to the part. And that makes the whole system about respect and permission and choice. Choice—that's the Swedenborg word. It really makes it all about choice.

Jonathan: It's so—I don't know—the word that comes to mind is civilized. There's something just wonderfully polite about it all and respectful. I mean, truly, it's beautiful. Just a little bit that I've dipped my toe into IFS, experiencing a session myself, it was amazing to see how the parts respond to that hand-over. "Here, you make the decision." I mean, that changes everything.

Bob: Yeah. They're used to being pulled around, and they don't like it. They dig in their heels and fight and cuss. There's a great Milton Erickson story. He was raised on a dairy farm in the Midwest. When he was about twelve, there was a big storm coming, and his dad was trying to get all the cows in the barn. One calf had gotten a little too big for Dad, and Dad was trying to pull it in. Milton started giggling. His dad got really angry at him and said, "Okay, Milton, you think you're so smart, you do it." Milton went behind the calf, grabbed its tail and pulled it away from the barn, and the calf ran right in.[59]

Another thing, when I was learning Gestalt therapy, I was down there with one of the teachers and a bunch of my peers, feeling quite proud of myself. I was complaining about a resistant client. The teacher said to me, "Bob, there is no such thing as a resistant client. There are only bad therapists." I was devastated. My face turned bright red, but I haven't forgotten it in forty years.

---

59 Milton H. Erickson, *The Collected Works of Milton H. Erickson*, vol. 3, eds. Ernest Rossi, Roxanna Erickson-Klein, & Kathryn Rossi (Phoenix: Milton H. Erickson Foundation, 2008).

Chelsea: All of this reminds me of the non-pathologizing approach of IFS. What does it mean if we're not broken? Everything shifts when you start to think about IFS in that way.

Jonathan: To return to something I mentioned earlier, I think of it as "the new evil." Evil is not evil the way we usually think about it, in Swedenborg's framework. When we identify with things so strongly, that's what does us in. He writes about how even if you did something evil, if you could see that that wasn't you, or see a distinction between you and that, you would not be culpable, even if you did it. So it's different than saying, do this, and that's a good person, and do that, and that's a bad person. For Swedenborg, it is more about your relationship to either one of those actions. If you're grabbing the good or the bad, you're not admitting that there's this inflow, this relationship with the Self, where the good things come from, and hell, where evil and falsity come from. As it's generally thought of, the locus of evil is focused in the wrong spot; the trouble really comes in when we take on either the good or the bad stuff and misattribute it to ourselves.

Bob: As I said before, Dick has defined enlightenment as shifting your sense of identity from the group of managers who run your life, which is what we usually identify as, to the Self, the observer. I think that's very much what you're saying here, Jonathan. If you identify with either the good or the bad, you're down there in the realm of the managers and the other parts; you haven't made this shift up to the Self who can never be damaged or dirtied in any way.

I want to go back a little bit to this idea that all parts are good when we find the good intention. In a lot of jurisdictions, still, that's considered malpractice. You can lose your license for acting on that. For example, if you start dialoguing with these parts, you're accused of colluding with the delusions of your client, and you could lose your license. If you start acting sympathetically toward suicidal parts, you can lose your license.

There are some jurisdictions where you have to get the client to sign or otherwise recognize a "no suicide contract," which is a very disrespectful demand to a part, so this idea is very revolutionary and still very upsetting to a lot of people.

I also want to underscore how crucial this idea is that parts are not their burdens. Just the recognition of "this isn't me" can be so important. I want to tell a little story here. This woman went to an ayahuasca ceremony and got a really nasty energy in her. Driving home from that ayahuasca ceremony, she went completely, floridly psychotic, and was picked up by the police, and institutionalized. Her parents came out from the Midwest to take her home; on the car trip home from California to the Midwest, they had to stop and have her hospitalized four times, because she'd become so psychotic she would fight and try to jump out of the car at freeway speeds. They got her home. She had a cousin who was sort of a psychic, and the cousin said, just tell that thing, "I have nothing here for you but love. I have nothing here for you but love" as a mantra. The woman said, "I felt it coming back, and I repeated this phrase over and over; it went away and never returned." She came to me later for clean up, and I said, "Well, sometimes they're allergic to love." She said, "No, I think what it was is that I finally realized it wasn't really me, and then it lost all power." So that's just what you were saying, I think.

Chelsea: It's an odd paradox where what gets us in trouble, what brings the burdens on, is when we attach them to ourselves, when we think that they are us; and we think that we are the source of goodness and love too—we think that it all arises in us. That's what ends up being problematic. So the spiritual path is letting go and surrendering your identity—"I'm not the evil inclinations coming up in my system, and I'm not the source of the love and the goodness that's flowing into me." That can seem threatening to our sense of self, but what Swedenborg says is that the more that we lean into that and become more and more like a prism, where we really are a gem that can let the light through—because we're not holding on to either one—our sense of self becomes more precise and pristine—our sense of our identity gets clearer the more that we let go and open up (see *Divine Providence* 42–45). I find it to be one of the most fascinating paradoxes of this work in how that plays out in our lives and in our interactions with parts.

Bob: Dick calls IFS a constraint release model. It's not about building up a spiritual muscle, going to the gym and building up a muscle, meditating ten hours a day, and so on. It's not that at all. It's all constraint release. His fundamental belief is that Self is there, undamaged, undirtied, and all we have to do is help the clouds part. When they part, who we are just shines forth. I have aligned that with kenosis and apophaticism, and the Hindu phrase *neti neti*—not this, not that—which seems very much to line up with this not trying to claim the good or this disidentification. What word does Swedenborg use for that?

Jonathan: One expression that he uses is a Latin phrase *sicut a se*, which means "as if from self." A very important appearance is that we seem to be autonomous beings. We seem to have our own independent life. We seem to be completely cut off from everybody else. There's no divine anything flowing into us. We're just our own life forms and we do what we want. What he says the case is, though, is that we function *as if of ourselves*, but actually we're drawing on these other energies or what he would call an inflow from the spiritual world that comes in. We have a choice about yes to this inflow, no to that inflow, and so on.

It is very important emotionally to feel that sense of autonomy: "Hey, I've got to figure my life out. Nobody's going to do this for me." Or, "This is my life. I have to plan. I'm worried about whether this will work out or not. And I'm planning this and thinking that." But it's also very important to have the cognitive realization that of myself, I can do nothing. There's kind of a dissonance, in a way, between a cognitive recognition and the appearance.

There was one time I was sitting in the sun on a very cold day, but I was out of the wind, against a wall, and the warmth was just immediately on my skin. I realized when I closed my eyes, I honestly could think the sun was right here. There was no ninety-three million miles between us; it was right here. And yet cognitively, and if I opened my eyes, I realized, no, that's very far away; that's radiant heat and so on. I could tell what was going on. If we didn't have that feeling of a sense of selfhood, then there's no game—we're just automata. Both are important, and yet the risk of having us feel so much like we're independent life forms is that we'll get all tangled up in it, take ourselves too seriously, and not be able to separate from it. One of Swedenborg's phrases for a simple form of repentance is, "I am thinking about this, and I am intending to do it, but because it is a sin, I am not going to do it" (*True Christianity* 535). That's kind of like looking down on your thoughts and intentions and saying, "I notice I'm actually planning this, but I'm not going to act on it." That's enough to break the connection. A part might be planning something, but with Self-leadership, we guide our system not to behave that way.

The Function of Evil and the Role of Evil Spirits

Jonathan: Going back to the nature of evil, and how it is flowing into us from the spiritual world, Swedenborg says we *need* evil spirits. Evil spirits can be helpful to us in our process of rebirth, of shifting our identity to Self and creating alignment in our system.

Part of what they do to help us out, Swedenborg says, is at these times of spiritual crisis or temptation, they inflame—they exaggerate our symptoms. They heighten it all, and then angels are countering that.

In *Divine Providence* 21 he addresses the function of evil, and why there is evil.

> The Lord's divine providence works things out so that what is both evil and false promotes balance, comparison, and purification,

> which means that it promotes the union of what is good and true in others.

So balance, comparison, and purification.

The balance is the balance between heaven and hell that puts us in a state of equilibrium, because if we didn't have that equal and opposite force, it's just like the atmosphere at fourteen pounds per square inch. He says, "Every one of us is kept in that balance as long as we are living in this world, and this is what gives us our freedom to think, will, speak, and act, the freedom in which we can be reformed." (*Divine Providence* 23).

The second one is comparison.

> We recognize the quality of what is good only by its relationship to something that is less good and by its opposition to what is evil. This is the source of everything in us that is perceptive and sensitive, because this is what gives perception and sensitivity their quality. (*Divine Providence* 24)

In my own experience, when your heart and mind are in a riot for whatever reason, you really think, *This is not how I like to feel.* You get clear you don't want to live there, mentally.

Then the third is purification.

> This happens in two ways, by temptations and by fermenting. Spiritual temptations are simply battles against the evil and false things that breathe forth from hell and affect us. These battles purify us from things that are evil and false, so that goodness in us is united to truth and truth to goodness. (*Divine Providence* 25)

Ironically, evil spirits try to make us more like them, but then they also shame us for what we've done wrong—like a corrupt cop who plants drugs on someone and then arrests them for it. But that strategy by the evil spirits works against them, since we can recognize it as a hallmark and move away from it.

Swedenborg also explains that,

> Spiritual fermenting happens in many ways both in the heavens and on earth, but people in our world do not know what these processes are or how they happen. There are things that are both evil and false that are injected into communities the way agents of fermentation are injected into flour or grape juice. These serve to separate things that do not belong together and unite things that do, so that the substance becomes pure and clear . . . . These useful functions are provided by the Lord through the union of what is evil and false. (*Divine Providence* 25–26)

One of the divine rules is, there should be nothing ever that's not useful. So in an odd way, evil spirits are useful; their efforts are used to help others with their decanting process.

Chelsea: It's a clarifying process. He uses the analogy of fermentation and describes it as a corresponding process to what we're going through.

Jonathan: The best things float to the top and the dregs go to the bottom.

Bob: I think this could become a key metaphor, this fermentation thing. It's very unusual and unique. What a great model for healing that the modern therapy world has lost.

That would be something I think Swedenborg could contribute to the IFS world: an expansion of the IFS model of healing. There's also this fermentation going on.

Chelsea: Yes, I think it's similar or could be applied to what is being found about psychedelics in the research today. There is often intense fear that comes up, and people want to initially resist these states, but Roland Griffiths (1946–2023), the late neuroscientist and psychedelic researcher, talks about how what you want to do is welcome it and open up to it, because then the very thing that's creating all this noise, all that fermentation, suddenly it opens up and there is a flooding in of new perception around love and connection.[60] It's fascinating that psychedelic experiences seem like a microcosm of the long-scale healing that we're doing in our life. And IFS sessions also reflect that same process.

It's cool to think about layering on that model of fermentation to an IFS session. It could help you welcome the negative mind states that come up and be present to them, knowing that's the way this works. The fermentation is happening; this is part of the process.

Bob: A quote I really like that I recently discovered is from Marcus Aurelius, who we don't think of as a therapist: "What stands in the way becomes the way."[61]

Chelsea: I want to underscore how the quote Jonathan shared pinpoints the useful function of breaking things apart that need to be broken apart and uniting the things that are meant to be united. It's interesting to think about how that happens in an IFS session too. The breaking apart or separating seems like the clarity and insight, the releasing of burdens and that kind of stuff. And then the uniting is the connection of Self to the part with love and compassion, literally bringing the parts closer to Self in the imaginal realm, and inviting them to invite in the qualities they desire after they have unburdened.

Jonathan: I would like to throw in a scripture that occurs to me. In Hebrews chapter 12, it quotes something from Haggai 2:6 and then explains it:

> At that time his voice shook the earth, but now he has promised, "Yet once more I will shake not only the earth but also the heaven."

---

60 Tara Brach, "Meditation, Psychedelics, Mortality: A Conversation with Tara Brach and Roland Griffiths," tarabrach.com, January 18, 2023, https://www.tarabrach.com/meditation-psychedelics-mortality-conversation/.

61 Marcus Aurelius, *Meditations*, trans. Martin Hammond (New York: Penguin, 2015), 5.20.

> This phrase, "Yet once more," indicates the removal of what is shaken—that is, created things—so that what cannot be shaken may remain. (Hebrews 12:26–27)

Part of what's going on is shaking it all up because you find out this thing is firm while the rest falls off.

Bob: This one is also important: "Times of trial occur when we are actively regenerating. . . . " (*Secrets of Heaven* 5036:2). Now, in IFS, we talk about tor-mentors. People who torment us are our mentors. They bring out the parts we most need to see.

> . . . (no one can be reborn without undergoing trial), and they're brought about by the evil spirits around us [tor-mentors!]. At such times we are brought into the state of evil that is ours, or rather the state of evil characterizing the part of us that is most our own. (5036:2)

So it's right there, in both of those quotations. I think this is exactly what he was talking about.

I think something that Swedenborg can contribute to the modern world is this idea of fermentation as a model for healing. We need that because it's so organic.

I think one of the worst things about modern mental health is that it tends to be what I would call mechanomorphic—it's modeled on a machine. But healing is a growing process, like a vat of yeast.

The Role of Truth in Freeing from Burdens

Chelsea: Something that is occurring to me with regard to what it's like working with parts in IFS has to do with the role Swedenborg describes truth having. According to Swedenborg, truth has power; truth is what you need to see falsity, to break things free. Truth is the form of love, but it's almost like truth does its work and lets love in, as if truth makes a pathway for love. It makes me think of negotiating with protectors. Letting truth make some inroads seems like the way Self's witnessing allows for parts to change their minds, which then allows love to reach the exiles they are protecting, and allows Self to imbue the whole system with love. So there's some interesting interplay there.

Jonathan: It's very striking what you write in your book, Bob, where even for the unattached burdens, the light is not going to hurt you. For the UB, it has a transformative effect.

Bob: Yeah. It's only your own fear that hurts you.

This idea of how falsity and evil are not real or living relates to one thing I tell people over and over again in this work with UBs: they lose all power in you once you're not afraid of them. It's really true. You can see these great big snarling monsters and then all of a sudden, when that person has been able to welcome all their scared parts in and love 'em up, the monsters are no longer dangerous. These great big snarling demons can destroy people's lives if you're scared of them, but when you're not scared of them anymore, they're absolutely powerless. That's a very powerful parallel between Swedenborg and IFS.

Jonathan: It's beautiful to see the real healing that happens for people out of those truths. It sounds like from what you've written, the therapist stays in touch with that truth and helps the person connect with it inside themselves. Jesus said, "The truth will set you free" (John 8:32). I don't know how all those healings were done, but somehow Jesus was able to release the demons.

The Particular Burden of Trauma

Bob: There's one thing I want to mention because I haven't seen any parallel in Swedenborg myself, and you guys know that end so much better than me. A particular kind of burden, maybe the most common burden, is when a young child is abused horribly and there's absolutely no way for that child to continue living with all that emotional pain. So that pain is encapsulated and encysted and formed into a mass, which becomes a burden until sometime later in that person's life, when they have enough strength and resources to deal with the intensity of that kind of pain and terror and betrayal and all sorts of other things that are part of that burden. Is there anything in Swedenborg about this kind of thing? Because sin is not going to be anything like that kind of burden. It's a whole different thing. So is there anything like that?

Jonathan: The only thing that comes to mind immediately is what I said before about the fact that you cannot face certain trials until you're equipped with certain concepts. There's kind of a quorum of understanding, perspective, and so on, that we need and then you are ready to deal with something like that.

Bob: Does he say what happens if a person is given this kind of trauma that they don't have the tools for?

Chelsea: He describes people whose rationality has been impaired. And remember, his understanding of rationality is this freedom and agency in yourself to start growing and developing as you were designed to in relationship with the divine inflow. I feel like it's a bit clunky the way he writes about it, but I like giving him the benefit of the doubt. What I've taken him to mean is that he is really describing people who are traumatized or the parts of us that hold or react to our trauma. When you're traumatized from a young age, you experience limited agency in your own life. You're mainly acting from all of this pent-up pain and suffering that hasn't had an opportunity to be processed. He writes that evil doesn't cling to you in that condition. It's similar to how he writes that children haven't developed their rationality yet to be able to be spiritually culpable for what they do. So he talks about it in terms of the evil you might get involved in not clinging to you. I think of it as though we're not the one in the driver's seat, when our whole lives are just being driven by this pain and suffering (or in IFS terms, blended parts) that we have had since we were a kid.

You eventually get to a point in adulthood where you have what Jonathan's describing—enough love and wisdom—like this quotient built up so that you can start to engage your freedom and rationality fully. Then you can start doing real spiritual work, which is healing those parts of yourself.

Jonathan: He mainly talks about the kinds of things that they do in the world of spirits to deal with things. He talks about people who become so much wiser and get this perspective where they get released from the pit they were in. He says that for a lot of people after they die, it's like awakening out of a sleep (*Heaven and Hell* 506:1). They just come to a greater understanding and perspective and wisdom.

Chelsea: I might just add something quick to that work in the world of spirits. IFS resonates so much with what Swedenborg says he was seeing happening in the world of spirits. One of the skills that angels have, because it's just the nature of divine consciousncss, is to be able to open up for people why they did things, and then why that, and the why, and the why, and the why. And you just go through this infinite depth of understanding of all of the reasons behind your life. You can go through your whole life's history and revisit all the things that happened, but you're viewing it with this angelic lens, seeing it all from love, and understanding everything and why it happened.

Jonathan: He says that angels know so much more about what we're thinking than we do. We don't realize why we have certain thoughts. The angels could tell you, "Oh, well it's three layers deep: you were reacting to this, but then you also were concerned about that; and then this was bending this way," and that's how it ended up in this simple thought of, like, "Maybe I won't go tonight." We're down on this outer layer. So I love that idea of angels being able to look at those purposes.

There's a beautiful statement in which Swedenborg says that "gold is still gold whether it shines next to the fire or its surface is blackened with smoke" (*True Christianity* 595:4).

He definitely has the image of people coming to life in the other world. I have assumed that this extends to mental illnesses.

Bob: I think that quote is perfect for this. There are no bad parts, but they carry burdens.

Parts are valuable even when they've got these terrible burdens. Including burdens of hatred, suicidality, shame, or harmful sexual inclinations—doesn't matter. There's still gold in there.

All parts are welcome because all parts have gold.

Curiosity Is Key

Bob: Curiosity is the most important of the 8 Cs. You can't proceed without curiosity. You can do therapy quite effectively without compassion. You don't have to like the person at all, but if you've lost curiosity about them and their system, you're dead in the water. You can't do a thing. So I've come to think of curiosity as almost the panacea.

If you think about it, curiosity cures fear. It's like you could have two reactions to something. Something comes up, it's big, and you're afraid of it, or you're curious and orient toward it and move toward it. What does Swedenborg say about curiosity? Does he talk about it?

Jonathan: That's a really great question. It does seem to me that fear and curiosity are mutually exclusive. I can't be in full-blown anxiety and be curious at the same time. It's a great little hallmark: Am I in the right state?

Chelsea: I could do a search for curiosity, and I don't think that would exactly come up or be meaningful in what Swedenborg wrote.

Bob: So it might be the wrong word for him. He might have another word.

Jonathan: I think there's a little translation issue there. Go ahead, Chelsea.

Chelsea: What jumped to my mind is that Swedenborg associates a lot of good qualities that occur when you have trust in providence, and I think curiosity would fall within that. Trust in divine providence is a core piece. Swedenborg has a lot to say about how trust is core to our spiritual awakening or enlightenment. When you have trust in providence—this trust in your partnership with the divine—then it's just a fountain of all the good feelings of joy, delight, usefulness, and insight. I would just think you could throw curiosity in there, even though I don't think he tags it as such. In other words, if a part is feeling curious, that's Self-energy being in that part. So if you turn that around, if we are ever having curiosity, there's this trust in this larger divine picture, even if it's on a subconscious level.

Jonathan: There's a phrase that has driven me and other translators crazy forever trying to understand what he means. It's *affectio veri*, "affection for truth." The way we've been translating it lately is "desire for truth." I think that correlates in a very interesting way, because he is always mentioning that. I mean, that is the bomb. If you have that, you're doing great. It's kind of an interest, a passion, wanting to know. And sometimes he adds "for its own sake"; the truth for its own sake, or for the sake of what's useful. In other words, it's not, "I want to know what's going on so that I get rich, or I want to know what's going on so that everybody admires me." It's when, even if I don't like the answer, I just want to know. That seems to align with curiosity.

Bob: Oh, definitely.

Chelsea: That's very cool.

Bob: From what you're saying, Chelsea, curiosity might be how you operationalize trust. Curiosity is operationalized trust.

Social scientists are often trying to get these big concepts and operationalize them so that you can test them. For example, Roland Griffiths and his staff operationalized a definition of mystical experience that you can quantify.[62] So it might be something like that.

Chelsea: Curiosity is how you operationalize trust. That is amazing. I think that's exactly true.

Bob: The more I think about *affectio veri*, the more I think that's curiosity. It's right on the nail of how IFS talks about that.

Jonathan: I love that connection because it's a phrase that a lot of people don't quite know what to make of it. Swedenborg talks about it a lot, but we're always wondering, what is he talking about? We've wrestled with this. So I love making the curiosity connection.

When I was younger, there was a big debate about, is it the affection *of* truth or the affection *for* truth? Because it's this vague genitive, a case that links two nouns in any number of ways; and so which way is it going? Some people would say, well, it's the affection *of* truth, which is the effect that truth has

---

62 Frederick S. Barrett, Matthew W. Johnson, and Roland R. Griffiths, "Validation of the Revised Mystical Experience Questionnaire in Experimental Sessions with Psilocybin," in *Journal of Psychopharmacology* 29, no. 11 (2015): 1182–1190.

on you, even though "effect" is spelled differently there. But others said, "No, it's objective genitive. It's *your* affection for truth." As we worked with it, on the NCE, we realized that substituting words like *longing* worked, because in his framework, he'll use the word "love" when you're talking about a higher level, and then he'll use the word "affection" when referencing a lower level, but they're one of a kind. So sometimes he'll talk about a love of truth, and we thought, *Well, how is the love of truth different from the affection for truth? It doesn't make sense*. But what finally clicked in my mind was if the affection is a longing or desire for something you don't have, that makes sense. You love something you have, but if you long for something you don't have, it's something that pulls you forward. It's an interest. I think it fits very well with the idea of curiosity because you don't know the answer. What is this doing here? Is this part of you?

Chelsea: It makes sense that it comes from a love for truth. It reminds me of the pairing of "being" and "manifestation," which Swedenborg makes (*True Christianity* 21–22). There's the eternal love for truth that just *is*, but then in the flow of time, how that unfolds is that you have this affection for it, this drive for seeing what's going on, with that love inside, or a longing to get to that love.

Jonathan: And Swedenborg describes the lack of it as well. He talks about when people die and go to the other world and become spirits, they're taken to different environments to see how they respond (*True Christianity* 281:3). They might be taken to someplace where there's a lively conversation going on about spiritual things or something like that. Some of the people get lit up and their hearts are burning, and other ones are like, is it time for lunch yet? They're bored and they want to leave. He expresses that as "no affection for truth," which to me means they're not interested.

I want to call it a starter kit. It's something that pulls you; it's even what little children have. It's what makes them learn how to crawl. They're like, "What's on the other side of the table? Can I go there? How does this work? There's a world out here."

Bob: Am I understanding you right that it's this affection for truth, this curiosity, that leads spirits either toward the heavens or lets them fall into the hells?

Jonathan: It seems like a key component. It's certainly used as a kind of diagnostic tool or as an assessment of what you are like. What do you respond to?

Chelsea: A sorting mechanism.

In Swedenborg's understanding, the world of spirits, like we described before, is a sorting ground, an in-between state where we all spend some amount of time before we find our true spiritual home. Any insight you might get from that kind of a litmus test would probably just be like, "Oh, okay, let's guide this person." This person's going to get guided to another area where we're going to work on them in a different way. Angels don't want anybody to go to hell; they never give up on people. They're like, let's try a new situation and find that *affectio veri*. Let's just keep going until we find any little bit where there's some willingness to be opened up.

Jonathan: Right, the lack of it is not a deal breaker necessarily. They can try to awaken it in various ways, but it's a telling thing if there's none of it.

Chelsea: Yeah. Like no pulse.

Jonathan: No interest.

Bob: Therapists who go to meet a client and think they know what's going on with that client—they always mess it up. And that's why these people with these strong diagnostic categories in their head do so much damage. They're not curious.

Reflection and Perception: The Opposite of Blended and Burdened

Bob: One other question I have is about Swedenborg's conception of perception. There's all this stuff in modern medicine about the default mode network and how that creates repetitive thought rumination. There's what they call the predictive coding model of perception or predictive processing. It basically shows that if you've got a certain mindset up here, it's what you'll see out there in the world.

Your brain selects in very complicated and sophisticated ways what comes through to you. So this idea of perception and cleansing the doors of perception—what does Swedenborg say about perception?

Jonathan: He says that it is a very high angelic quality. And to him, it's a kind of intuitive knowing. He says everybody has access to it, but often it's kind of clouded in our minds. It's kind of a "Ding!"

He says that we are often better at having those insights when someone else is talking. I'm just imposing my own thing on this now, but what he says reminds me of how some people just play their tapes. When they're talking, they're just playing their tape. But when they're sitting in church, or they're in a session, or they're watching a movie, or something moves their heart, or they see something, something goes "Ding!" and they intuitively see some truth.

It's not a process of cogitation: E equals X and Y, and if we subtract two, then we might get to the answer. It's just an instantaneous knowing, and a very powerful thing. He says this is a much higher state than faith. He says the highest angels don't even want to talk about faith. We have a maple tree in the front of our house that is just a blaze of red right now. It's peaking.

It's so gorgeous. Faith would be like saying, "Do you believe that there's a maple tree out there?" No, I *see* it. It's right there. Perception is just seeing; it's a kind of intuition. This is a very high state.

He says there are lots of angels who don't even have this. They're still thinking things through, but the highest layer of angels can see things intuitively. That's what Swedenborg says it means in the New Testament when Jesus said, "Let your words be yay, yay, nay, nay. Anything other than that comes from evil" (Matthew 5:37). It's just a simple, "That's correct. No, that's not right," and being able to tell, no matter how dressed up it is—how fancy, how scary, whatever it looks like.

Chelsea: When I think of perception, it's the constraint release principle again, because perception is something that exists within the inner self. Everyone has the ability to have perception, and so the higher or deeper you go, the higher angels have the most amazing perception; they can see and understand things super deeply.

We can open ourselves up to it more and more. It's what we're designed to do. The key, Swedenborg says, for starting that process is reflection. You have to start reflecting on yourself or reflecting on anything. Reflection is this special superpower that different levels of our minds have so that we can examine something and consider the nature of it. By practicing reflection, you open up perception.

Bob: Is that the same thing as unblending from a part?

Chelsea: Yeah!

Bob: Reflection and unblending would be very parallel processes. They both lead to Self.

Chelsea: Exactly. And then that opens perception; it's just going to happen.

Jonathan: It's having the perspective of being able to see, "Wow, I pretty much acted like an idiot yesterday afternoon when that thing came up," but you're not in it now; you're reflecting back and seeing.

Bob: You unblended from that.

And in IFS language that leads you to Self, and I guess in Swedenborg language, it leads you to perception.

Jonathan: Swedenborg talks about meditation. Meditation and reflection, where you're lifted out of your daily life, and you're looking down on it. A huge part of Swedenborg's own practice was reflection and breathing; I think that was a lot of where these insights came from.

Bob: That is so parallel to unblending, to achieve Self. Looking down on your own life, that's getting all the managers to step back; getting all the firefighters, the exiles, to give space, and coming up to the position of Self.

Chelsea: There's some amazing passages in Swedenborg about reflection.

He writes, "When we do not reflect on the things in our own mind, or our motivation—how we are thinking, what we are thinking, what we are doing, what is motivating our actions—without reflection we know nothing, except that we are, and nothing else, not what we are" (*Spiritual Experiences* 734).

Later in the same work, he makes the following observation: "When I was in conversation with angels, it happened that we were thinking about reflection, or paying attention to something, and the fact that only reflection causes spirits and angels to know what they are, that things are as they are. Reflection constitutes the essence of thinking, for without it the thinking has no life by sensation" (*Spiritual Experiences* 2221).

In one place, he states simply, "Without reflection, there is no life" (*Spiritual Experiences* 2228).

I love that connection of reflection with unblending. Reflection necessitates unblending, because if you're reflecting on it, you're creating this distance.

He talks about reflecting on your own evils and abstaining from them as sins. In a traditional Christian framework, you might think of reflection as being, "Oh, I'd better feel a lot of shame over this." Or, "Oh, I'd better get rid of these evils." But if you're reflecting on your evils, it means bringing curiosity to them.

Abstaining from them as sins, I think, is to get to that sense that they're not you. As Jonathan said before, the "new evil" is thinking that the evil is yours. The core "sin" is just thinking that it's you. Abstaining from them as sins is recognizing, I'm not going to do this because it isn't me.

Jonathan: *Secrets of Heaven* 7479 is striking to me because he writes of spirits, saying,

> They were surprised that there were so many evil spirits around me and that these even talked with me. I was allowed to answer that this was permitted to the evil spirits so that I could learn what they're like and why they are in hell. The reason being that hell suits the way they live their life. I was also able to say that many of them were people I had known while they were alive in the world, when they had been settled in positions of high rank, caring about nothing but worldly advantages. I added though, that there was never any spirit, not even the most hellish who could harm me because I was under the Lord's constant protection.

So that seems to fit well with what we're talking about, both of not being harmed, and also being able to be curious.

Chelsea: Taking reflection to the next level, Swedenborg often witnessed angels doing this work with newcomers to the world of spirits. He describes this process in which the angels facilitate the individual becoming aware of themselves, bringing new awareness to who they are on the inside that they maybe didn't have any awareness about before. Then contrasting that with who they were and who they think they are on the outermost levels of themselves. There's this going back and forth and even being brought into different states. Swedenborg calls this ability "opening a person's inner memory." Angels have this power or skill, which they receive from the divine flowing in.

Swedenborg describes that we have an outer memory and an inner memory. Something happens when angels open a person's inner memory to them and then they bring the person back out into their outer memory. Then they go back into their inner memory and then back out. This going back and forth wakes the person up and leads them to new, greater awareness, so that they start to know themselves. It opens the choice of who they want to be. What do they want to let go of? What are they wanting to choose? And that's what seems to guide them on their path; it seems to be a key way that angels serve people on their journeys. That interesting skill of opening a person's inner memory really sounds akin to what's happening in IFS, going from our outer awareness to insight and back out again.

Bob: In DID (dissociative identity disorder), which they used to call MPD (multiple personality disorder), each of the alters has a distinct memory system. They often remember different things. All trauma disturbs memory. The first book I edited was on trauma and memory. It's a really important topic. I would say the first phase of helping someone heal from massive trauma is helping them get their memories back and get clear about what really happened.

When we are assaulted with such force that it creates intolerable emotion, we encapsulate that emotion and bury it deeply in some psychic basement, and someday when we're a whole lot stronger and able to handle this, it'll come back up. And that's very much what happens in trauma survivors. They get to a place where either they can't go on or this stuff starts coming back up because there's some sense in the whole system that there's now enough strength to deal with this. If you could just amputate this stuff, that would be great, but you can't; it's like you have all these rocks you're carrying around in a huge bag. So that idea of opening up the memory to the inner memory and moving back and forth is very aligned with current trauma therapy.

Chelsea: It's amazing to hear you draw that parallel. It is relational as well, relating to our memories in a new way. We often think of memory as ideas or thoughts, but really the memory is the feeling, the whole somatic experience, all the emotion—that's a part of the memory. And so to be going into that and relating to it differently, bringing it back out, is an amazing process.

Bob: Let me say some more about that because I think what you're hitting on is super important. Some people divide memory into two basic categories: procedural memory and narrative memory. Procedural memory is how you know how to ride a bicycle or drive a car. Narrative memory is a storyline; a story you can tell. For some bizarre reason, most Westerners think narrative memory is reality. If you can put a story on it and put words to it, it's real; and they think that procedural memory stuff is airy fairy—not reliable; weird. But really, you rely on your procedural memory for survival every day. It is much more reliable than the narrative memory.

You couldn't swallow food unless you had the procedural memory of how to swallow. You couldn't drive a car; you couldn't walk. This is much more reliable than narrative memory. Another thing about memory that is not that well known is Dr. Bennett Braun's BASK model: behavior, affect, sensation, knowledge. He worked early on with major trauma survivors. He said, when these memories started coming back to people, often they had no knowledge of what went on with them as a child. That is common for major trauma survivors. They often would come back fragmented into this BASK. They might say, "My arm just keeps doing this [waving arm back and forth]. I don't know what that is." And then they would explore that and realize they were trying to get the abuser to go away. The memory came back through only a behavior in their body. Or it might be only a sensation, and they say, "Oh, I don't know, I'm having a hard time swallowing, and I can't breathe." It was a memory of suffocation coming back only in sensation. It can also come back as affect: people would be overwhelmingly scared or overwhelmingly frightened.

Jonathan: Seemingly for no reason at that moment.

Bob: No reason that they knew about.

Jonathan: You're riding a bus and suddenly, you're terrified.

Bob: Or it could come back as knowledge. I've heard people describe being tortured in a voice like the morning news. Well, not even the morning news—a statistical table, just totally flat.

So memory can also be fragmented in that other way.

Chelsea: So we were talking about blending, and it seems as though blending is a memory taking over or blending with the Self so that all of the part's BASK is kind of managing or filtering the experience in the present moment for the person; that's the way that memory can cloud our vision.

Bob: The thing that IFS adds to this is, it isn't just like a memory fragment: it's a person.

Chelsea: Yes.

Bob: A whole person, a part of you, who comes up and takes you over and hijacks you. That's why having the Self witness that person is so healing. Because if you just have it coming up and taking you over once in a while, that's a disaster. But if you can form a relationship with it, that's a pathway to healing.

Chelsea: So often with the fragmentation you're left with a sensation, and most of your parts don't even know what the other pieces were. They just have the sensation. But the Self can connect with that part via the presenting sensation, as a trailhead, and then the part can reveal its whole experience to you—all the aspects of its memory. It was limited to being just a tingling, but then it can be its whole self, and that's part of the healing: letting that be witnessed.

Jonathan: Swedenborg talks about a psychological meaning of Noah's ark. There was this tide of water that covered the entire earth, but he does not believe that that story literally occurred. He thinks that it was a psychological event about the mind and the heart of the people at that time.

The mind was protected and lifted up in this ark covered in pitch, in tar. But he says, psychologically, over time, the pitch and the tar break down and that tide starts to leak in. It comes to mind as fitting what you're talking about. You get some feeling that's so huge, like, "If I'm going to survive, I must have a little craft and just be on the top of this thing. Because I can't deal with it; it's destroying all life on the planet." Part of what's odd about it to me is that in the Noah story, in the Bible, the pitch doesn't break down. They don't sink, and it doesn't leach into the boat, or we never hear about it, but Swedenborg uses that concept as a platform to talk about this psychological process and the idea that the pitch and the tar are only good for so long. They shield you from the overwhelmingness of the situation (see *Secrets of Heaven* 741 and 751).

And then when you're ready for it, as you say, just a little bit breaks down so that now you get a little bit of muddy water showing up on the bottom of the boat. Or even if it's a lot, it's not the full tide. It can be overwhelming, but still more manageable than the whole thing.

Bob: People are typically in a much better situation.

Jonathan: They have enough development in their other parts, or however you'd put it in IFS terms, that you've got some other resources, and now you're ready to take this thing back out of exile.

Bob: Yeah, it is. Everything about how you've said these angels help heal by opening a person's inner memory, that is so twenty-first-century therapy-land.

Jonathan: When angels evaluate you, when you go to the other world, to understand who you are, they look very carefully at your body, especially the palms of your hands. They listen to your words, and they can read your body. They can see everything you've been through. They can see who you are, what you care about, the quality of your understanding, and so on, from looking at your spiritual body. Your physical body's in the grave, but they still take this next outer shell and read it. It almost sounds to me like our spiritual body is a videotape. They can just put it into the player—to be old-fashioned, to date myself—but you put it in there and you can just play the person's life by looking at this, drawing things out of that memory.

Chelsea: There's a lot of really great stuff that Swedenborg writes about the inner and outer memory.

Jonathan: A big topic.

Chelsea: In his work *New Jerusalem*, he does a synopsis of a lot of major topics, and one of them is the two types of memory. As he describes them, he says, "The earthly memory that belongs to the outer self and the spiritual memory that belongs to the inner self" (52).

So he distinguishes them that way. And he says,

> Human beings actually have two faculties of memory, an outer memory and an inner memory, or an earthly memory and a spiritual

> memory . . . . The contents of our outer memory are in an earthly light, while the contents of our inner memory are in a spiritual light . . . . Every least detail of everything we have thought and said and done as well as what we have heard and seen is inscribed in our inner memory. That memory is our book of life. Our inner memory stores the [truths] that have become part of our faith and the goodness that has become part of our love. (52)

This sounds like procedural memory: "Our inner memory also stores things that have taken on the force of habit for us and have become part of our life" (52).

He then distinguishes the inner and outer memory. He says,

> Knowledge of worldly and spiritual things is stored in our outer memory. That information is extremely dark and tangled compared to the contents of our inner memory. In this world our ability to speak our various languages depends on our outer memory. Angels and spirits speak from their inner memory, so they have a universal language such that no matter what country people come from they can talk with each other. (52)

I think that's very interesting in terms of IFS, that these principles are universal; to think that the language of the inner memory that is spiritual is something that we all have.

Getting Managers On Board to Explore More Deeply

Chelsea: Another piece I was wanting to bring up is the therapeutic process overall. Negotiating manager fears is a big part of getting these parts to be willing to get to know the Self; they have a real fear of what's going to happen if they allow that. Swedenborg writes:

> Here at the outset, a few words need to be said about this union, the union of the outer, earthly self with the inner, spiritual self. Our outer, earthly self is in control from the earliest stage of our

> life, and we do not know the inner, spiritual self exists. When we reform, therefore, and start to change from superficial, earthly people into deep, spiritual people, our earthly part at first rebels. This is because we learn that our earthly self needs to be yoked—in other words, that all our cravings have to be rooted out, along with any justifications. Left to its own devices, our earthly self thinks this will annihilate us, because it is fully convinced that the earthly dimension is everything. It has no idea whatever of the boundless, indescribable realities on the spiritual plane. When the earthly self thinks this way, it recoils and refuses to be subordinated to what is spiritual. That is what is symbolized here by fear. (*Secrets of Heaven* 5647:2)

And so he even says, "This is what is symbolized here by fear." It's this real experience that the parts in our outer self think, "I'm going to be annihilated." That's one of the manager fears in IFS. Schwartz and Sweezy list the most common manager fears that come up over and over again, and one of them is this fear of being annihilated.[63] I'm going to cease to exist. I'm not going to be here anymore if I open up to the inner self.

Bob: I like in that quote where it goes, "Our earthly part at first rebels."

Jonathan: Yeah, until what, like seventy?

Bob: One of the major advances in IFS over the previous kinds of parts work, like voice dialogue, psychosynthesis, ego state therapy, is Dick's insistence that we get permission from the protectors. We don't go to the exiles, the hurt parts, without permission.

There are lots of things we can do that will just blast by the protectors, especially hypnotherapy and sometimes EMDR or

63 Schwartz and Sweezy, *Internal Family Systems Therapy*, 146.

psychedelic work. You really can just blast right past them. In old-fashioned therapy we did that all the time. We blasted by the protectors, went to the hurt ones, thought we were healing them, and then the client would flip out later and it would all backfire.

But Dick says, no, you have to get their permission. Treat them with respect and get their permission, because it's a delicate ecology. So that addresses this very point. You get them to go along with your explorations. You don't drag 'em by the neck.

Jonathan: A Biblical example of that which comes to mind, which has really struck me, is that when the prodigal son returns, the older brother has been very responsible; the younger brother has been very irresponsible—spent all the money, lived riotously—but not the older brother. The older one gets very upset and says to their father, "Come on, I've been with you all this time, but you haven't had some feast for *me*. I've been here holding down the fort. He's been out there ruining everything, yet you're being all loving to him." And what strikes me is that the father, who I think in IFS terms would represent the Self, comes out, leaves the party, leaves the son who's been found, and spends a lot of time with the older brother.

He reasons with him; talks to him: "Hey, think of it this way. Everything I have is yours. You're with me every day. Isn't this great? Don't you see how this is great? Now we have him back."

The older brother has kind of a manager role and feels like, well, what about me? And rather than be dismissive, or bypass him, the father leaves the party and goes to him. It's very striking.

Bob: Yeah. That's befriending the protectors.

Jonathan: Yeah. Getting them on board, working with them. That's right. Swedenborg talks a fair amount about consent being essential to the forming of a relationship. Mutual consent. And what we're talking about is the relationship between parts and Self, so the need for mutual consent is part of it.

Bob: I'm so glad you brought consent up here. That's just the same. We never force a part; we always ask permission.

Jonathan: I really like that spirit in IFS about looking at the parts as having freedom and autonomy. They are able to say, "I'm worried about you talking to that exile. I don't want that to happen." In fact, Swedenborg talks about the fact that little children, like two-year-olds, as is widely known, say no a lot. He says that is important for our development to learn to say no; so we start to practice that very early. He says the same happens for children who die and grow up in the other world. There are certain spirits that'll go and try to egg on the kids to do this or that; challenge them, to encourage them to practice saying, "That isn't so" (*Heaven and Hell* 343). You need to be able to say no in order to have your yes.

Bob: Some people will never look into their inner world at all. Very often the most intellectual and well-educated people are the most difficult because they insist on *thinking* about stuff rather than *relating* to it.

A lot of times kids get this much quicker: "Oh, you want me to relate to my imaginary friend or somebody?" They're right there. There's no problem.

I think people who like to think about things can be very, very difficult. That's why a lot of times some of the clients are the most difficult ones who've done sort of traditional analysis for ten years. They know everything about their childhood and everything about how this part relates to that. And it didn't help at all. Unless you really can rope them in, in a very gentle way, they're just going to go off into all these theories that don't help.

Chelsea: Right. And that can be a manager who's gotten really good at thinking, "I know this system really well. I know how it works."

Bob: Ask them something and they've got all these theories they've known for years, and it doesn't change a thing.

Jonathan: Have you found ways to work with that and go deeper?

Bob: I try to recruit the intelligent manager parts. Usually what I do is something like this: I say every good analyst, every good scientist, and every good skeptic knows that there are two major phases: data collection and then analysis. And if you start the analysis too soon, the analysis is faulty, and the data collection gets messed up. Isn't that true? Then I say, we're still in data collection. Could you please help us with data collection? There's a lot to do here. We really could use your help. We need to be aware and track all the person's sensory modalities in the inner world. Sight, hearing, sound, body sensation. And there's other sensory modalities we have that we're usually not conscious of at all. For example, we are aware of magnetic fields around us, and there are many others. Would you please be willing to help us with this?

We are recruiting the skeptic, telling it we need your intelligence. You're super important. Please come help with the data collection.

There's lots of other things you can do, but that's one.

I think respect is a word they don't use in IFS formally, but it really encapsulates 90 percent of IFS in one word.

The other thing you can do with people like this is you just get them paying attention to the body.

"Oh, you have a part of you that's really angry. How does that show up in your body?"

"Well, my fists get like this, and my shoulders are like that."

"Oh, get really curious about your shoulders. Does that sensation there move around or pulse or vibrate? Or is it really stationary? Is it hot or cold?" You just keep going. Get them down in their bodies. Then all this theoretical stuff has to drop away.

They have to come into real-time present sensing. Then you ask them, "How do you feel toward this part?"

They've been curious about it for five or ten minutes. They're going to say, "I'm really curious." You've seeded curiosity. It's almost irresistible. So those are two ideas, but it's a big issue getting people down out of their theorizing parts.

Jonathan: What I love about asking those sorts of questions is that you want to answer, but the only place you can find the information is in the direct experience, because it's not in any theory. No theory will tell you whether it's hot or cold. The only place you can go to find out whether pain in your shoulder is large or small is to feel it. I love it.

Bob: It's the turn to the inner self. It gets them in the inner world.

Chelsea: I like what I read in your book, Bob, about little compassion drops: not too much love; don't overload the system. You really have to work to just allow that, and that's enough for this goodness and energy to start the process.

Bob: Planting those yeast cells for the fermentation process to happen. Exactly. That's a great model for me. I want to be a seed planter, like Johnny Appleseed, and trust that it's an organic process that will grow if it's just given a little.

5
POROSITY AND THE INFLOW OF SPIRITS

Although we have touched on the presence and influence of spirits up to this point, we now turn our attention to porosity directly and discuss how to navigate this phenomenon from the perspective of IFS and Swedenborg's experiences.

Defining Porosity and Who Influences Our Inner World

Bob: I think Swedenborg is a million miles ahead of the modern West regarding the idea of the porosity of mind—that demons and angels are talking to us or influencing us all the time. In IFS, we've come to recognize the presence and influence of unattached burdens and guides, but Swedenborg is way in the lead here. I think it's really important; I think the next major revolution in psychotherapy is an understanding of how porous our minds are.

I just reread one of Chico Xavier's novels. They're all about dead spirits in the afterworld interacting with this world. His novels have been translated into some twenty languages and have sold between thirty-five and fifty million copies worldwide. They're not intellectually sophisticated at all, but they do seem to be very much in the direction of Swedenborg. Some of the spiritists even say, well, Swedenborg came ahead of us, and he knew this stuff.

Jonathan: Wikipedia calls Swedenborg the father of spiritualism. It's got his picture right there on the article.[64] I was very interested in that. Bob, I saw an interview you did with someone named Ruth, I think. I was very interested to see that she had five links to websites below the interview and the third or fourth one was swedenborg.com, the Swedenborg Foundation's website, without any explanation.

I have some thoughts, if it's appropriate at some point, about the relationship of the Swedenborgians to the spiritualists and spiritists. The Swedenborgian churches historically don't like that association.

Chelsea: I've been fascinated by that history as well. There are several interesting historical intersections between the spiritualist movement and the formal organized church—the religious organizations—of Swedenborgians. Historically, the organized church has understood itself as this distinct new church that is the physical organization that represented what Swedenborg was talking about, this "coming of the new church" (*Survey* 71, 116–117). A recurring subject in Swedenborg's works is the coming of the "new church," which has been understood in different ways by different readers. They understood that they were it, and that it was their job to fend off anything that appeared to be like it, but didn't have it right in their estimation. All through the nineteenth century, you have these spiritualist movements come up, and if they ever claim Swedenborg, the church people kind of go after them. They say things like, "That's not it! We know what's really going on in Swedenborg. This is what it is."

---

64 "Spiritualism (movement)," *Wikimedia Foundation*, last modified August 4, 2024, https://en.wikipedia.org/wiki/Spiritualism_(movement).

Bob: It reminds me of all the different Hasidic rabbis. They all had their own point of view, and they fought each other viciously. It's like that in psychotherapy. There are all these schools. There's IFS; there's SE; there's EMDR, DBT, ACT, and so on.[65] They should be natural allies. The closer their ideas, the more they fight!

It's similar with the spiritists and spiritualists. For spiritism, Brazil is the primary home of it now, with the Philippines being the secondary. They all depend on Allan Kardec's work. And they don't like the other spiritualists.

Jonathan: I was thinking that if you had four points about spiritualism, Swedenborg would totally agree with three of them. Just off the top of my head, (1) the idea that we immediately survive death and still have the personality that we had; (2) the idea that we're in a better world and that we become wiser or develop in some way, if we're open to it; and (3) the idea that we're built from creation to have contact across the veil. All fine, but when spiritualists say therefore we can get information about God and about what we should be doing in our lives from these spirits, Swedenborg says that's overly simplistic.

Most of the spirits around us are basically us; the reason they're spiritually associated with us is that they think the same things we do. They're not at all likely to tell you anything new. The type of spirits who are most eager to communicate with certain types of people are the worst. Swedenborg says no spirit would dare and no angel would wish to teach us about theology (*Divine Providence* 135); the reason is to not take away our freedom.

It can be dangerous for people who aren't prepared or protected to communicate with spirits. The analogy strikes me with what people have discovered about psychedelics over the

---

65 SE: Somatic Experiencing; EMDR: Eye Movement Desensitization and Reprocessing; DBT: Dialectical Behavior Therapy; ACT: Acceptance and Commitment Therapy.

decades: if you don't take care of the environment in which they are taken, they'll magnify whatever's going on; it can be a difficult experience, but under the right circumstances, it can be healing and very positive.

So Swedenborg's position is nuanced because he's pointing the whole human race to connection with the spiritual world. To him, the state of heaven on earth has angels being in touch with people on earth so completely that you hardly know who's died and who's still in the physical world. And the two sides are working together.

Part of Swedenborg's answer to spiritualism is not to look to spirits as an authority, as it says in the book of Revelation a couple of times to John when he tries to bow down and worship the angel (19:10, 22:9). The angel said, "Basically, I'm just like you, I'm your fellow being; worship God." Swedenborg is strong on the idea that we need to cultivate our own direct connection with the divine. That's who can help you. The other ones are just a few years ahead of you in the cycle, so they don't have as much to teach you in that same way.

Bob: IFS has this idea of guides, which people often interpret as guardian angels or something like that. And that we can learn from them. Very much so. So what would Swedenborg say about that?

Chelsea: I think partly why Swedenborg can feed very different communities of people is because he wrote so much, and you can see it in different ways depending on how you interpret it or where you focus.

One thing he writes that aligns with guides is in his work about describing the people of other planets and the spirits of other planets (*Other Planets* 1, 123). In contrast to us, he notes that they're in a much better spiritual condition than we are on our planet. He describes very much of a guide role the angels who are already on the other side play; they are helping the people on this side. And remember that for Swedenborg, angels are essentially just unburdened humans. All angels were once people. So as you develop in this world, you have open communication with these guides, with these people who give you insights.

> On all other planets, divine truth is revealed directly by spirits and angels . . . . This takes place within families, though, for on most planets humankind lives in separate families. This means that the divine truth revealed in this way through spirits and angels does not spread much beyond the family in which it was received, and if new revelations were not constantly occurring, the truth would become distorted or be lost. (*Other Planets* 120)

It sounds a lot like what I know about Indigenous spirituality from the Diné. What insight or revelation they receive from the other side is very customized to their life and their immediate community. You wouldn't necessarily go out and say, "Everybody else has to believe this!" But these spirits provide even daily insights and support, and then help you transition at the end of your life. He suggests that that's where we're headed in our collective community here as well.

> We have been created in such a way that while we are living among others in this world, we could also be living among angels in heaven and they could be living among us. In this way heaven and the world would coexist and work together in us. We would know what was happening in heaven and angels would know what was happening in the world; and when we died, we would cross over from the Lord's kingdom on earth into the Lord's kingdom in the heavens. This would not be like passing from one kingdom into another but like passing into the same one we already inhabited during our physical lives. (*Other Planets* 135)

So he gives that example of the way spirits and people interact on other planets—very much of a guide-like role; that's available to us, but how do we tap into that? That's what I find fascinating about IFS: it has a really practical way of understanding and connecting to these guides.

I love that it almost doesn't matter what spirits technically are, because whether you think of the guidance as coming from a higher part of your own self or that you're tapping into wisdom that appears as this other guide, the facts are the same. You are accessing insight that you weren't feeling like you could get yourself. It really feels like it's coming from outside of your frame of reference.

Jonathan: Swedenborg often paints with a broad brush. He'll make a sweeping statement, and then you look at another passage and that sheds a different light. There's an irony in his saying what I just said—him being relatively cautious about people getting taught by spirits—because he learns from angels all the time. It's a huge part of his process; hundreds of pages. "The angels said this, and then the angels pointed out that, and here's how the angels think of this." There's a lot of angelic teaching going on.

He partly wants to emphasize, first of all, what kind of spirits are angels? One of the things that he says about angels is that they respect our freedom tremendously. No angel would tell you to harm another person. So if you get any kind of message like that, you know it's not from an angel.

The more the communication takes the form of command and control, the more that's a sign of a hellish or evil thing, and not to be obeyed; whereas angels would lay out options or suggest something, but not be offended if you choose not to do it. Swedenborg says repeatedly that we're supposed to sift everything through our own freedom and rationality. We can ask ourselves, "Does this make sense to me? What do I think would be the outcome if I tried this?" Whatever we hear from spirits or angels, we then need to make sense of it and decide for ourselves what to do.

Digest of Traits of Lower and Higher Order Spirits[66]	
Lower Order Spirits	**Higher Order Spirits**
Lie, make false promises, and give misleading advice	Respect the person's freedom; do not oppose the person's will
Tease, torment, attack, and harass	Are emotionally powerful and supportive
Cause anxiety	Withdraw if they cause fear
Cause pain in the person's body	Often communicate using visual symbols
Impersonate and deceive	Teach and instruct; serve as helpful guides
Limited to the individual's own memory and experiences	Possess knowledge far beyond the person's comprehension
Undermine the individual's will, act against it	Do not stir up material ideas but influence the person's inner motives
Cause delusional ideas and false beliefs	Tend to be nonverbal

66 Van Dusen, *The Presence of Other Worlds*, 138–156, drawing from his own and Swedenborg's observations.

Digest of Traits of Lower and Higher Order Spirits[66]	
Lower Order Spirits (Cont.)	**Higher Order Spirits (Cont.)**
Conceal their personal identity	Do not conceal their identity; honest
Oppose God and all religious practices or beliefs, or claim to be God and all-powerful	Identify as emanations of the Divine or similar
Attempt to possess and control parts of the person's body	Support the person's spiritual growth
Act through the person, leading to strange behavior and speech	Communicate directly with inner feelings
Attempt to destroy the person	Carry an almost inexpressible ring of truth
Seek to subjugate the individual and others	Help the person feel a desire to do good
Suggest acts against the person's conscience and threaten if refused	Help broaden the person's values
Cannot reason sequentially or think abstractly	Richer and more complex than the person's normal experience

Chelsea: Our freedom and rationality is so key, and angels are respecting that. Consent is also a huge part of it at the level of porosity. In *Heaven and Hell*, Swedenborg writes a ton about the roles of angels. The whole heaven that he describes is not that they're off doing their own thing. It's very much about helping the people in this world. He describes several different jobs and roles that angels have, and a lot of them are about helping us in this world, but it's not necessarily with us being conscious of it (*Heaven and Hell* 387–394).

Jonathan: Some angels are involved in government, and some are managing the hells, and some are greeting people after they die, but it sounds like everybody also gets assigned a human or two to watch over. Across the board, they're all sponsoring people on earth in their spare time, you could say. And their greatest delight is to help us out and move things forward. But they never get credit for it because we don't realize that we were in a bad mood, and then we happen to see things in a different light. Most of it is happening without our conscious awareness.

A while back I mentioned how some spirits come to Swedenborg and say, "We've always been with you." And Swedenborg says, "No, you just arrived." And he kind of wins the argument (*Secrets of Heaven* 5859). They feel so one with him. They're in his memory. They know his languages. So it seems like almost the definition of what you are as a spirit is kind of fluid. They get confused! The higher angels, not so much. But spirits, who I think are people who've died in the last ten or twenty years or less, have a lot of confusion about who they are or what's going on. It's for a protective function as well.

Bob: In earlier sections, we've talked about the Swedenborg phrase that seems perfect for IFS: "distinguishably one." How are parts part of the Self? Well, they're distinguishably one. I mean, it's just perfect. But what happens when we bring that to the level of porosity?

I've had a theory for a while. I think they're wrong about consciousness being the hard problem. I think consciousness is a semi-hard problem. The real problem is personhood. How does "distinguishably one" happen? That's much harder than consciousness on its own.

The Boundary between Us and Spirits

Jonathan: Since we've started these conversations, I've really been wondering that myself. When Swedenborg first had spirits present in his thoughts, it was such a shock to him. He really thought this was his own interior private space. He was dumbfounded: "How do you know what I'm thinking?" And as we've said, that had always been his big quest, to find the origin of thoughts and feelings. But it's gotten me pretty profoundly confused; my sense of self works on a daily basis, but what is going on? What is actually me? Are these habits and these desires actually me? Where does a person begin and end?

I've wondered about this in connection to UBs. Swedenborg says every thought and feeling we have is mediated. There are also possessions that he talks about, which is a different category, and yet to him, every thought and feeling we have is influenced by spirits. He writes of how when the immediate influence of spirits was taken away from him, he slumped as if dead, like a marionette (*Secrets of Heaven* 5849; see also *Secrets of Heaven* 4067:2; *Heaven and Hell* 302; *True Christianity* 118). Yet he also holds that our thoughts are unique to us; our own identity is an operative factor. All the influence is mediated through our own nature and through the filter of our memories, our unique experiences, and our point of view; we know that even different children in the same family grew up in a different family, in effect. You have your own unique perspective.

But there's an element of smoke and mirrors. It's unshakeable. You never get behind the mirror. In fact, the closer you get to God, as I mentioned before, the more like yourself you feel. It's a deep mystery, but what's useful about it is the type of work you're doing, Bob. Otherwise, it's only a fascinating philosophical discussion. But if you're going to help somebody who's stuck, or who's in pain, this is helpful information to have.

Chelsea: That's what I was thinking about. In *Secrets of Heaven*, Swedenborg writes how spirits take on our full memory. We have spirits associated with us but in a way that preserves our distinct identities. We relate to parts of us, but these parts also have spirits present with them. When you read what Swedenborg writes, it blows your mind in terms of the expansiveness of our interconnection.

> Spirits possess everything in our thought and will, and angels possess what is even deeper, which means that we are bound tightly to them. As a result, we cannot help sensing and feeling that we ourselves are the ones thinking and intending.
>
> Communication in the other world works the same way. In a single community, where everyone is similar, each member believes that what belongs to another is his or her own. When good [spirits] go to a heavenly community, then, they immediately enter into all the understanding and wisdom of that community, so thoroughly that they are completely convinced it exists inside themselves. The same is true for a person on earth, and for a spirit with that person.
>
> What flows in from spirits from hell is evil and falsity, but what flows in from angels from heaven is goodness and truth. The opposing inflows keep us in the middle and therefore in freedom.
>
> Because more of the angels' inflow comes by an inward way, it is not as perceptible outwardly as the evil spirits' inflow.
>
> Furthermore, angels by their very nature are completely unwilling to hear that goodness or truth flows in from them, only from the Lord. It upsets them if anyone thinks otherwise, because they have a clear perception that this is so. They love nothing more than willing and thinking under the Lord's power rather than their own.
>
> Evil spirits, conversely, grow angry if told they do not think or will on their own, because this goes against the kinds of pleasure

> they love. It makes them even angrier to be told that life does not exist in them, it comes from elsewhere. When the fact is demonstrated to them by personal experience (as it often is), they concede its truth, since they cannot argue with experience. However, a little while later they deny it and want never to have it confirmed by experience again. (*Secrets of Heaven* 6193:1–2)

What is the value of knowing this in clinical practice? How does it help?

Two things that come to mind is knowing that we're deeply interconnected. But then also it brings a level of freedom because, when you know about inflow, you have freedom in how you relate to these parts. It's not just determined. There's an influence going on that can be shifted in some way.

Jonathan: I think that's really crucial what you just said. The scripture that came to mind is that what you bind on earth will be bound in heaven (Matthew 16:19; 18:18). What you unbind on earth will be unbound in heaven. And I think there's something about binding here. If the system were not so beautifully designed, it could be overwhelming.

In the case of UBs, I think a lot of what those kinds of spirits want to say is, "I'm part of you," and make you believe it. Part of what I see happening in IFS therapy is saying, "No, actually that's not true."

We have a choice about this. I think what we essentially are is a choice. It's not like you have infinite choice or unlimited freedom, but I think you can move away from certain behaviors and find yourself in different spiritual company, because certain behaviors attract certain company.

You also move naturally through different spiritual company as you go through life. Swedenborg talks about the fact that in infancy, we have certain kinds of angels with us, then different ones in childhood, and then different ones again as teenagers; as we go through the stages of life, we're changing these spiritual associations (*Heaven and Hell* 295). So even there, it is not like we're locked in; but some of the people that you've been treating, Bob, have been stuck for a long time. Or they've had this thing in there for, you know, twenty years or something. Or even multi-generationally, which is incredible.

Bob: What the importance is, the clinical importance—that this isn't just some intellectual, heady discussion about this idea of porosity and the idea that there's stuff inside of us that's not part of us, or our personal life history—is that you treat it very differently.

We welcome everything that is from our own lifetime. It might be carrying all these burdens. It might be a raging addict; it might be suicidal; but we welcome it, and we help it shed those burdens.

For stuff from outside of us, we help move on. So it's a very, very, very different thing.

I think that's the most significant reason to know about this, because a lot of people who don't know about unattached burdens try to integrate them into the person's system. That's like burying a parasite deeper into the person's soul. I think that's the crucial difference.

Dick's most recent book is titled *No Bad Parts*. That's true—there are no bad parts of you. But he is not upfront about the fact that there's also stuff in there that's not part of you. And that's where you need the idea of porosity.

Chelsea: There's this concept that Swedenborg describes, and this connects to "who do you meet in the inner world," which is that we have associate spirits. He often uses that term: our "associate spirits." He makes a distinction between those spirits who are associated with us versus these spirits that come in with an agenda and want to get something out of us (see *Secrets of Heaven* 6189–6204). One analogy might be that associate spirits are like the bacteria that is always on our skin, and we need it to live, while the other kind seems like a foreign microorganism that causes us harm.

He says that the ones that are just with us—our associate spirits—are just like our own personal aura. Those are the spirits who are just happily in the flow of our love and connected to our parts. But they are distinct from these entities, these UBs, these other spirits that try to manipulate us.

Bob: Spiritists and spiritism have this idea of soul groups. This sounds like the associate spirit idea.

What you can tell about unattached burdens is, they're parasites. They feed off negative emotions, and they do their best to create far more food for themselves. The images I've seen in people's minds are of coma farms or farms of spirits that have shackles and chains on their ankles and are being made miserable, so there's lots of food for the UBs; in whatever representation, they're clearly parasitic and are feeding off human negativity and pain. So that's quite different from the soul group and really different from guides. Even though they are known to disguise themselves as guides.

The classic archetype would be the antichrist. What does Swedenborg say about the antichrist?

Jonathan: Interesting. He does not talk about it much. He doesn't believe in the classic antichrist idea.

Chelsea: For Swedenborg, all of hell—the energy of hell—is the opposite of what is divine love. You can think of hell as one giant burdened system.

Bob: How does he envision the highest, most intelligent, most devastating energy of hell?

Chelsea: He says just like how heaven all at once looks like a single human being, hell all at once looks like a single monster. But then it has these levels to it, which are full of all the different spirits who have aligned themselves with that energy.

Jonathan: Sometimes he sees groups of spirits turn into a big lion, or take on a form that's larger than themselves.

Bob: This idea you two are talking about now is super important. This is parts in the whole; parts and Self. That's the distinguishably one concept again. I think that is more of a core mystery than consciousness.

Jonathan: I love your insight about that, because everybody's sweating about the consciousness thing. But this is beyond that; the personhood question: where do you begin and end?

Bob: All living systems are semipermeable. They have these semipermeable membranes around them. If you look at modern physics, our bodies are 99.99 percent empty space.

Auras of Connection

Chelsea: It might be useful to say a bit more about auras. In physical terms, everything has an energetic vibration. You can feel your pulse, for example. But Swedenborg is saying something spiritual happens that way as well. He writes how love is what unites everyone in the other world.

> Heaven is divided into many overall communities and into smaller subgroups, but goodness still unifies them. Religious truth there accords with goodness, because it has goodness as its origin and its goal. If heaven were divided up along the lines of religious truth, not of goodness, it would cease to exist. There would be no unanimity, because the Lord could not give the inhabitants unity of life, or a unified soul. This is possible only where there is goodness, which is to say, where there is love for the Lord and love for one's neighbor. After all, love unites everyone, and when each individual loves what is good and true, it is common ground received from the Lord that unites them all. Therefore it is the Lord himself who does so. Love for goodness and truth is

> what is called love for one's neighbor, because one's neighbor is a person with goodness and therefore truth. In an abstract sense, one's neighbor is goodness itself and the truth that goes with it. (*Secrets of Heaven* 4837)

Love is like a vibration, and that's how you get associated with other spirits. That's how you get "distinguishably one." Your love leads you to and creates the connection; love is what unites us.

That's why our freedom is so critically important. Swedenborg makes these claims and then IFS, to me, makes it so practical because you're using the ideas in a way that creates effective change for people.

Bob: Going back to the vibrations you were talking about, Chelsea. There's now hard scientific evidence behind this: hyperscanning. The brain-monitoring technology—fMRIs, EEGs, a bunch of them—is so advanced, researchers can put something that looks like a bathing cap on and they can scan your brain as you're walking around the room.

Scientists have done experiments in which they bring a bunch of people together and scan them all at once. These are called hyperscanning experiments.[67] The brain has a rhythm, and certain parts of its electrical field are doing certain rhythms at certain times. If two people are talking to each other, their brains' rhythms start to entrain; they start to match each other. If the two people make eye contact, the entrainment is much more powerful.

If the two people love each other—ooh!

They've done studies with storytellers. If it's a good storyteller, the audience entrains to the storyteller's brain. Then afterward,

---

67 Alejandro Pérez Fernández, Manuel Carreiras, and Jon Andoni Duñabeitia, "Brain-to-brain entrainment: EEG interbrain synchronization while speaking and listening," *Scientific Reports* 7, no. 1 (2017): 4190.

when they do tests of comprehension and recall, the ones who entrained the best have better recall.

They can also go the other way around, which is truly amazing. You can show people the brain scans and then can go, this one was talking to this one; this one, no. So there's powerful evidence of rhythmic entrainment of electrical fields around our brain when we interact. That's just one piece of evidence.

There are several others. They've been trying to figure out how psychedelics work. The main thing is, psychedelics downregulate the default mode network, but there are other people who think psychedelics influence brain rhythms.

Psychedelics might function by helping the inner brain synchronize with itself in terms of rhythmic fluctuations. This points in a really revolutionary direction. Consciousness may not depend on neurons and synapses; it might depend on the fluctuation of these fields and rhythmic entrainment. The most striking evidence of that is a professor at NYU named Rodolfo Llinás.[68] He's the world's expert on the physiology of the thalamus. He developed this theory that a lot of brain dysfunction comes from what he called "thalamo-cortical dysrhythmias." Basically, he came to believe that certain areas of the thalamus should be giving off electrical fields that synchronize with certain areas of the neocortex. This is measurable. He developed ways to stick electrodes deep into the thalamus and stimulate it.

Daniel Siegel has developed this whole field of interpersonal neurobiology. He says that our primary way to regulate our internal world is through our connection to others. That fits with what the hyperscanning studies are finding. And it all fits back with these other studies about the internal synchronization of rhythmical pulsations of our electrical fields, which goes back to vibrations.

---

68 Rodolfo R. Llinás, *I of the Vortex: From Neurons to Self* (Cambridge: MIT Press, 2002).

Chelsea: I've heard about how our nervous systems regulate; that it's the proximity to somebody else who is in a state of a regulated nervous system that we then map on ourselves. It's like the mirror neurons kind of thing. But what you're saying takes it to another level of that vibration, which I feel is perfect to bring up for this conversation to get a sense of what Swedenborg is describing, not in material terms, but that there's something—what Swedenborg calls spiritual substance—that is operating in this same way, and that is what is inside of us.

When we go inside—when we go into the inner world—that's how things are operating there.

So we ask the question to Swedenborg, "What is possession?" In one sense, we are always possessed by spirits. You have to start actually making distinctions within the word *possession* because it's really about what the nature of the possession is. If we're possessed by good spirits and angels, then everything's good. That's sort of like how we're designed to be; we can't avoid having this interrelationship going on. But of course, we usually use possession in negative terms, which Swedenborg would describe as a possession by the quality of a negative aura, the negative energy hell, of what's not loving, that then either enters our system in the form of burdens, which is through association, and in that case the evil spirits don't know that they're with us. Even the evil associate spirits that are with us are there for our purification, balance, and comparison, as we discussed earlier. But beyond that, we can get into the circumstance that a spirit is manipulating a part or parts of us in a conscious way. Swedenborg says that evil spirits dwell in our affections, that is, in our emotions, feelings, and desires (*Heaven and Hell* 295). It sounds so much like what you describe in your book, Bob, about how exiles that have feelings of shame or longing for belonging, companionship, will bond with a UB who is offering a sort of counterfeit version of those things.[69]

---

69 Falconer, *The Others Within Us*, 94.

Jonathan: Part of what I think makes the difference is what their purpose is. You know who they are. It's part of the nature of the angels that they support your freedom. They don't want to interfere. They're just there to help; they are a benevolent presence. Whereas what these certain kinds of evil spirits are doing is more like marauding for their own gain. They're not there to support your sense of freedom.

Swedenborg talks about changes of state in the brain (*Divine Providence* 279, 319). What he describes seems to line up with the changing brain rhythms you described, Bob. It has struck me for years in performance situations. You get a concert or an opera or something like that, and all these people file in and they're all in their own separate headspace. If the performance is really awesome, though, you reach a certain point when people say you could hear a pin drop; it's as if everybody holds their breath at the same instant. That whole room has turned into one organism. I think it must have something to do with what you're talking about. The brains are in sync. Something happens and you can tell in a way; everybody can tell we were all one. It's been amazing to me to see how that oneness can happen with any random group of people, under the right circumstances. They can come together and have that moment. And it feels great.

Chelsea: Swedenborg describes something very similar to this which he calls gyres or choirs or choral circles. He says that's how people get organized and get in the same flow (*Secrets of Heaven* 3350, 5182). And it's through this sort of amazing way which also sounds like the brain rhythms and entrainment on a collective scale. Swedenborg also describes the flow and movement of energy in the brain: "A perceptible view of its flow or circular motion was granted to me, the demonstration lasting several days. From this experience I could tell that the form of the brain matches the pattern of movement in heaven" (*Secrets of Heaven* 4041). He's describing this before there was any instrument to detect it besides his own interoception. He says that is the pattern of heaven that's implanted in us.

But again, if we are living in a world of that vibration, what do I do with that information? IFS gives us a pathway: you center in Self and ask your parts to unblend, and amazing things can happen.

Bob: It's important to recognize that our membranes are semi-permeable often in a very good way. We can work with this kind of resonance and rhythmic entrainment in a way that's beneficial to everybody.

But jumping back to how we tend to think of possession as a negative thing, in my research, that's just modern twentieth-century America, and even here it's not really true.

There is much more energy devoted to trying to establish contact with good spirits. You think of all the hours in prayer and all the meditation groups and on and on and on. That way outweighs the "let's get rid of the parasites" negative possession. But we tend not to use the word possession for contact with good spirits.

I think we need a word for that. Tanya Luhrmann uses the phrase spiritual presence experiences;[70] that term overarches the whole spectrum, which is useful because I think they're fundamentally and structurally the same experience. And we miss this when we label one as possession and bad, and the other as God-contact and good.

Jonathan: This is just a quick interjection, but the fact that solitary confinement can be so destructive to so many people's mental health supports that, doesn't it? That some people can somehow hang on, but a lot of people are never the same.

---

70 Tanya Marie Luhrmann, Kara Weisman, Felicity Aulino, Joshua D. Brahinsky, John C. Dulin, Vivian A. Dzokoto, Cristine H. Legare et al., "Sensing the Presence of Gods and Spirits Across Cultures and Faiths," *Proceedings of the National Academy of Sciences* 118, no. 5 (2021): e2016649118, https://doi.org/10.1073/pnas.2016649118.

Bob: It permanently cripples some people; however, there are other people who it almost turns into saints.

You look at the yogis in Tibet, where they get locked in a cave with no light and nothing for three years, three months, three weeks, three days, and three hours. And they come out of there saints. Nelson Mandela in South Africa was locked in solitary confinement for most of his twentysomething years in prison, and what happened to his soul?

I think when there's nothing around you for your internal rhythms to resonate with, whatever is in there is going to get way exaggerated; it's going to run off the rails.

Jonathan: I've assumed the ones who turn into saints are able to connect with something within, because I think it's equally important that they're connected to something, but they're able to find a resource. I even read a story years ago about someone (it might have been Terry Anderson in Lebanon) who was held hostage on threat of death for years. It was very trying. He never knew when it was going to end. When he was back safe and sound, he was very grateful but said that he still sometimes missed the presence of God that he had felt in captivity.

So he was very close to something, but I don't know what that difference is.

What You Let in through the Gates

Jonathan: Going back to Swedenborg's description of spirits, they fall into a couple of categories. There's a whole bunch of them around him. And I just found interesting evidence that they were not even all European (*Secrets of Heaven* 5858). They were saying they knew his language. And he remarked that it was interesting that they only knew the same amount that he knew about his language; they didn't know any more than that. They didn't actually know that language. They were just using his knowledge of it.

But he had this group that he was with, and some of them were unsavory types, but he said, it's not only not harmful, it's also beneficial to be around them under the right conditions. He had thousands of these spirits around him. But then there were these other ones who came in and inflicted pain in his teeth or caused him to not be able to think, or gave him pain in his groin or his bones. And so it does seem like there are two different kinds; there's his own associate spirits and this other kind that attacks. I don't know what you'd call them to distinguish them, and I don't know that anybody's really studied this in that way.

Bob: Clinically, I've come to believe that there's only one portal or one doorway, and you either pull the veil aside and you're open to both the good and the bad, or you close the veil down. In other words, it's hard to make the membrane selectively permeable. What does Swedenborg say about that?

Chelsea: Swedenborg uses the image of a city to describe our minds; there are gates to the city that can be open or closed. Some face in a heavenly direction, others a hellish direction. Going on a bit of a tangent here, what determines the openness and the porosity to the hellish ones is letting in the stuff from heaven: we can open the gates to heaven in our minds, and that comes in, and then that allows us to close the gate to hell. If that's happened, the spirits still can come up to the gate, but they're not allowed to come into the city anymore.

But you can still communicate with them through the gate. Those qualities of love that are coming in from the divine make you safe. The quality of what creates safety in the inner world, in terms of possession, is the love that we have. In IFS, they talk about needing to have a critical mass of Self-energy present before it's safe to work with parts. You don't want to start messing with the system if you don't have enough Self-energy present. It can backfire on you.

Swedenborg says a similar thing, that in his time period it wasn't safe for people to go into the inner world as much as it was in the past because he said there was so much hatred inside (*Heaven and Hell* 249; *Secrets of Heaven* 784, 9438, 10751). I found that so remarkable because the nature of evil spirits is to just hate other people. If you're full of self-hatred inside, you have to build up resources or fill a reservoir of love and compassion, and then you'll be able to safely be in the inner world and do work there.

Jonathan: At the end of Ezekiel, there's amazing stuff about this temple that the prophet envisions in the future (Ezekiel 44), and about how the gate will be open to the east. To Swedenborg, the east means love.

Swedenborg often quotes the line we shared earlier, "Let your word be yay, yay, nay, nay" (Matthew 5:37). He describes his spiritual process of trying to assess the nature of the input. Is this good? Is it contributing to peace or is it teaching me something I need to know? Is it just trying to belittle me?

Through his veil, he definitely gets both kinds of input, but he's doing a lot of "no" to this and "yes" to that. That's how he sees his function in a way: through doing a lot of yessing and no-ing, he feels that he becomes more and more himself. People would argue with him saying there must be nothing left of you—what are you if you're just saying yes and no to whatever is flowing in? And he said that he was finally more himself than ever (*Revelation Explained* 1147:3).

Bob: Let me try and summarize this and clarify it. In Swedenborg's thinking, there definitely are separate gates to the city, but the process of opening one gate and closing another is a complex, long-term thing. You have to learn and develop. We can't give people three or four bullet points that will help them do this.

Jonathan: I think that's accurate. And I think in a way, his explanation of the whole reason for God coming into the world embodied in Jesus was to be able to create a safe way to connect with heaven that didn't also bring the hells right in. Basically, the way he describes it, there was a time in ancient times when people were very open to both influences, and it got to the point when it was worse to have both open than to have none. And so it shut down, because that's better than having evil spirits running amok with the human race. I don't mean shut down in the sense that nothing would happen, but I think there was much more connection in these ancient cultures, as much as there are in some of the non-Western cultures that you talk about in your book.[71]

The whole accomplishment of Jesus coming into the world was to set it up so that being close to the Lord, having some sort of connection with the Lord, would provide safety. Even if you're walking through the valley of the shadow of death, as Psalms 23 puts it, you're fearing no evil because you've got this presence with you; which to me relates a lot to the way that the Self allows you to deal with these things that are really trying to scare you and have successfully scared the client.

Bob: Can I summarize this to see if I've got you? In Swedenborg's thinking, a major reason Jesus showed up was to help us open the gates toward heaven without opening up the gates toward hell.

Jonathan: Yes. Or even if the gates of hell are open, the Bible says they will not prevail against "the church" (Matthew 16:18); according to Swedenborg, the church means a person's heart and mind. This is ironic because even a lot of readers of Swedenborg have been uncomfortable with anything about spiritism, while in a healthy way, according to Swedenborg, if you have a purpose, that's exactly what heaven on earth is; it's what we're going for—we want and need to have that connection now. He warns against the dangers of messing around with no purpose in that realm, but a lot of what he lays out is how to get that connection, what it feels like when you've got it, and how you

71 Falconer, *The Others Within Us*, 197–222.

can tell when you don't have it. So I think that is a big part of his project too.

Chelsea: What I take away from Swedenborg on this is that there is a protective mechanism that is built into the way we're designed. To shut off the inner world, to have our consciousness only focused on the outer world is a protection that can be necessary when you don't have enough connection to love. Swedenborg says when Jesus came into the world, redemption was "a matter of gaining control of the hells, restructuring the heavens, and by so doing preparing for a new spiritual church," or religious environment (*True Christianity* 115). All of that was so that enough spiritual light could get into our collective consciousness, so it would be safe to go inside again. So you could open up, and there'd be more connection to love.

There's a developmental piece to this. Earlier, Bob, you said you think learning how to navigate this realm is our only real safety and is the source of our healing (see p. 64). I think developmentally, in early childhood, and especially in infancy, we are totally open. As we grow older, we are meant to be outward focused, as a safety protocol, since we are just full of whatever we were given, whatever came into us from heredity and spiritual association; we don't know what's going on on the inside, and we've got all kinds of devils in there and attachments and all this kind of stuff, but not the tools yet to deal with it.

But then when we have enough of a sense of self, when we have our own rationality—that term he uses to mean our ability to make the yay/nay choice—then our purpose, meaning, healing, and everything is to start going in and sifting through all the junk that's there, and find all the gold, basically evaluating those connections that we find. In IFS, it's getting to know our parts and seeing what's in our inner world. Even if you don't think in any of those terms, it's about reflecting on the thoughts and feelings that are flowing in, assessing their quality, and deciding what we want to act on.

This is the design of our development. It's a useful context to know when you need to bring into balance a system that's been infiltrated in devastating ways, but it is also the developmental process for us to go into our inner world, get to know ourselves, start to make choices, and exercise our freedom.

Bob: Many of the spiritists believe that the more light you shed in this world, the more you will be attacked by demons or whatever we want to call them. Does that come up in Swedenborg? Anything like that?

Jonathan: Yes, he definitely talks about how you face challenges. First of all, there's no point in you going under assault if you're just going to cave. Under the care of divine providence, which as Swedenborg says, is a constant force in reality, there'd be no point. You need a certain understanding, I would say "ego strength," before you go through things like this. And then the first of what he calls temptations, or trials, or crises of the spirit, are of the mind. They're more intellectual, about who God is or who you are, on an intellectual level. They can be quite painful. You're no longer sure that what you thought was true is true. Later on, it becomes about the heart, and those are really, really intense, because that's attacking what you love. So that's a different level that he says comes later.

So it does tend to build over time. Like, "Congratulations, you got to level three, now you get a more painful experience." Ha! But it's always monitored. It's always regulated. It's a spiritual process and is always only as much as is beneficial or can be beneficial to you. There's no senseless torment just for the heck of it—even though it can feel that way!

Working with Porosity

Jonathan: Swedenborg doesn't lay out a recipe in a specific way of saying, "Hey friends, here's how to deal with your evil spirit problem." He tends to show you himself functioning in those situations and how he's feeling, or what he's saying, and what's going on. Then in other passages, where he's not talking about evil spirits, he says, it's all about love. Secondarily, it's about faith; it's primarily about being a good person.

You have to piece this kind of thing together from what Swedenborg says, but I've gathered that your purpose is very, very important in navigating the inner realm and interacting with the porosity you find there.

I think it's both that you're approaching this from a kind of love and also that you have a clarity of "What are we doing here? We're trying to help this person." That's part of what protected Swedenborg. He talks a lot about purpose and how important it is. He says the highest angels have to do with purpose, and the middle angels have to do with means and the method, and the outer angels have to do with results.

Chelsea: Love is purpose, wisdom is the means, and usefulness is the result. The purpose of the divine, according to Swedenborg, is to save the human race. It's interesting to reflect on that being the purpose of Self, too, if those two equate. How do you save the human race? By connecting to love. Swedenborg talks about love and intention so similarly. Love is this power, this driving force, that has an intention. And divine love's intention is to save us, which means to free us from evil and falsity.

Jonathan: It's not just a feeling.

Chelsea: I think that's really interesting to connect with Self. In IFS, I've heard it said that Self doesn't have an agenda, but it really does: the agenda of Self is healing. In an emergent way, Self spontaneously knows how to accomplish healing in the moment. It has all the wisdom necessary to do that.

Jonathan: I found a passage the other day that said that divine love is exactly that. It is the desire to save the entire human race

(*Secrets of Heaven* 2253, 6495:1). That's it. It's not like it's this, and that, and six other things. That's it.

Chelsea: Swedenborg says we become our authentic selves when we align our will with the divine will. So we participate in the purpose to be helping, to be assisting in that saving.

Jonathan: That's something we do with our own freedom and our own apparent autonomy, to say, "I choose to align myself with this"; that's what's binding on earth. And then things get bound in heaven.

Bob: It could be of immense value if you guys could pull up specific recommendations from Swedenborg about how to learn to do this yes and no process—how to learn how to open the gates to the east and close down all the other ones.

Chelsea: Swedenborg has so much interesting stuff about how to do this or that, but you really have to piece it together from what he says. He is not exactly didactic; rather, he's describing the territory.

Jonathan: A lot of people who go to the other world think that you should avoid evil spirits at all costs. They were sort of horrified that Swedenborg had thousands of them around him at all times. But I happen to think those spirits were probably also very funny. He probably enjoyed them to a certain point; they're amusing.

Bob: I don't think you can avoid them.

Jonathan: I think it was very instructive, because parts of himself are the connection points. The evil spirits help to bring out what we might not be aware of. Our connection to evil spirits can activate under certain circumstances. Then you get to see, "Oh, I totally have X in there." I think it's for their benefit as well, as you say in your book, Bob; as you're dealing with the UB, you're also trying to head them in the right direction.

Bob: Yeah.

Chelsea: To your point that we can't avoid them: we're surrounded. Swedenborg describes how their presence is necessary for our freedom. We talked about evil as burdens before, but the same is true of evil spirits in general. We really do need to always have both so that we can be developing our sense of self through our choices.

Bob: A Tibetan lama helped me. He did some empowerment ceremonies for me, to support my work. One of the things he said was that evil spirits are like bugs outdoors at night. "They're always here, but they don't bother me anymore." He was just waving his hand. "They're always here."

He said, "It's no surprise that bugs come to light. The more you do good work in the world, the more bugs. No problem."

In the IFS world, and in my world, the number one safety is whether you are scared of them. The fear. It's not so much hate; it's fear. The number one way to work with negative spirits is to find any parts who are scared. You don't shut them down. You love them up and welcome them in. And then look for more parts who are scared. What does Swedenborg say about fear in relation to the demons?

Jonathan: In his own stories of his spiritual experiences, he often mentions not being afraid. He quotes that scripture that I think comes up a number of times in the Old Testament about how they shall lie down and none shall make them afraid (Leviticus 26:6, Psalm 4:8, Proverbs 3:24, Isaiah 17:2, Zephaniah 3:13).

He talks about times when he does find the spirits kind of terrifying. I'm thinking of one time where an evil spirit comes up, and they are outside the house. He's inside the house. He closes the window. He still talks to them, but he closes the window (*True Christianity* 80).

The way he puts it in his Christian vocabulary is that the Lord kept him safe. "They couldn't harm a hair on my head," he says, which is another Biblical expression that he often mentions. It seems like he attributes that to the Lord, like a blessing that protects him in that situation. He talks about people trying to hurt him, but they can't. Eventually they'll be taken away, but he'll still get to see, "Wow, the hate is really coming in here," or "They're really trying to do this or that to me." He is witnessing it.

Chelsea: In these passages about communicating with spirits on the other side, he writes that you have to have that safety inside. Safety is goodness and a belief in the Lord. We can be raised to heaven only through goodness inspired by love and faith. So he says that's what creates this safety (see *Secrets of Heaven* 6724). The presence of love creates safety, and then there's no fear. You can turn that into the practice that you do so beautifully in IFS, where you look for where the fear is, and you take that as an indication that it's lacking love. Ask yourself, "How do we bring that presence of Self to those places?" Then that affects the transformation. IFS says in practical terms what Swedenborg is saying in conceptual terms.

The Nature of Evil Spirits

Bob: I want to talk about the honesty of evil spirits. I don't think they're honest, but there's one question they seem to have to answer honestly, and that's, "Are you a part of me?"

For some reason it doesn't seem they can lie about that one. I was saying that as an absolute fact one time in one of my lectures. A very powerful woman from Nigeria with a deep voice yelled out, "They lie! They lie!" I asked her more about that. She said, "They lie about everything. And they can lie about that too. And sometimes they've been in people, and people's families, for so many generations, they've forgotten who they really are."

Jonathan: I think, in some cases, they truly believe themselves, so they're not lying in that sense, even though what they're saying is lies. They have an agenda.

I'm interested in this business of an honest world after death (see p. 29) and how exactly that works. Part of the way Swedenborg describes it is that you can tell when they're lying by the sound of their voice. They just don't sound right. So there are signals. They have the option of being quiet or saying something, but in that world, you can't just lie through your teeth in the same way the material world allows us to.

I'm still working on understanding how honesty works in the other world because there's such a commitment to dishonesty on the part of evil spirits—they're very fond of particular lies about reality. Some of the spirits Swedenborg talks to are so bold as to tell him that God checks with them before assigning people to heaven and hell (see *True Christianity* 660:7–10). That's the way that they see everything, and they firmly believe it; they'll be honest about that. But it's ridiculous.

An additional point I want to throw in real quick, because I think it does figure into IFS work, is that Swedenborg says that no matter how committed evil spirits are to what is evil, their intellect is always capable of being raised up. He's able to have conversations with them where they have some perspective. I felt that from some of your sessions, that at some point they're able to get the perspective of, "No, actually I'm not essential to this person. Actually, I have nothing to do with them."

Chelsea: I think with the honesty of evil spirits and demons, it might be less that they are honest, but more that they have to be so in the presence of heaven's light—in the presence of Self, in the presence of those qualities; it is so perceptive that you can't be fooled. The more Self-energy that you have, the more this is the case. The evil spirits might think they're being deceitful, and parts can be gullible to that—parts can believe that. Swedenborg says the way things appear is part of the issue. What leads to falsity is that we believe that things are the way that they appear. We're always having to interface with this falsity of appearance. But in *Secrets of Heaven* 1640, he says if they're deceitful, these spirits, "then the general and specific type of their deceit can be detected in every word and thought even if they're not lying at the moment." So even if they're telling something true, if they're just a deceitful person, it comes across.

And he says it's true of all other vices and obsessions. Even before they've said anything, you can feel that they're deceitful. It's just the way that thought translates in the inner world.

Bob: I think that applies only if you're closely connected with Jesus in Swedenborg's language or profoundly in Self, in IFS language.

Jonathan: He has a chapter in *Heaven and Hell* on the powers of angels (228–233), and one of the points he makes is that they can see through whatever deceitful spirits are up to (*Heaven and Hell* 229).

Bob: I've lost battles with UBs or whatever we should call them, and the people have chosen to believe the UBs. The metaphor that works best for me for the attachment to many of the UBs is cocaine or meth addiction. There's a big rush and then an even bigger payback.

Jonathan: Yes. They're feeding off that negative energy. Sometimes I feel like I can feel it in myself. I'm in a bad mood, and I can feel that something wants me to stay in here and is kind of talking trash in my head and wants to keep the party going. Swedenborg talks about spirits that can drain you so much that you can't get out of bed (*Secrets of Heaven* 5721:2, 5722).

Bob: I think the connection to these negative spirits is the archetype of addiction.

Jonathan: There's a lie in it somewhere. You get something out of it, but then the cost is higher; it goes up and you get less of it next time, and you become more and more enslaved. Swedenborg talks about that slavery. You're just enslaved to this thing, and they don't care about you (*Secrets of Heaven* 2890, 6390:1, 8293).

Chelsea: Swedenborg says, when describing repentance, that you begin by reflecting on yourself; you begin sifting through the stuff inside and deciding what you want and don't want to be active in you and in your behavior. He makes the point that our behavior in the physical world holds a lot of power for our spiritual associations. Action on this outermost level has an impact. One of the key ways that we start shifting stuff in our inner world is to start using our choice, our determination, and our agency to change our behavior in the outer world. Then that loosens the control of whatever sort of inner demons might be influencing us that we're not aware of. That creates a certain level of safety that gets deeper and deeper.

You may get to the point of having a very good-looking outward behavior, in terms of how you act in the world, but then you start looking at the inner level, at your inner intentions. He says it's very natural at first to become overwhelmed by all the evil you find in yourself. Maybe you go inside, and you find parts who aren't willing to let go.

Part of something that Swedenborg says that's helped me is that it's meant to take a while, and it's this very, very careful surgery that divine providence is orchestrating. In the same way that we have parts, and Self is working with them, we are part of the divine, and the divine is never forgetting about us and all of our parts. Trust the process. It's okay for things not to suddenly be turning a corner. That's not a reason to lose hope.

Jonathan: A lot of people in a Christian context think, *Okay, Jesus, take all my evils away*. Swedenborg says if that were to happen all in an instant, we would fall down dead. Angels will actually defend some of our evils (*Secrets of Heaven* 761). They'll sometimes actually keep that in place because we're not ready yet. I found that idea challenging when I encountered it, but it makes sense in this context that higher wisdom knows when you're really ready. What astounds me is that, when there's a letting go, there's a real letting go. It's not like "I'll be back in three days." It changes the relationship.

Chelsea: One thing about the levels of our mind is that we are never seeing the whole story. Our consciousness is aware of maybe only one level, but there's a whole process going on in the deeper levels that impacts what's happening on the lower levels. There's a purpose to things being the way that they are. At those times, when something just isn't going the way that we think it should, we can consider letting go of what we think should happen.

Sometimes there might be a protection in some sort of evil staying attached, because that holds part of our spiritual life and we're just not ready to connect to love more deeply. He says the feeling of love is incredibly painful and even torturous to parts of us, or rather to the evil in us, which might be a burden or a UB. If there's a lot of that in us, then it'd be the most unkind thing to suddenly push somebody into a love-filled room.

Jonathan: Swedenborg hints that we should pick one thing at a time (*True Christianity* 525). I don't know how that relates to IFS practice, but it sounds like it's sort of focused on one area per session; that's plenty of change.

Bob: The unattached burdens are actually doing us a big favor. I compare them to the ants in the kitchen. The ants are obviously not trying to help, but they show you exactly where you spilled the food. They can't help themselves. I think in that sense, you don't want to rip these things away and leave all the spilled food. The UBs will show us all the parts who are really hurt, really vulnerable, really needy. They'll lead us there with this incredible radar that they have, because that's their food. They need that to survive. So they are good at finding that. We can make use of that, and therefore we wouldn't want to just rip these things out.

Jonathan: It really shows you, okay, here's an area that needs some help.

Chelsea: And it's serving a critical role in maintaining a balance. I think that's a good word for what Swedenborg means by our freedom. Even if we have these attachments to evil and falsity, they are critical to the whole picture of us, for a time, as we're going through this incremental change.

Jonathan: As we said, one of the functions of evil is fermentation. He'll say how an evil spirit will come into a group, and then it'll draw certain impurities to itself. It'll bring things out and clarify the group (*Divine Providence* 25; *Revelation Explained* 677:3; *Spiritual Experiences* 1054, 5222). We actually get some benefit from that presence that we wouldn't have without it. That's not what you instinctively think about evil spirits.

Bob: You know what this reminds me of? Remember, like back in the 1930s, the medical community used to think the ideal environment was totally sterile. Completely wrong. We need bacteria all around us. And now in hospitals, they have these things that introduce good bacteria into the air systems. Totally sterile environments create dysbiosis, which makes us incredibly ill. So we need that.

Chelsea: Perfect. It serves a purpose for a time, even though ultimately, it's like, "No, this is not love. There's something bigger, and you'll get to that."

Keys to Finding Freedom and Safety from Demons

Bob, you were saying fear is an indication of a part not feeling safe. And then we discussed how you need to connect to love to become safe. Swedenborg writes in *Secrets of Heaven* 6202 about spirits he sensed in the area of his stomach. These spirits flooded him with worries. He could tell where the worries came from. These greedy spirits flooded him with anxious concern about the future. He says, "I was allowed to scold them, telling them that they correlate with stomach contents that are undigested, bad smelling, and therefore nauseating."

So he has this inclination to scold the spirits, right? And then the next sentence, he says, "I also saw them driven away and when they were gone, the worrying stopped completely." So it didn't stop when he scolded them, it seems. He puts it in a passive action—that they were driven away. He explains in other places that the only thing that drives evil spirits away is the presence of love. One example is *Secrets of Heaven* 1398:

> There were quite a few spirits around me who were not good. An angel came, and I saw that the spirits could not bear his presence, since the nearer he came, the farther away they went. I was surprised but was able to see that they could not linger in the aura that he carried with him. This too showed me, as other experiences have done, that one angel can drive away tens of thousands of evil spirits, since evil spirits cannot abide an atmosphere of mutual love. Still, I could tell that his aura was being moderated by his associations with others. If it had not been, all the spirits would immediately have scattered. This once again shows clearly what kind of perception exists in the other life, and it shows how people join together and separate in response to their perceptions.

When love is present, they leave of their own choosing. They're just like, I don't want to be anywhere near this.

So angels don't push evil spirits away, it's just the presence of love.

Jonathan: I just want to tack something onto the end of that. I just found a passage the other day where he has beautiful things to say about angels from the highest heaven just being able to walk through the hells.

> In the other life there are some who possess more truth than others. This gives them so much power that they can go anywhere in the hells without danger. At their presence the inhabitants of the hells flee in every direction. (*Secrets of Heaven* 8200)

I didn't remember him saying that before, but their presence of love is so great that it's just absolutely repellent to harmful intentions; nothing can touch them. They're unassailable.

Bob: Does Swedenborg have specific advice or direction for people who are dominated by demonic energies or have a great deal of that in them?

Jonathan: In Jerry Marzinsky's work, the primary thing seems to be to convince people that they are not the voices, and that the voices don't even have their best interests at heart. If people are really willing to see that gap, it's a game changer. His work is to help them learn how there's a distinction between them and this thing. That's the whole game, as far as I can tell. Getting connected with the Self is how that can even happen, but I love this insight about creating space; creating a gap between you and this thing.

Bob: I think this is key. Just the realization that we can have things in our mind that are not part of us can heal and reduce human suffering vastly. Yet, American academia and the therapeutic establishment resists this idea with everything they've got, and destroys the careers of people who dare espouse it.

I've seen people get healed from these possessions, or whatever you want to call them, just when they realize, "Oh, that's something foreign to my mind. It's not me. It's just like my obnoxious aunt who'd never shut up." That reduces the pain.

Chelsea: When we talk about the nature of UBs and what their tactics are, what to be on the lookout for is if you're feeling intense personal guilt and shame. You can pause and say, is this really coming from me? Swedenborg describes how evil spirits influence us to try to get us to feel that way. It feeds them for you to continue to believe the shame, and believe that there's no way out, and that you're just broken. That's their power—how they fool us. And this might be their influence into a burden a part of us has, or a UB, but in either case, the value is in recognizing that it's not really you.

Jonathan: Swedenborg talks a lot about what people go through after they die. Some of these processes are called devastations. There's a great passage in what I was recently editing about people who, in their earthly lives, had the basic attitude that the thing that they loved the absolute most was eating stolen meat (*Secrets of Heaven* 7248:1).

They would raid other people's land, steal their cattle, and then eat that. This was their chief delight. Then he watches those people being broken down and becoming spiritual (*Secrets of Heaven* 7250–7251). One of the key parts of devastations is that you get led to the depths of despair; reaching this point is what allows for the evil and falsity to be removed from your spirit. It's really, really intense what he describes.

There are things about coming to understand a particular truth. He's definitely big on the idea that the truth has the power to deal with these things. Using the truth in your mind to contrast against the negative messages can be helpful.

Chelsea: There's no giving up, there's no "all hope is lost." No matter how impaired a person might seem, or how completely overrun and devastated, probably the biggest thing that the demonic forces want to convince you of is that there's no hope. That's their biggest weapon: to say, "Don't even try."

No matter how full you are with them, they're not you. You are allowed at any time with your own consciousness to say,

"You are not me." Declare that with whatever shred of power you can muster, even if you don't believe it.

Sherry Swiney has the "That's a lie" program,[72] which is just to chant that mantra, "That's a lie. That's a lie," about whatever the demonic forces are telling you.

Bob: Strengthen that muscle. I think this thing you're saying about "not you" is super important, Chelsea, and I'm glad you're underscoring it, because one of the most important contributions of IFS is that parts are not their burdens. In therapy, everybody used to think the part was its burden, and we tried to amputate the part, and this caused nothing but bloodshed and disaster. So this realization that they're carrying something that's not theirs is crucial. It's very significant.

Chelsea: Swedenborg makes this distinction between temptations around truth and temptations around goodness and love. The attack on love—that's the demonic forces that really want to convince you that you don't matter. They get into your feelings. It can be helpful to know that they're going to make you feel like you really don't matter. They're going to make you feel like you have no connection to love. Whatever we feel, we think we are, and their attack on our feelings is the nastiest, toughest temptation or spiritual crisis. But that's where it's most critical to say, "I am not this," then you go through a slow process of actually getting to feel the reality of your connection to love eventually. That's the consolation that comes after the fact.

Jonathan: They're not you. All evil is from hell. All goodness is from heaven. Swedenborg keeps coming back to that again and again and again. We've talked about the inner self being undamageable. A lot of what those spirits are trying to do is to attach

---

72 Sherry Swiney, "The 'That's a Lie' Program," *Keyholejourney Blog*, July 21, 2016, https://keyholejourney.wordpress.com/2016/07/21/the-thats-a-lie-program/.

things that are not actually attached, to say, "There's only one of you, and you are this whole thing. You're this thing you did in the past," or, "You're this thing that somebody did to you." So the ideas of freedom and rationality, and how providence is playing a long game, can be helpful. Also Swedenborg says several times that it's possible to bring good out of everything: nothing's allowed to happen that cannot be turned to good (*Secrets of Heaven* 6572; *Spiritual Experiences* [38a]; *Divine Providence* 295). It can benefit you to emphasize that whatever is happening can have a good outcome.

Chelsea: Evil spirits will use how you feel against you, but there's power in saying, "This is not me," even when it doesn't feel that way. In *Secrets of Heaven* 4353:3, Swedenborg makes this point:

> The act comes first; our will to do it comes afterward. What we do at the urging of our intellect we eventually do with our will and finally take on as a habit. At that point it is infused into our inner, rational self. Once it has been infused, we no longer do what is good from truth but from goodness, because we start to feel a certain bliss and to sense something of heaven in it.

It is an important tool to understand you're not going to want to do this, but this is what you need to do. Take these actions, declare what you know is true, and eventually things shift.

Bob: There's a line in AA that captures that idea in their typical blunt way: "You can't think your way into a new way of acting, but you can act your way into a new way of thinking."

Chelsea: Swedenborg would say you act your way into a new way of willing, which is really an inflow of the divine will, experienced as your own.

Another point is that if somebody is feeling aware that they are overrun by demonic spirits, that's actually a good sign. If you're feeling okay, then it's invisible to you, but if you're feeling like, "I've got so much evil inside," that is evidence of an awareness you're having that is separate from the evil.

In *Secrets of Heaven* 3696:2 he says,

> At first, when we are being reborn, we experience a tranquil state, but as we enter into our new life, we also enter a disquieted state. The evil and falsity we previously absorbed emerge into the open and agitate us. In fact, we eventually suffer trials and harassment inflicted by the Devil's crew, which constantly strives to destroy our new life. Nonetheless, there is a state of peace at our center. If there were not, we would not fight. In the struggles we go through, we keep our eye on that state as the goal, and if we did not have it to aim for, we would never have the strength or power to fight. It is also owing to this vision that we conquer. Since it is our goal, it is also the state we enter after our struggles or trials.

If you're feeling like you're being harassed by "the devil's crew," that actually means you have this peace at your center, and you're already in a better state than you were before, on an inner level. It's counterintuitive because it still feels like crap.

Bob: I have another little slogan from AA for that: "The real moments of enlightenment are not 'aha' moments. They're 'oh no' moments."

Death and Rebirth

Chelsea: An aspect to porosity that could be useful to discuss is the subject of death. Porosity, in Swedenborg's terms, is such because there is life after death; there is a spiritual world we all enter when our physical life in the world ends, and that same spiritual world is what we are a part of right now via our consciousness. The spirits we interact with inside of ourselves right now are people who have died.

The nature of death is important to understand in order to grasp the nature of healing. In Swedenborg's terms, he describes the cycle of our rebirth, or our process of regeneration. He's using the Christian term, alluding to when Jesus told Nicodemus that he would need to be born again (John 3:3, 7). The cycle of our growth—of our healing—is always dying and rebirth. Swedenborg says that in "people who are regenerating, the Lord dawns in every moment" (see *Secrets of Heaven* 2405). I don't know if I hear people remark on it as much coming from just the healing standpoint, but maybe they do. It sounds counterintuitive, but healing actually means dying, while knowing that there's life after death. You experience renewal, and you are transformed and become a new thing. Swedenborg uses the image of a butterfly and says we can see "our earthly state in the caterpillars, and an image of our heavenly state in the butterflies" (*True Christianity* 12).

You might think dying and healing are opposites, yet spiritually speaking, dying is actually the healing process.

I'm curious about this in terms of IFS. I've experienced it personally, but I wonder in your experience, Bob, if parts often feel like they're dying when they're letting go of a burden. Or in the case of protectors, when they don't like the idea of letting go of the way they've been operating, it can feel like dying. Swedenborg says when angels hear mention of death, they think of life (*Last Judgment* 25). When there is enough Self-energy present, and the healing happens spontaneously and protectors are less reluctant to let go of their burdens, they just slough them off.

I've had parts who have felt like, "I'm going to surrender to death here," but then they are surprised that they don't cease to exist. They're bracing themselves, thinking everything's going to go away, but then they actually find life on the other side.

Bob: I love the metaphor of dying as a part of healing, and I don't think it's in IFS very much.

Dick is really concerned about making IFS academically acceptable. Death as healing is not academically acceptable these days. What he does talk about is unburdening, which is perhaps death of an identity, or something like that.

He sort of gets around it by framing it that way, instead of going right onto it. There's a man I really like named Eduardo Duran. He's a Native American psychologist who works mainly with PTSD clients. I just heard him talk about suicide. Suicide rates on the reservations are somewhere between twenty and a hundred times above the rest of the United States. He said suicidal thinking is all about transformation. He says suicidal thinking is a spirit: it's conscious, it has an intention, and it's also the spirit of transformation. So thoughts of death mean transformation: it's not about killing; it's about healing. Welcome it; it is visiting you. Ask its name, and offer it a gift. The presence of suicidal thoughts means the need for some way of life to die—the need for major transformation. He says it requires spiritual and ceremonial healing.[73]

Chelsea: In your own experience, clinically, do you find that the unburdening process, or maybe it's the surrendering of some protector parts, ends up even having a dying quality to it?

Bob: I have a meditation that I made up that is like this. I call it "dissolve." Basically, you have the person, or a part, go out to some beautiful place in nature, lie down, say goodbye to everything, let their body die and dissolve, and let all the flesh start dissolving off their bones. Then let the bones dissolve to sand. Your sense of identity doesn't disappear—it shifts to something larger. Does it shift to the sky? Or the land you're lying on? Or the horizon? What does it shift to? Let that dissolve and be an act of expansion. And then at the end of the meditation, come on back; bring the much larger sense of who you are back into you. And a lot of people find that very, very peaceful.

Jonathan: Another word that might be more acceptable to IFS that Swedenborg uses a lot in this context is "despair." He

---

73 Eduardo Duran, *Healing the Soul Wound: Trauma-Informed Counseling for Indigenous Communities* (New York: Teachers College Press, 2019).

says that it is important for these processes, especially the most intense, to continue to the point of despair because there's something you learn at that moment of despair (*Secrets of Heaven* 1787, 2694, 5279, 7155, 7166). People may pray to avoid the despair; they don't want to go there, but the despair is the magic.

He doesn't use that term for it, but that's where transformation happens quite quickly—that point of despair. I've certainly experienced that in my own life: I've longed for something, but then finally came to the sense that it was so hopeless that things were never going to change. I might as well just live with whatever it is, because all this desire I have for it to change has just amounted to nothing over all these years and all this effort. Often not right away, but a few weeks or months afterward is when I notice, "Oh, it changed."

Bob: In IFS language, that going to despair would be getting the managers to stop trying to do it. They get out of the way and let Self do it.

Jonathan: The managers are the ones who despair. Yeah, because they feel like they've failed. Right. All their managing effort hasn't worked.

Chelsea: It does seem like the managers are the ones who need to reach a point of despair and go through a dying process. When they're willing to let go, they find that Self is real, and they still exist. And there's the possibility for a fulfilling, expansive sense of who they are.

Bob: I think "die" scares a lot of people. If you want to scare new therapists, say "suicide." All their sphincters will tighten up and they'll behave like idiots.

Jonathan: That's right. It's visceral.

Bob: I have another story about this issue. Did I tell you guys the story of Milarepa?

Milarepa was a Tibetan monk, a famous monk yogi who had been a murderer and tried to reform. His lama gave him a very hard time and made him do all sorts of stuff. But anyway, he had this meditation cave high up in an inhospitable mountain. One time he went away to do yogi business, and when he came back, the cave was totally full of demons—nasty, nasty demons. He goes up to them and says, "Welcome, welcome." Half of them disappear just like that. Then he goes inside the cave, and only the bigger ones are left. He says, "Oh, let me make you dinner." He prepares them all food. With that, they all disappear except the worst one, the biggest one, with a green face, huge fangs, dripping saliva, all that stuff. So Milarepa looks at him, smiles, goes over, and puts his head in the demon's mouth. As soon as he does that, it too disappears.

Chelsea: The idea of putting your head in the demon's mouth—that's surrender.

Addictions

Bob: I want to go back to the subject of addiction for a moment. The problem with addictions is, they work.

I was working with a man once who'd been an alcoholic, and then a junkie, and then had been clean and sober for about sixteen years when I met him.

I said something about, "Well, you know, addictions work a little, and then they cause so much trouble." He started yelling at me, "You idiot! That disrespects the thinking and mind of every addict!"

The problem with addictions is they really do work. If you snort a lot of coke and drink a fifth of whiskey, you don't feel pain. You're out of the pain. You eat enough, you don't feel any pain. Then there's a big payback, and you have to keep increasing the dose. A lot of people don't care if it kills them. Does Swedenborg talk about anything parallel to addiction?

Jonathan: He does use the word addiction occasionally. What he says about internal possession seems to fit the bill. He talks about obsession and things like that. He says there are particular spirits who are very focused on the body or the outside layer, and that they need to be with people who are going through these things because that's what they love the most.

> Everything whatever that exists in a person's mental life and feelings, evil as well as good, has spirits, and societies of spirits, who exactly interact with it. Just one such case was, when I was taking pleasure in some unimportant details, either in regard to writing, or eating or drinking, or something else, like while buying things I had desired in times past, and for which I had acquired a liking. When those enjoyments recurred, then there were spirits, and societies of spirits, that had exactly the same enjoyment, so that they were much more desirous than I myself, even to the point that they could hardly control themselves, without almost perishing, if they were not indulged and given those things—even though they knew they were of no use to them, but to me. So there is not anything mental or emotional in a human being that does not have societies of spirits that indulge and favor it. (*Spiritual Experiences* 2169)

Bob: That's the spiritist understanding of addiction too.

Chelsea: For Swedenborg, though, he wouldn't isolate addiction as this certain category over here, but rather it's just the reality of what we're all dealing with all the time. Our urges and our desires even come from spirits with us. He describes it over and over again, being like, this spirit really wanted me to choose this teacup and not that teacup, and this spirit really wanted me to choose this piece of clothing and not that one.

He says to just pay attention. "Who wants that? Is it what you really want?" Any craving you have is definitely coming from spirits that are with you but then you get to decide, do I want to say yes? I want this to be me too. I'm going to choose this.

Or you can say, "Oh, these are just cravings that these spirits are flowing into me with." And then that opens up other possibilities for action and behavior.

Jonathan: I think you hit it on the head there with the word "craving." The Latin is *cupiditas*. There are several different words, but that's one of them that he uses, or *concupiscentia*, which means a strong and growing craving.

To him, people get addicted to thoughts.

Bob: "Polyaddiction." It's a relatively new phase of addiction treatment.

One thing I want to say about addiction that I think is super important diverges from IFS. Dick says the best way to recruit a guide is to be completely in Self. That's the safest way. You get all the parts to unblend, and that's how you get to Self. But in the 12-step tradition, and in many other traditions, people meet the higher power when they're absolutely destroyed; when they're in the gutter and they've lost everything, and everything has fallen into a pool of feces. That's where they meet guidance, and the higher power, and spirit, and all of that. So these two things don't fit together so easily.

Jonathan: Swedenborg talks a lot about what he calls temptations, which we've mentioned, which is not like, "Oh, I'm so tempted to try this." We've sometimes translated it as spiritual crises or trials. They are horrendous experiences that get you to that point of absolute despair. At the point of despair your strength fails (*Secrets of Heaven* 7155).

I often picture the end of a rope, when your ability to hang on fails; then you fall. He says you fall spiritually, and then God picks you up. I've reflected a lot on that because you learn a lot at that moment. There's a love there; there's something merciful when you had nothing. It wasn't because you were great or that you were doing everything right. It's when you're at your worst and you fall, and you can't sustain it anymore, and then something rescues you and picks you up. That is an awesome moment.

Bob: That sounds exactly like hitting bottom in AA.

Jonathan: Swedenborg says that these kinds of trials are the only way of a certain kind of spiritual advancement. They really help to break up that proprium that we were talking about earlier. Shake up your sense of identity and get you on a different footing; make you more open.

Chelsea: That was his firsthand experience. That was his process.

Another word he uses is the consolation that comes after you've gone through the despair. And that's this precious moment when there's an opportunity for falsity to be removed and fall away, and you've been softened to be able to accept goodness and love.

In a similar way to IFS, Swedenborg's paradigm also doesn't match with the Western idea of mental illness, because really anything that we're going through is some kind of spiritual trial or crisis. If there's suffering, it could be coming from environmental or spiritual world stuff, or it's your own active addictions or trauma, but it's all in this framework of what he calls regeneration; the process of rebirth or healing. Whatever happens, it's possible for healing to begin from that point.

> The state of rebirth for each of the senses, and for every attribute on the earthly plane, and for every attribute on the rational plane as well, has its progression from beginning to end. When it reaches the end, it starts all over, beginning with the final stage reached in the earlier state and continuing to a further goal—and so on. Eventually, the pattern switches, and what had been last becomes first. For instance, when both our rational and our earthly planes are being regenerated, the phases of our first state advance from truth that leads to faith to good that is done out of charity. The truth that brings faith seems to play the leading role, and good that

is done out of charity a supporting role, because religious truth looks to charitable goodness as its goal. These phases continue until we have been reborn. Charity, which had been the goal, then becomes the starting point, where new states commence, heading in two directions: deeper within and further outside. The new states move deeper within toward love for the Lord and further outside toward religious truth, continuing beyond that toward earthly and even sensory truth. This last kind of truth is then gradually reduced to correspondence with goodness from charity and love on the rational plane, and the process brings them into heavenly order.

That is what is meant by continuing advances and developments right to the end. These advances and developments are unending in people who are being reborn, stretching from their infancy all the way to the end of their life in the world, and beyond to eternity. Yet the process can never regenerate us to the point where we may be called perfect in any way. The elements needing rebirth on our rational and earthly planes are numerous and even limitless, and each of them has unlimited offshoots, or advances and developments, reaching both deeper inside and further outside.

We are completely unaware of this, but the Lord knows absolutely all of it and provides for it every moment. If he let up for just a second, all development would be disrupted. What comes first looks to what comes next in an unbroken chain and produces a series of consequences to eternity. Divine foresight and providence clearly covers the very smallest details, then. If it did not, or if it took only a general sort of care, the human race would perish. (*Secrets of Heaven* 5122)

Jonathan: He talks about the opportunity for rebirth or healing sometimes happening in connection with worldly crises too. You lose a job, or somebody dies.

There's a culture out there of "Be excellent, live your best life, be one hundred percent every day." But it doesn't take into account the kenosis aspect. Swedenborg writes a lot about "exinanition" or emptying out. Having been so exposed to his works, it makes me feel different about going through crises, because I feel that there is something good that could come out of this. It's not that God wills it, but rather that God can make it transformative.

The Spiritual Aspect of Physical Illness

Bob: People argue that a whole bunch of mental illnesses are organic in nature. There's some kind of biological cause. They say manic depression or schizophrenia has a biological thing going on, and therefore all you spiritual people are stupid and have your heads wedged somewhere where the sun doesn't shine.

I think there's some truth to there being a physical component. But I think it's much more like Dick with his asthma button and his migraine button that we discussed before (see p. 56). People who are high on the schizotypal scale have a button in there that their parts or spirits can push, and it will give them certain kinds of experiences. So this way, you get to have both the spiritual cause, the spiritual meaning, and the spiritual depth to all these experiences, and there's the biological side to it.

We all have a different set of buttons inside us. The citadel model of mind denies the spiritual side entirely.

Chelsea: These physical bodies are time-limited. Swedenborg had strokes toward the end of his life, and that's what took him out eventually.

There's a breakdown that happens undeniably in the physical body, but coming back to the centrality of us having freedom, there is also the potential for us to explore what spiritual healing is available to us through whatever we are experiencing. How can this be helping me in my life process? But it's not like you're missing something if you don't do that. There's just this spiritual potential to any of those buttons being pressed, which will have an impact beyond your earthly lifetime.

Jonathan: Swedenborg might say, if you want a mental illness, here's a great way to get one: just believe you are isolated in your mind and watch the suffering ensue.

Chelsea: A huge shift happens when you say, "I'm not just me; I'm not just this person." When you start to open up to that idea, huge potential for healing and newfound freedom opens up.

The other thing he emphasizes is the importance of knowing about life after death, and believing in life after death. Not about believing it's a certain way after death, but rather just that your consciousness will continue after death.

It's kind of a parallel to the citadel model of mind: the belief that your life begins and ends with the timeline of what occurs in this world. It connects to the porosity of mind. There's porosity because we are spiritual beings and because consciousness is eternal, not time-bound, not material world-bound. That is also key to being okay. He would say that's also the cause of mental illness, to think that it's only this world, this life. Two core things: life is not only physical, and it's not only isolated.

Bob: IFS brings this revolution that our minds are not one unified thing. They're made up of all these parts. And then if you go a little further, which is where I go, our minds are not this citadel; they're porous, and all these other beings, or whatever you want to call them, are coming in and out all the time and influencing us. Without them, we really wouldn't exist, which is very Swedenborgian. If you take those two concepts together, it totally revolutionizes mental health.

It sounds like Swedenborg might've been there a couple hundred years ago.

Chelsea: And I think Swedenborg would add that you're also not running out of time; that's maybe a way to put it.

The Role of Ancestors

Chelsea: I am curious to put it to both of you, as the resident Swedenborg person and the resident IFS person: What is the role of ancestors as part of our porosity discussion? How does that show up? What does that spur in your thoughts?

Bob: In IFS, there's a quite developed set of ideas about what they call legacy burdens, which have their scientific basis in epigenetics. There are very specific ways to deal with this, to find out what's the legacy burden and what comes from a person's individual lifetime. Then you help them get the legacy burden out of their body and pass it back through the ancestors.

There are also cultural legacies—legacy burdens and legacy gifts.

I also think that there are reservoirs or lakes or oceans of suffering that are back in our history that need to be drained or that can be used by the unscrupulous to cause pain.

Chelsea: I've heard of the process of giving it back to the generations, and how that might be visualized in different ways for people or experienced inside in different ways. What's your experience with ancestors or deceased loved ones showing up for people in doing this inner work?

Bob: There are three different ways. Dick is the minimalist. He just says, what's important is you get the person to recognize it's not theirs; it's not from their personal lifetime. Get it out of the person. That's enough. Other people, best represented probably by Kay Gardner, pass it back three generations because they believe that's as much as most people can remember. Ann Sinko and many others and I pass it all the way back the lineage up to where it first came in, and then up out of the first ancestors to try and clear the entire lineage. This is more shamanic. Some people are going to complain, "Oh, you're so woo-woo." But I actually think it's very helpful for a lot of complex reasons.

I've seen sometimes that there's healing that happens to the mother. When a client of mine did a big legacy unburdening, her mother called up after and said, "I'm feeling a lot better. I don't know what happened." Very often I have seen, for people after a parent has died, that you can ask, "Would you like the spirit of your grandmother to show up?" And they show up very often in a very emotionally meaningful way for the person. Usually it seems that when most people die—not all—they unburden, and they become much more Self-led. Usually that presence is very, very positive.

Sometimes, if you call it forth and it's not positive, you just send it away again.

Chelsea: I've heard it used in a way where it's like, you might invite the next generation up to come take the burden back. If the person can't feel like they can get rid of it themselves, you might invite the generation that it came from to come relieve the person of it, and that seems to help the inner work. What are your thoughts on that?

Bob: I wouldn't want to give any power to the previous generation. What I typically do, and this comes more from Pia Mellody, is guide the client to get everything that's not theirs out of their body, and have them turn around and hand it back to their parents, saying, "Take this. It's not mine. I can't heal it for you. You can't heal without it." You take it and pass it back where you got it from. Then I would ask the client, "How is that for you? Did they do that?" If they won't take it, I tell them they can just be like a boulder in the stream. That stuff can keep going around them and keep going back. It would be nice if they could take it—it'd be really good for them—but it won't interfere with the person's process.

I really don't want to give anybody else any big power inside a client's system.

Chelsea: That's so interesting. That makes sense.

Jonathan: I can't think of ways in which Swedenborg specifically addresses this, but it makes me think, again, of associate spirits. They're spirits that think a lot the way we do and feel things the way we do; some are good, and some are evil. It has seemed to me that it's very likely that some of these are ancestors. I think because we're dealing with some of the same issues, we got them from them.

Our hereditary evil is tendencies that roll down through the generations. Swedenborg says that hereditary evil comes from our parents and grandparents. I've thought for myself that these associate spirits could be ancestors or relatives who have died.

Bob: There are also legacy blessings, or heirlooms as Dick calls them. Family traditions that are really, really positive. Most cultures have ancestor worship, or at least ways to honor them. They tend to get overlooked, and the focus tends to stay on the legacy burdens. I think that's because in IFS, we focus on people's illness and pathology.

Chelsea: How does that show up clinically, like in sessions, and become functional?

Bob: In all sorts of ways. I know one woman for whom many of her ancestors had profound spiritual connections. She could have a profound spiritual connection much more easily than other people.

Chelsea: Something that's occurring to me that might be useful to note here from Swedenborg is even when it comes to an idea of family, Swedenborg talks about it as a correspondence. What does it mean to be spiritually family with somebody? It's not necessarily our biology and our DNA. It certainly plays a part, but spiritually we get connected to our family. Family in a spiritual sense means who we are aligned with in love and wisdom, our understanding, and our purpose, our usefulness. That's our family. So if you think about it that way, then what it means to have spiritual ancestors probably goes beyond just who you have your inherited evil or blessings from.

I'm thinking of how Swedenborg describes spiritual communities like stars and constellations and galaxies (see *Secrets of Heaven* 1808). Your spiritual associations might function like ancestors for you. The people we meet in the other world might not really be our family, but they feel like family to us because we have that alignment (see *Heaven and Hell* 46).

Bob: Things aren't necessarily biological at all. The Brazilians and the spiritists talk about soul groups, and how we're reincarnated that way. I think the things you were mentioning, Jonathan, are exactly legacy burdens.

Porosity and Reincarnation

Chelsea: I would love to spend time on reincarnation from an IFS and Swedenborg perspective.

Bob: IFS doesn't talk about this.

Do you know the work of Dr. Ian Stevenson? He was the director of the department of Psychiatry at the University of Virginia medical school. He got interested in reincarnation and decided to study reincarnation in children.

In our society, when a child claims to have experience or memory of a past life, we tell them they're crazy, and to shut up. Stevenson mainly studied cultures that had some belief in past lives. He was doing this for ten or fifteen years when the man who founded Xerox learned about his research and funded him. Stevenson quit his tenured professorship and devoted the rest of his life to studying this stuff. He has produced an incredible body of data.

He'd get a report from some village in India of an eighteen-month-old child claiming to have been born in another village. He would go there, would record the information—he'd have translators—and then they'd help the child get to the other village and they would interview the family that the kid said he came from, and they would have the kid identify objects from the previous life. He covered 8,000 to 9,000 of these cases, but he called 1,600 or more proven. These proven cases were ones in which there were so many details from the previous life that the kid knew that it seemed true beyond a reasonable doubt.

For example, in one case in Thailand, this kid kept bugging his grandma, who he lived with. He said, "I was born in that other village. I was shot when I was riding my bicycle. I was a school teacher. I want to go see my family." Finally, grandma gives in, takes him to the other village, they get off the bus and the kid walks quickly by the shortest route back through these unmarked streets to a house and knocks on the door. These old people come up and he says hi. And they say, "Yeah, our son was a school teacher. He was riding his bicycle to work one day, and he was shot and killed." Then the little kid says, "Where's my necklace? Where's my necklace?" And they bring out this necklace with two buddha beads on it and a bunch of other beads. He's upset. He says, "Where's the third Buddha? What did you do with my third Buddha?" And they go, "Oh, we gave it away."[74]

There are 1,600 cases like this. Amazing. And there are several in the United States now, some of which are incredibly famous, with book-length documentation.

Dr. Jim Tucker took over Stevenson's work after he died. And it's still going on at the University of Virginia Department of Perceptual Studies, which also sponsors near-death experience research.

One of the final projects was about reincarnation and biology. Stevenson's book on this is two volumes and over 2,200

---

74 Ian Stevenson, "Cases of the Reincarnation Type, Vol. IV, Twelve Cases in Thailand and Burma," *The Journal of Nervous and Mental Disease* 173, no. 1 (1985): 63.

pages.[75] He describes a case in which a kid is born with birthmarks that match the death wounds of the person from the previous life. There are 210 of these cases with photographs of the kids' birthmarks. There are autopsy diagrams from their previous existence. One kid was born with four fingers missing on one hand; they go back and find the person he claimed to be a reincarnation of and that person had lost four fingers in an agricultural accident. The same four fingers.

Chelsea: Does he say anything about how the children themselves integrate this reality that they know about themselves?

Bob: *The Journal of the American Medical Association* is as uptight a journal as you can find in the United States today, and their chief book review editor reviewed Stevenson's work and said, this is incredibly careful, unemotional, well-documented research carried out over a period of thirty-five years; it cannot be ignored.[76]

And what has happened? It's totally been ignored. Because it does not fit our current worldview.

Jonathan: When I was in Minneapolis recently after giving a talk, one of the audience members came up and said that when her son was four years old, they were going by a gravesite and he said, "Well, that's where I'm buried." That was the first time I'd heard a story face-to-face. She had all these details. In his case, it stopped when he was still very young. I am curious about this. It's astonishing. I especially have nothing to say about those marks and things like that.

---

75 Ian Stevenson, *Reincarnation and Biology: A Contribution to the Etiology of Birthmarks and Birth Defects* (Westport: Praeger, 1970).

76 Lester S. King, "Cases of the Reincarnation Type, Vol 1: Ten Cases in India" in *The Journal of the American Medical Association* 234, no. 9 (1975): 978-978.

Swedenborg is generally against the idea of reincarnation. As he understands it, we have a life here, and we die. We go to the other world. That's it. We don't come back. But there are things he says that to my mind could explain some of what is experienced.

As we've covered now, Swedenborg says that angels and spirits are with us all the time. Generally the way it works is, they cannot flow into us with their own memory. But then in the very next sentence he says, and when they do, it's the experience called déjà vu. So he talks about how they're so close with us that there can be a memory leak.

I wonder if it's some connection like that, if they're not actually the reincarnation of the person, but that person is so present with them, especially when the young mind is so open and doesn't have a whole sense of identity yet. When a mother cries, the child just starts crying. You don't even know the difference between you and other people.

Swedenborg says that kind of connection is something we have with spirits all the time. We just don't realize it. You would think if you were the reincarnation of that person, you would want to continue their life, but very often they end up having their own different life.

Bob: One of these reincarnated kids in India went back and married the wife from the previous life. Even though there was a major age difference.

Jonathan: Swedenborg talks about individuality, but his whole model is extremely porous. If we cut off the influence of angels and spirits, we'd fall down dead. We wouldn't have any mental activity going on. It's all kind of mediated. He talks about the fact that every single thought we have is the product of tens of thousands of angels. In other words, a thought is a very complicated thing to have. It takes a ton of beings; it comes cascading down through this whole realm. You can have one thought and a whole bunch of people are having it.

Chelsea: If we could put a kind of spiritual lens on what any of these case studies were experiencing—if you could suddenly just open up the spiritual side and see behind what's going on here—I am curious about what that is.

The paradox of identity is that it is a core part of who we are, and yet it's the one thing we need to not be identifying with, not identifying with the evil or the good that's flowing into us.

> People who do not know any better cannot help seeing the good they do as their own and the truth they think as their own. The same applies to those who take credit for the good they do and feel that it makes them deserving. . . . Still, the proper method is for us to do good as if on our own. . . . We should do good as if we were doing it on our own, but when we reflect on the good we are doing (or have done), we ought to think, acknowledge, and believe that the Lord working in us is actually doing the good.
>
> If we abandon all effort because of the kind of thinking mentioned, the Lord cannot work in us. He cannot act on those who rid themselves of every capacity for receiving the power to do good. . . . The reality is that what the Lord animates in us is that which seems to be ours. . . . It is an eternal truth that life is not ours; but if it did not seem to be, we would have no life at all. (*Secrets of Heaven* 1712)

And yet, through doing all that Swedenborg just described in that passage, we get this thing called identity that is very distinct.

In an unpublished draft for *Divine Love and Wisdom*, Swedenborg describes how a fetus develops in the womb and how the spiritual body and the spiritual mind are getting developed at the same time.[77] According to Swedenborg, during our whole lives in this world, we are developing as a vessel. And the

---

77 Emanuel Swedenborg, *On the Divine Love and the Divine Wisdom*, trans. Samuel Worcester, rev. John C. Ager, in *Apocalypse Explained*, vol. 6, trans. John C. Ager, rev. John Whitehead, ed. William Ross Woofenden (West Chester, PA: Swedenborg Foundation, 1994–1997).

vessel that we are exists for eternity. We get this eternalness to us because of our connection with the divine. Touching down in this material universe is what creates a new vessel. Then all of these things that are existing forever—these vessels of love and wisdom, these wills and understanding—are semipermeable membranes of identity. We live in this soup of the spiritual world, this amazing network of interconnection.

Bob: Am I right in thinking that all the demons and angels previously had a body, whether on this planet or some other planet?

Chelsea: That's one of his core principles. Once something has been brought up through this outermost level, it takes on an eternal nature as itself.

Jonathan: He says there's nobody else up there.

Bob: The spiritists insist that we all reincarnate in soul groups, that there's certain families or larger groups that go through all these generations and permutations. That would seem to be like all these various small heavens in certain groups of interacting beings.

Chelsea: Yeah. One fundamental thing that Swedenborg talks about is that when we think about spiritual things, you have to remove all sense of time and space. Time and space don't exist in the spiritual world. Time is only a function of this material reality, and it's part of what makes material reality confusing.

When thinking about soul groups, or communities in heaven, or reincarnation, how do you relate to that when you think of it outside of time and space? Each of our own unique identities have had or are having this timeline where we were born and then we died or we're going to die, and somehow it mattered, even though it all actually fundamentally exists outside of time and space.

Jonathan: Swedenborg uses the analogy of an egg. Your infancy is an egg to your childhood. Childhood is an egg to your teenage years. Teenage years are an egg to your adult years. Your adult years hatch into your old age. But he says that's just an egg too. After you die, you keep going through this hatching forever, so that no matter how far along that course you are, you're never beyond the egg stage compared to the limitless things that have yet to come (*Secrets of Heaven* 4379).

Now that's a mindblower. That's not a linear, static kind of view of what a human being is. I don't know what he means, but I love it. It's almost beyond reincarnation, which could be described as circular or spiral. That hatching is kind of a birth again and again and again, but always moving forward into something new.

Another analogy that's along the same lines that he uses a lot is that we're like a seedling that grows up and then gets branches, gets leaves, and then develops into a trunk, then bears fruit, and then all those germinate and come up. So we become a grove of trees, and then we become a whole forest of trees, and then we become a whole grove of forests, and then a forest of forests growing without end (*Secrets of Heaven* 2657:4; 5355; 5804:2). So every person—every individual—is like that. But what is that like?

Bob: If you think we're a little further down the thing, our soul group in the spiritist language could be the grove growing from some tree.

Chelsea: Yes! If we're a seed, we are connected in both directions. It's what we're a part of and it's what we become. In IFS, it's possible to meet these beings who tell you that they're a part of your history, and yet they're there with you. How many groves of forests are we interacting with here?

Swedenborg says, as angels get higher in heaven (which means opening to love more), they feel more interconnected with all of heaven and all of heaven is interconnected with them. So when you think of that forest of forests, these angels feel like everybody is my story, from such a deep sense of interconnectedness.

Jonathan: He describes in one place that some of these angels know everyone in heaven (*Spiritual Experiences* 4670).

Chelsea: Right. They don't just feel connected. They actually know they're connected.

Jonathan: And he specifically says that our wisdom is a function of how much outreach we have to other communities in the heavens. So people with not much wisdom, they're just sort of connected to the group next door in effect. Our outreach grows over time. So as we're in the other world, we make more and more connections—synapses or whatever you'd call them—just reaching out. We're drawing on this huge pool of input, so in what sense is that my own wisdom?

The opposite of what we're talking about is that Latin word proprium again, meaning just what *is* yourself. To Swedenborg, that is this idea that I'm this thing and this is where I begin and end: "This is who I am. I know what's what," but that's not understanding what's going on.

I think Swedenborg is laboring on every page to try to convey, "I thought so too until my mind was blown by these experiences I've been through, and now I've found out that these beings know my thoughts. I can't even tell if I'm thinking their thoughts or they're thinking my thoughts or who's doing what to whom." The idea that I'm just this guy right over here is the key fallacy. That lowest sensory level is to think that I'm separate from everybody else.

Bob: So this idea of proprium could equate to Tanya Luhrmann's concept of the citadel model of mind.[78]

---

78 Tanya M. Luhrmann, *How God Becomes Real: Kindling the Presence of Invisible Others* (Princeton: Princeton University Press, 2020).

Chelsea: I think it lines up very well.

Bob: It also matches Isabel Clarke's billiard ball theory of mind.[79] Both of them say that this belief in the isolated nature of our minds is at the core of mental illness and our vulnerability to psychosis, because if you have this thought that everything inside your mind is yours and private, you get an odd thought coming in; you think you're shattered. You fight like hell, and then you collapse in a pile, and you go have a psychiatrist give you the Western curse, and then your life is toast.

Earlier Chelsea asked, what do you do with these kids who have reincarnation experiences? How do they integrate it? Stevenson did not study this at all. He was purely data collecting. Carol Bowman, an American therapist, made how to deal with reincarnation experiences in children clinically her life's work. She said the absolute worst thing you can do is deny the reality of all these experiences. Which is what we do. This is the last thing you want to do.

From an IFS perspective, you follow a client's belief system and system of metaphors and their language, and there's really good clinical evidence as to why we should do that. I remain agnostic. It allows you to accept people's reality and be curious about it in a way that won't lose you your license.

Jonathan: It's simple and brilliant. Why try to impose a different vocabulary on somebody who's already got a whole system in their mind?

Bob: While in the West, as therapists, we're trained to impose this whole rather ugly, hideous language on people, which is beyond unfortunate.

As I've said, we do have concrete scientific evidence for legacy burdens: things coming down through a person's lineage and

---

79 Isabel Clarke, *Madness, Mystery and the Survival of God* (Ropley: O Books, 2008).

affecting them—that's the whole science of epigenetics. When people experience past life stuff—whether it's spirits, or UBs, or a past life, I just go with whatever the client says. It seems to be mainly people who died in tremendous distress, often with hatred and vengeance on their mind. Like people being burned to death at the stake, and in their attempt to cope with that pain, they're just vowing vengeance. Those seem to be the kind of past life experiences, or whatever you want to call them, that show up in people and need help.

There's a wonderful tradition from Korean shamanism, because they know these things happen. They say that to help these spirits move on, you have to witness their *han*, which is an emotion Koreans have that we don't have, or rather, we have it, but we don't have a name for it. It's injustice and anguish and pain, but it's without vengeance. You have to witness that spirit's suffering and then it can move on.

I had a client who had this memory of being in a basement stone cell in a prison with just straw on a stone floor and rats and stuff. It appeared that everybody who'd been in the castle keeping the prison left. He was just left there starving to death in the basement and died there. He was looking out the barred opening, and there was an oak tree on a grassy field, and he died with all this hate and vengeance for the person who'd betrayed him and the army that was keeping him in prison. But what he really hoped was, he just wanted to be able to get out of that prison cell and die under the oak tree.

We were able, in the imaginal realm, to help that spirit go and get under the oak tree and die there. It was able to release all its hatred, and it stopped whatever it was; it stopped bothering the client.

Chelsea: Sounds like whether or not you would say, "Oh yeah, these are people who claim to have been reincarnated or have reincarnation experiences," whatever it is, they end up across from you in a therapy room or on a Zoom call, and you're going to approach that story like a part until you're maybe asking the part, "Are you a part from outside of the person?" And then whatever the answer is, you just go with that. It comes down to, even in the case of a part, witnessing the suffering and bringing the curiosity and compassion.

Bob: Yeah. But the big difference with a part is that you welcome it into the system. You form an enduring Self-to-part relationship with it. Whereas if it's something that's not part of the system, you help it go on to where it's supposed to be.

But see, like with that case—with the guy in the prison—it seemed to be medieval or the time of the crusades, but I don't need to know if that was a past life or if that was an unattached burden or anything else. I don't need to know anything about that. I don't need to try and make that judgment.

Chelsea: The protocol is the same.

Jonathan: Get to the oak tree and help him release his hatred.

Bob: Witness his hatred and betrayal and all that. Yeah. And get him to the oak tree.

Jonathan: I'm just thinking of a phrase that Swedenborg says that no falsity or evil can be removed unless it first appears (*Divine Providence* 278).

Bob: In IFS that's witnessing, yeah!

Jonathan: Of course it would be so attractive if this stuff would just melt away, like there was some pill you could take and you lose weight while you're lying there in bed or something. As if it could just melt away when you're unconscious. But I think it must have something to do with the Self. It's never removed unless it appears. You've got to look at it. You've got to somehow witness it.

Chelsea: Swedenborg uses the analogy of a wound that has to be opened up and purged before it can really heal.

Jonathan: If it's closed over, it could turn into gangrene or whatever. It must be allowed to drain.

Chelsea: I love bringing that topic to this subject because from a more managerial sense you could think it has to appear so you can understand it, so you can fix it. So you can fight it off, or cut it out. But who's doing the removing? It brings my mind back to our discussion of *affectio veri*. Something appears, then there's this affection for truth: witnessing and validating with curiosity and compassion. In IFS, they talk about re-experiencing histories. Basically you get to play out the past differently. You get to have a repair.

Bob: "Redo" might be the word you're looking for. You complete the witnessing and then you ask the part, "Is there anything you want us to do with you or for you back here before you go?" "Reparative" is another word for that.

I think there's a problem with this. These things used to be called change-history techniques. It's dangerous because so many people with big trauma don't trust their memories in the first place, and they have amnesia. Big trauma is always accompanied by amnesia. So when you ask them to go back there and make new memories, you can be causing a problem, in that everything gets opened to doubt and derealization and the idea that "Oh, well, I just made all that kind of stuff up." I'm very leery about this. It's something that's come into the forefront—the redo or reparative experience. It was a very small part, if there at all, many years ago. And I think it's potentially problematic.

Chelsea: It makes sense that there'd be a difference between witnessing and a redo. The witnessing itself is reparative.

Bob: Another primary technique I use with these kinds of past life clients comes from Brian Weiss and Roger Woolger. Basically what they do is they say you go back, and whether it's a part or whatever it is, you help it go through its death experience. And then you say, "What happened right after you died?"

Usually what you hear is something like, "Well, I went and found somebody else to attach to because I couldn't go up to the light because I knew they'd hate me or send me to hell." A lot of times beliefs in hell are a big reason why these parts won't go on.

"So you died this horrible death; what happened right after that?" And then you help that spirit go up to the light or go to a more appropriate place.

6
THE PROCESS OF HEALING

Through our whole journey of exploring this material, we've discussed what the inner landscape is like, the nature of parts and Self, and the importance of their relationship; we discussed the nature of burdens, and the porousness of our minds. Now, to round it off, we explore healing itself.

What Is Healing?

Chelsea: An idea that has struck home for me is that healing is different from a physical cure. The root word in healing means whole—to become whole. What is the spiritual reality of healing? There's something to that. Why would healing even matter if we're nothing but these biological, isolated beings who are born and then die? Does it really matter so much that we have a good day while we're here? The whole idea of healing feels like it's leading to something that goes beyond just a physical life, and beyond our personal identity—it impacts community, or why would we care so much about it? There are a lot of things Swedenborg says about it. I just want to serve up the topic and put it to both of you. I'll chime in if I have anything to add.

Bob: In terms of Western psychotherapy's model of healing, when they have recognized parts at all, most of the people doing the parts work thought healing was putting all the parts in a blender and making a nice mush.

IFS says, no, absolutely not; that's wrong. Parts are not the product of trauma. They are natural and very valuable. We don't want to get rid of any of them. Parts are not their burdens. We want to get the burdens off them. So the image of healing I like the best, and a lot of other IFS people use it too, is people start out as an internal civil war, often vicious. Often, it's so bad it actually kills them. So in healing, you convert that civil war into an orchestra or a great improvisational jazz band, or a choir. A sports team is another metaphor a lot of people like. But you need the violins and the trumpets; you need a bass player and a drummer. You don't want those players all mushed together.

Jonathan: As we've mentioned, Swedenborg talks a lot about what you're calling the civil war between the inner and outer self. He describes it as being kind of a war, and the winner takes all. Great things happen if the inner self wins the battle: the outer self becomes compliant and cooperative and is a great asset. But that battle goes on for a long time.

What occurs to me is a couple of things in terms of what I was talking about before about the pit and what happens after we die as parallels to healing. There's this awakening that happens after death. People realize, "My feelings matter, and thoughts are important." He says a lot of people end up in this underground realm, as he describes it, which as I say, is characterized by false beliefs. You may be a good person or good-hearted, but you're really entrenched in some unhelpful perspectives. I can't help but think those false beliefs are perspectives about yourself, perspectives about God, or perspectives about the great questions of life.

A person might have a very judgmental, harsh view of God inside. Gradually, you start to realize there's tremendous mercy here. There's kindness. So the real truth is a component to our healing journey. If somebody could really hear the message, "No, you're fine; you don't have to beat yourself up about this," or what we've talked about several times in these sessions, how you have a part of yourself that's indestructible (see p. 24), that in itself is a healing experience, if a person is really able to take that in. No, you are not tainted by what happened to you or what you did. Or no, it's not all over because of this and that in the past, or whatever it might be. A falsity might be the thought that you're a horrible person or that you've been shafted over the course of your life, and nobody ever treated you well. I think the truth, the way that he describes it, and the state that people are in when they come out of the pit, sounds to me like healing. They experience what Swedenborg describes as consolation, which you mentioned earlier, Chelsea. They're weeping, and they can't believe it, and they're exhilarated. They really didn't think it would go this well for them. It sounds like a pretty huge healing of the stuff that happened in the course of their lives.

Chelsea: Whoa, what happens "after death" in Swedenborg's terms is psychotherapy as IFS now. It is about sorting and processing, building new relationships and connections, removing burdens and helping parts connect to Self and become their natural, beneficial selves.

Jonathan: Another angle on what healing is from Swedenborg's perspective comes from what he writes about the story of the Good Samaritan and the man who falls among thieves (Luke 10:25–37). What is put in the wound is oil and wine. Swedenborg says that oil means love, and wine means a particular kind of spiritual truth. Water corresponds to truth, but it's not going to clean; it's not going to disinfect your wound. Wine, he says, is more like a spiritual truth that has that kind of energy in it. I picture hydrogen peroxide or something that fizzes. But you need to put both of those things on: if it's just wine, then it's, "Ow"; but the oil is soothing. That's all very broad brush, but I think that's got something to do with healing. And it's interesting to note that the oil is put on first and then the wine. So the oil would be the love first, and then a little shot of disinfectant in there, of new clarity.

Chelsea: What I hear in what you're saying is the role that truth has in healing. Something that occurs to me about what Swedenborg says, which is also in Buddhist teachings, is that truth is really the reality of what is. Being present to what is, and accepting what is, is healing because reality is always better, as Byron Katie describes in her book *Loving What Is*.[80]

Reality is always better than what we think it is in our heads. So much of our suffering is on account of delusions. When we experience and touch reality for what it really is, whether you're doing that through meditation or whatever, it's a lot better. You're going to be met with what reality is, which Swedenborg says is love and truth. That's the only thing that's real. Everything else is relatively unreal. It's cool to think about interfacing with the truth, with reality, as inherently healing.

Jonathan: Swedenborg talks about people who are so hardened in their ideas that it's as if their spiritual body has a thick callus, almost like bone, in their brain (*Heaven and Hell* 466). He talks about this guy who got that way, apparently partly out of pride and partly out of thinking that memory made him an extremely wise and amazing person. All he had was a power of memory, but he got very fixated on this idea that he was one of the most intelligent people on earth. Swedenborg sees this guy undergo what I could only call a kind of operation to bust up this bony callus in there. Swedenborg said that after the operation, the person was like a little child. He was like an infant (*Spiritual Experiences* 4749). So some of the healing would be busting up the calcification, the things that have gotten hardened in somebody's spirit, to try to soften them up.

---

80 Byron Katie and Stephen Mitchell, *Loving What Is: Four Questions That Can Change Your Life*, (New York: Harmony Books, 2002).

Bob: Two words in Swedenborg I sort of thought might be equal to psychotherapeutic healing were *redemption* and *consolation*. What is healing compared to redemption? I am wondering if there are other words that should be up there in that group. I'm also wondering if the Latin words he uses for redemption and consolation translate directly into English, or if the English has got a whole bunch of different connotations.

Jonathan: I think those ones are pretty good translations. Like redeem in English and in Latin has an idea of buying back or some sort of exchange. And consolation is very much the same in English. Redeeming is being rescued from hell, and hell can take various forms for people, but I think it's what we've been talking about: people being burdened by either these false notions, or addictions, or what he would call evils or compulsions, like a delight in hurting people.

Chelsea: With Swedenborg, you end up quoting the Bible because he's referencing that so much. So this topic is full of all these different Bible connections. For example, "take the water of life freely" (Revelation 22:17) is what comes to my mind, and "my yoke is easy and my burden is light" (Matthew 11:30). It's so counterintuitive to our minds that life is so good and that healing is actually so free and available to us. And all it is, is letting go and surrendering.

It's interesting to reflect on the parts of us that think it's so hard to believe that healing is actually available to us, or that this goodness—this love—is actually free, and we can take it freely.

Bob: Are there more words beside redeem, redemption, and consolation that Swedenborg would use that are somewhat parallel to healing? Or are those the big ones?

Jonathan: Where my mind goes is the opposite end of the universe a little bit from a single word, which is the entire sweep of the narrative of the Old Testament. That's not one word, but the whole story of slavery in Egypt, getting out of Egypt. Then you wander in the wilderness for a while, and a whole generation has to die. Another generation comes along, then you get into the holy land, but it's full of enemies. You have to fight.

Another word that Swedenborg would use is *regeneration*. Regeneration is very related to redemption. He would say that Exodus is a story of regeneration; it's this long gradual process by which we're brought to freedom.

Chelsea: I think it's useful to bring up the Bible here because when you say regeneration, you might just think of an escalator. It can conjure pretty boring images of progress. But the stories of the Bible are such rich human histories that reflect different spiritual states that we go through.

I was mentioning IFS to a Swedenborgian friend of mine, and they said, "Oh, yeah. That's how we're always relating to the Bible. The Bible is a reflection of all the parts of ourselves and their story." That's what Swedenborg is always teaching. All the characters in the Bible are parts of you. But IFS takes it beyond metaphorical.

Jonathan: And the Bible is about how there's a divine presence interacting with all these parts, just like Self. You have the children of Israel, but you have the tabernacle in the middle of it, and the sense of the presence of the divine. It gives you a different way to look at the Bible, to think about the characters as parts and think about the Self in relation to these parts, and how there's a reworking of these relationships.

Swedenborg talks a lot about the fact that the two main things that Jesus did was teach and heal. The ailments he healed correspond to spiritual states of being, similar to how we were describing the ancient practice of knowing your neighbor and what would help (see pp. 123–124).

Bob: I've heard it said that Jesus was primarily a healer and only a teacher secondarily. The reason we hear so much about his teaching is because the people we hear from are teachers.

The metaphor of healing I gave you for IFS is only the first stage, but it's what you can present to the general public. It's a very spiritual program.

A minister I have studied was talking about exorcism and where the evil spirits get into us. I don't know the Old Testament passage, but there's evidently a quite detailed description of the Temple of Solomon and how all the various small rooms are arranged around a central space. He said that is specifically a model of the human personality and it shows us where the demons can get in. Half of his little book was about the Temple of Solomon and how that's a model of the human personality. Does that kind of stuff fit with Swedenborg?

Jonathan: Swedenborg talks a lot about the temple and the tabernacle as a map of the divine mind, the human mind, and how human beings and the Divine connect.

Chelsea: People try to compartmentalize religion and spirituality apart from psychotherapy, and yet it seems like they're coming together more and more. Swedenborg understands the Bible itself as a manual for our spiritual healing. It can become methodological and functional when you put all these pieces together.

Something I really appreciate about not only IFS, but other relatively recently developed therapeutic techniques like EMDR and brainspotting is that they are based on the idea that our brains intuitively know what healing looks like if given the opportunity.

Whether you think of it in evolutionary or spiritual terms, it's to the benefit of the brain to accomplish healing. It's energetically taxing to deal with the effects of trauma on a physiological level. Our systems want to heal, and they have the blueprint for it inside.

As we quoted earlier, *Spiritual Experiences* 2487 is about this idea of how that inner part is undamaged. It has an elasticity. It gets attached to things that are twisted and not great, but it's always wanting to return to its state of integrity. And that's how it remains unharmed. It doesn't matter how stretched out it gets. A major paradigm shift is to trust that there is something trustworthy inside of us; that it's not just broken, or damaged beyond repair.

I think that is what sets Swedenborg apart. He's not just making a claim and saying, "Yeah, you have this inner core that can't be damaged." He's saying, if you look under the hood, look how it operates. This is how it seems to operate. It's attached to these corrupt things on the outside, but it has this energy where it's always wanting to return to its state of integrity. So that's what reveals the fact that there is an undamageable inner core. It becomes something functional to use and test rather than just a tenet to accept. He writes of this purpose existing in the brain itself.

Bob: There are two things this might be equivalent to. One is the idea that there's no sin so horrible that it can't be forgiven.

And the other one is the idea that there are no locked gates on hell. That any spirit in there, when and if it somehow chooses to, can look up and start on a new path. There is something undamaged, no matter how far down you go.

I was pleasantly surprised to find this articulated in the Orthodox Christian faith. Metropolitan Kallistos Ware said there are no locked gates on hell, and anytime any spirit there turns to the Lord for redemption, they can find it. He said, though, there might be spirits down there who are so determined that for all eternity they will not turn toward the light. To me that's a very sympathetic description of self-caused going to hell.

Chelsea: That lines up with what Swedenborg says about how no one is condemned to hell. Heaven and hell, our place in the spiritual world, is what we choose; it has to do with our love and intention. Swedenborg says:

> In the spiritual world where we all arrive after death, no one asks what our faith has been or what our beliefs have been, only what our life has been, whether we are one kind of person or another. They know that the quality of our faith and the quality of our beliefs depend on the quality of our life, because life constructs a belief system for itself and constructs a faith for itself. (*Divine Providence* 101)

Jonathan: It feels like we're coming down the other side of the mountain in these conversations and thinking about what's most important. And I think it is the relationship of Self to parts, the humanness of every part, and the purity of that deepest level. And now we can add to that the inborn drive in us toward healing. He describes the stream of providence as a silent current. He did a lot of sailing in his life to get from one country to another. You can be feeling like you're sitting there, but the boat is just quietly moving along in a different direction. It's kind of like the hounds of heaven concept: that they're coming to get you and take you in a good direction. There's something in the lower self that I would say just automatically rejects that idea; it seems too good to be true—if I don't help myself, there'll be no help.

Chelsea: I feel like this connects to why is healing even possible? It's possible because there's that inner energy toward healing that's always active. That's something we can participate in rather than having to conjure it; it's always there. How do you get in that flow?

I was really intrigued—and I wonder how this might connect with IFS too—by *Secrets of Heaven* 6724 where it says the force of goodness on the inside is immensely more powerful than anything on the outside.

> When we are being reformed, the Lord anchors us internally in goodness and truth. Externally, though, he releases us to our evil ways and false thoughts and consequently to the companionship of hellish spirits immersed in the same kind of evil and falsity. They flap around us and make every effort to destroy us, but the internal influence of goodness and truth protects us so well that the hellish spirits cannot inflict the slightest damage. Any force that acts inside us is immensely more powerful than a force that acts from the outside. What is deeper, being more refined, acts on every single, solitary part of the surface and in this way bends the surface to its will. However, for this to happen the superficial level must contain something good and true for the inner influence to latch on to. That is how goodness can exist among evil and falsity and yet remain safe.
>
> Everyone being reformed is brought into this state. That is the way the evil and falsity to which we are prey are removed and the way goodness and truth are inserted in their place.

So on the inside, there's that goodness. If you recognize that it's there, if you're willing to even acknowledge it, then the superficial level must contain something good and true for the inner influence to latch onto.

As we said before, when you take actions with a good intention, or even just do something because you know it's good, even if you don't actually have the will inside yet, you take the action and the will follows. That is important because you're creating an external network for this inner goodness to start working with, to start creating that cycle, to start the siphoning process.

Coming from a Swedenborgian background, I find IFS so intuitive because Swedenborg talks about the cycle of our rebirth. Our job is just to get the bare bones in order. Like if you can help it, don't kill people. Try being nice to them. If you can do something that looks like goodness on the outside, from a sincere intention—even if you don't feel the motivation for it—do that because there are these principles at play inside. There's an inner goodness that wants to live in integrity. So we just set up those conditions on the outside and that starts the cycle of our rebirth that goes on for the rest of our lives. That is what healing is. We're going to be going through this cycle, and it is taking us toward healing, even when the appearances on the outside might not look that way.

Bob: There's this thing called healing by natural intention. There are some situations under certain conditions when they don't put sutures in a wound after an operation, but they can just gently move the tissues toward each other, with bandages or some other compression, and that wound will do what they call healing by natural intention. That's the same idea on a physical level. There's the bare minimum of what we need to do, and we can do a whole lot more than that, but that's enough.

Chelsea: And if it's happening on that physical level, then who are we to say it's not happening on the more subtle level of thoughts and feelings and perceptions?

Jonathan: An important piece of that, as you say, Chelsea, is that I think part of Swedenborg's project was to try to put different ideas and concepts in people's minds, because that would form a platform where something from within can work.

Everybody's got the same equipment under the hood. We've all got this goodness inside, but what we have down here, in our minds, can block it. Particularly if you have a completely materialist worldview, from Swedenborg's perspective. If you think there is no spirit, there's only flesh, there's only matter; there is no God, no afterlife, and so on, you'll still have angels with you, but it'll make it difficult for them to operate.

He talks a lot about this word "plane" or "level." You need to have a plane for inner qualities to operate into. There needs to be some receptivity down here, some home that these things have. Otherwise they just flow right on through. You've got nothing to catch it.

Bob: I want to challenge you two. Swedenborg says there's certain preconditions that will allow this healing to take place. Can you make an A, B, C, D, E, and F list of these preconditions?

Chelsea: I think that's what we want to do in this book! Or at least embark in that direction. A list like that would be very useful and it would take a lot of careful thought to create. I get the sense that one of those letters is what Jonathan is pointing to. It's like getting chemical reactions to occur. It's enough to read some good ideas, consume some content; or something a little more powerful might be to take some actions, create an atmosphere of some true ideas and goodness, or lean into some good intentions. Or take some actions that you've thought about that you think are good or kind, toward yourself or others. That's enough to catch this constant inflow of love and wisdom that is coming in and getting it to start acting in your system.

It's like weather system studies. People research how to catalyze cloud formation. If you can get clouds to start to form, then you can get rain, and you can help in conditions of drought. It's like there's a lot of water in the atmosphere, but you need those ideas to catalyze a cloud. Whether it's through reading or absorbing information or an output of doing good, kind, or loving things to yourself or other people, that can create that cloud catalysis; it can get the atmosphere to start condensing into this active thing. It's similar to the fact that the universe is dark, except in places that reflect the light, catch the light. That's what loving ideas or actions are in your mind or spirit.

Jonathan: Yeah, a list like that would take some work. Maybe that needs to be our next project!

Grief and Grieving

Chelsea: I want to talk about the subject of grief and grieving. I'm curious to ask about that as connected to the whole healing subject. Grieving is so important. People like Francis Weller in his book *The Wild Edge of Sorrow*[81] do a great job discussing this subject, but I'm curious if there's anything to explore from a Swedenborg or IFS perspective.

Bob: Great book.

Chelsea: Even in his preface, he uses the semipermeable membrane as an analogy of how we share our grief; our grief is not even our own, we are connected to each other.

Bob: I did one of his three-day-long grief rituals with him. And then I did another one that was a little shorter with two of his students that was also good, but nowhere near as powerful as working with him.

I think IFS is really weak with grief. It's one of the things IFS is not strong with. And I've come to have a lot of my perspective directly from Francis Weller, but I go farther than he does. I always go farther—sometimes this is good, and sometimes it's not so good. But anyway, I think this first part's from him: grief is actually a form of alchemy. It transmutes suffering into compassion. But the part where I go beyond him is, if you don't grieve, or if you grieve incompletely, or in some way your grief is unsatisfactory, instead of converting your suffering into compassion, it gets turned into bitterness, hate, and self-righteousness.

The corollary to that is, whenever I'm feeling bitter or hate-filled, I have to go look for what I failed to grieve.

Chelsea: Exactly. The negative states that we might find ourselves in could be connected to unprocessed grief in our system. To me, this points to how innocent it all is. It can turn into such nasty monsters, this negativity. And yet when you go to its core, it's like, "Oh, grieving had to happen here." And I think of how,

---

81 Francis Weller, *The Wild Edge of Sorrow: Rituals of Renewal and the Sacred Work of Grief* (Berkeley: North Atlantic Books, 2015).

for grieving to be healing—and I'm not speaking about this as an expert, that's why I feel like I'd love to bring Francis Weller into this conversation—what's needed is the power of having your story witnessed, which reflects IFS to me, when you're grieving in the presence of love. Our systems seem to require the presence of love to really feel safe to grieve; that's when something that didn't feel tolerable before can feel like, "Oh, I can feel all these feelings now."

Returning to the truth is being in a space where it's okay to grieve, and it's safe to grieve. You feel like it's going to be okay and then you can just let it all out. And that's what ends up being healing.

I'm intrigued to hear you say that you feel like that is a weak spot in IFS. I've been frustrated by the lack of clear handling of grief in a person's system in the model. It seems like there's so much potential to have IFS be this powerful way of being present to grief and yet I feel like I'm needing to chart my own path there. I don't know of other people who have systematically applied IFS to grief.[82]

Catharsis versus Witnessing

Bob: That brings up another very important issue for IFS. I don't know how this will tie into Swedenborg or if it does at all, but that's the difference between witnessing and catharsis.

Witnessing is not catharsis. Catharsis is sort of this hydraulic model of the mind that we've got a certain amount of an emotion in us, and if we spread it out into the world somehow, that's going to make stuff better. That doesn't work. People tend to need to do that over and over. Like the primal screamers. A

---

82 Since our conversations, I (Chelsea) have found that the late Derek Scott, founder of IFSCA and IFS therapist, made the subject of IFS and grief and grieving a focus of his work. See Derek Scott, "IFS, Grief and Loss," IFSCA, accessed November 2, 2024, https://ifsca.ca/videos/ifs-grief-and-loss/ and Derek Scott, "Self-Led Grieving: Transitions, Loss and Death," in *Innovations and Elaborations in Internal Family Systems Therapy*, eds. Martha Sweezy and Ellen L. Ziskind (Routledge, 2017), 90–108.

lot of those people were getting up every morning and doing their primal screams and driving the neighbors crazy. It didn't help really.

Witnessing is another process entirely, even though it looks quite similar sometimes. It's determined by the part, or by the griever in Francis Weller's language. How much do they want to be seen? What do they want to be known by another? It is not like emptying a bucket, but helping them feel they're not left alone with anything anymore unless they really want to be. They don't have to be alone with anything; there's somebody right there.

They sound similar, but they're very different in their process and in what they do and how they function. I think that's another big advance of IFS.

Jonathan: It reminds me of the truth and reconciliation commission in Rwanda, where they get people together and just tell the story. Nothing was going to happen, but it just needed to be aired. Just the truth. And it really helped people move forward in their grief.

I think the word "hydraulic" is one of the funniest things I've heard for a long time. "You got about a quart and a half in there and we've got a couple of pints out, but there's more to come." It just doesn't work that way. You can keep draining that for years to no effect.

Bob: Anything in Swedenborg that would be about catharsis or witnessing or florid emotional expression?

Chelsea: People often want to know what Swedenborg says about grieving, and honestly, it's just very thin. So I'm curious, Jonathan—anything that comes to your mind, or even just like an indirect application, and bringing in what you're saying, Bob, about catharsis and witnessing.

Jonathan: My main thought is that the eighteenth century was not a particularly safe place for feelings. It was a patriarchal era—lots of war, and not very touchy-feely.

But Swedenborg does talk about grief occasionally, and I feel like there are things that would address it, but they're not sitting right up on the surface.

Chelsea: It makes me think of Dr. Kristin King's work. She wrote an essay on the nature of feelings in Swedenborg's works, titled, "Reading What the Writings Say They Cannot Say."[83] She did an interesting study of all the places where Swedenborg says, "I can't tell you this, or this can't be put into words. Human language fails us, and I'm just not going to even try." Or the angels won't allow it. One of the things that she points out is about what Swedenborg calls the inner sense of the Bible. Swedenborg holds that there's an inner meaning to the Bible where the spiritual truth is; and the inner meaning has layers to it. He says the innermost meaning is the feeling itself, the emotion.

So you go beyond words and you're just in the feeling, and that's where the highest angels are. There's that beautiful verse in Romans 8:26 that says, "Likewise the Spirit helps us in our weakness; for we do not know how to pray as we ought, but that very Spirit intercedes with sighs too deep for words." You go into this other space or mode of being, and that feels like the liminal space of grief. You can't speak right to it. It's like an altered state of consciousness, to allow yourself into that feeling.

Bob: If I hear you right, Chelsea, you're saying that there are whole realms that Swedenborg says we can't write about. Specifically, the innermost realm of the Bible is feeling, and the highest angels are feeling.

---

83 Kristin King, "Reading What the Writings Say They Cannot Say," *New Church Life* vols. CXIX–CXX, nos. 8–9 (August–September 1999): 345–360; 393–410.

Chelsea: Correct. It seems the higher you go in heaven, the more deeply you are in touch with your feelings.

Bob: I want to mention one other thing. When I have clients who are grieving, I recommend three books. One is Francis Weller. The other two are C. S. Lewis's *A Grief Observed*—great little book—and *The Smell of Rain on Dust* by Martín Prechtel.[84]

Martín Prechtel was raised in a Guatemalan village and studied their shamanic traditions. Once when he was up at this men's group in Minnesota, he taught how when spirits aren't grieved appropriately, they can't leave this world and go on to where they need to be. He said, "I'm just looking at the couple dozen men in this room. You haven't grieved for any of your ancestors for hundreds of years. There's enough work just in this room to keep a shaman like me busy for lifetimes."

Chelsea: I gather that there is something critical about grieving in community or with others. You can be present to your grief in your own parts work, being present to the grief that parts hold, but it seems to get better and more effective the more people you have, the more presence, the more community. It's such a critical part of healing.

Bob: Dick and I had a disagreement once. He used to say that Self doesn't get sad. I said that when I'm in Self, tears often are pouring down my face. Now he's come around as saying Self does weep sometimes.

Joy-Pain

This reminds me of another idea I really wanted to run by you: the concept of joy-pain. Pia Mellody, for example, says that a characteristic of a spiritual experience is, you're intensely

---

84 Clive Staples Lewis, *A Grief Observed* (Grand Rapids: Zondervan, 2001); Martín Prechtel, *The Smell of Rain on Dust: Grief and Praise* (Berkeley: North Atlantic Books, 2015).

experiencing two opposite emotions simultaneously. Most often, it's joy and pain. Saint John of the Ladder said the same thing in the early seventh century: something along the lines of "Joy and pain are joined like honey in the honeycomb and this is a marker of spiritual depth."[85]

Does Swedenborg ever talk about something like joy-pain?

Jonathan: He talks about the fact that with any pleasure or joy, each of us has a capacity. It's different for different people. Whenever you have more than that, it's painful (*Heaven and Hell* 410). As you fill up with it, it will inevitably go to that threshold where it actually crosses over into being painful because our capacity is not that great. Something he doesn't say, but I'm thinking right this moment, is how that painful edge of that joy is like a growing pain. The next time you experience it, you'll be able to go farther, and then the pain moves a little farther out. So you can increase your capacity over time.

Bob: So it could be a symptom of spiritual growth.

Jonathan: Yes. And it begs the question that I don't think Swedenborg explicitly addresses: How do you increase your capacity for joy? Because some people can take more than others at a given moment in time.

Chelsea: That reminds me of something Pema Chödrön teaches. She says you meet your edge and soften.[86] It's hard to go to the furthest reaches of our capacity for joy. It's the most terrifying thing to parts of us, to be present to this joy. I feel like maybe part of that pain is that it is a part of our grieving. It seems like an acknowledgment. Swedenborg has written a lot about having

---

85 John Climacus, *The Ladder of Divine Ascent*, trans. Colm Luibheid and Norman Russell (New York: Paulist Press, 1982).

86 Pema Chödrön, *When Things Fall Apart: Heart Advice for Difficult Times* (Boulder: Shambhala Publications, 2000).

witnessed the last judgment in the spiritual world and writes of it as having been a spiritual event.[87]

In his description, he writes that when the presence of the Lord comes—when there's this light that comes—then everybody's grieving; everybody at first just falls apart. But it's actually the moment of salvation. They've been rescued. They're finally saved.[88] They're not in hell anymore, but that's when they're ripping their clothes.

The term I use for joy-pain is laugh-crying. Laughing with so much joy and yet crying like a grief release; it's like a moment of enlightenment that then also brings on this grief.

Jonathan: When people get lost in the woods, they often don't cry until they're rescued. When you're out there, you're just in it. But when you're finally safe and somebody's holding you, you can express the grief and pain.

Revelation 1:7 says God is "coming with the clouds and every eye will see him, including those who pierced him, and all the tribes of the earth will wail because of him."

Swedenborg talks about the grief that's going to happen when God comes, which seems so strange to me. Like, no, that's when you should be laughing. But there's something painful about that presence, especially at first. It reminds me of tears of joy. It's a relief but outwardly indistinguishable from being absolutely devastated.

Bob: This is really rich. You brought up the word "salvation," which is something we hadn't discussed as a Swedenborgian word for healing.

---

87 Emanuel Swedenborg, *Last Judgment / Supplements*, trans. George F. Dole and Jonathan S. Rose (West Chester: Swedenborg Foundation, 2018).

88 *Spirit and Life Bible Study*, episode 90, "Why Does the Second Coming Involve Sorrow?" written and delivered by Jonathan S. Rose, aired May 9, 2012, (mp3) http://640422ec8536d2c2516d-e7819cbb798e5e645cb0f80b-f20efc9a.r74.cf2.rackcdn.com/120509SecondComingSorrow.mp3

Chelsea: It reminds me of the Lord bending the heavens and coming down to save us (Psalm 18:9). That's a combination of redemption and consolation, so you just melt into a puddle, because you're being given what you need.

Bob: Does Swedenborg distinguish salvation from redemption, or are they synonyms?

Jonathan: I think the redeeming allowed salvation to be possible. If there's any difference between them, it would just be that there was a setting of the stage for redemption and then that allowed individuals' salvation to be possible.

Chelsea: That's a good point. When Swedenborg talks about salvation, he's often talking about it in conversation with the theology of his day and this dogmatic idea of salvation by faith alone.

He reframes it in terms of what Jesus came into the world to do. We weren't saved by Jesus dying on the cross, according to Swedenborg. It was the whole work of redemption that Jesus was doing by being in the world; he was walking the path, showing us the way. His process was our spiritual journey in microcosm, just like how the whole Bible is our spiritual journey in microcosm. Each of our healing stories—personal healing stories—is a microcosm of the whole collective of this healing journey. So there's definitely a fractal nature to healing.

Jonathan: I forgot that Revelation is not the only place that this grieving is said. In Matthew 24, there's a prediction in very similar language about the son of man coming in the clouds of heaven. And it says, "and then all the tribes of the earth will mourn" (Matthew 24:30).

This is *Secrets of Heaven* 4060:6 where Swedenborg remarks on this: "*Then all the tribes of the earth will mourn* means that everyone who possesses a loving goodness and religious truth will grieve. For this symbolism of mourning see Zechariah

12:10–14." Then he just explains that "tribes symbolize every facet of goodness and truth or of love and faith, so they symbolize people who possess those things. They're called tribes of the earth because they symbolize people in the church; the earth, meaning the church."

And then you go to Zechariah, and I didn't realize this, but 12:10–14 says,

> And I will pour out a spirit of compassion and supplication on the house of David and the inhabitants of Jerusalem so that, when they look on the one whom they have pierced, they shall mourn for him as one mourns for an only child and weep bitterly over him as one weeps over a firstborn. On that day the mourning in Jerusalem will be as great as the mourning for Hadad-rimmon in the plain of Megiddo. The land shall mourn, each family by itself; the family of the house of David by itself and their wives by themselves; the family of the house of Nathan by itself and their wives by themselves; the family of the house of Levi by itself and their wives by themselves; the family of the Shimeites by itself and their wives by themselves; and all the families that are left, each by itself and their wives by themselves. (Zechariah 12:10–14 NRSV)

So everybody will do their own individual grieving. It's interesting for him to say, to explain what this scripture means, go see this other scripture that I haven't explained.

Chelsea: And it started with the pouring on of a spirit of compassion. Like there's this pouring on of compassion, and then you're mourning.

Jonathan: And everybody goes into their own kind of individual grief.

Chelsea: That really connects grieving to healing. You can't avoid the grieving. Grieving is a sign of healing, rather than a sign of things getting worse. I think that would go a long way to have a cultural shift about that.

Jonathan: It's like the first wave.

Chelsea: When he says that people with love and truth will mourn, and will grieve—it's the ones who are tuned in.

Jonathan: What a fascinating conversation we're having. There's something really amazing about thinking about that; we're forewarned. It says it over and over again. This is going to come and y'all are going to cry.

CONCLUSION

Jonathan: What are the highlights? What are key points that emerged from this conversation, and which are surprising?

Bob: Let's go over those now. I think the idea of unblending is crucial. The distinction between inner self versus outer self and the inviolability of the inner self would be two more.

Chelsea: For me it's healing; the process of it.

Jonathan: There's an order to it. I think Swedenborg does lend clarity about the framework of how thoughts or feelings are in the human form and have autonomy. There's an order in there and a presence to the multiplicity: what that state of consciousness is, what spiritual light is, and how you see what's going on inside. Why is visualizing things inside effective? Because there's a whole realm that backs this up. And you're getting help. I mean, that's the spiritual piece. Healing is spiritual.

Bob: Another super important thing is the definition of Self or inner self. And what you said, Jonathan, about Hagar's vision, the hierarchy of seeing going all the way up to the divine.

Another incredibly useful concept is the idea of proprium, and how we take on burdens, but we are not the burden. Swedenborg can expand modern psychotherapy; this isn't an antiquarian adventure. There are treasures here.

Chelsea: IFS is brilliant. It is super functional. People are doing amazing work with it clinically. And yet in Facebook chats in IFS groups, I run across people wondering, "What is it really?" You try to look inside, and you can say, "Okay, I know from IFS that there are all these things, but how does that actually make sense?" It can kind of just feel like a black void or something. "Okay, somehow there are exiles in me and there are managers and Self or whatever." If I go to Jung, it kind of sounds like this; if I go to that guy, it sounds like that.

But Swedenborg gives you scaffolding; what he writes about builds a structure in your mind, and then you're able to have almost a three-dimensionality of your inner psyche that helps you literally see it better, to not just feel like it's abstract. Swedenborg helps you reflect on what all of this is in a way that expands IFS and gives it a little more context.

Bob: Another super important one: personalism and Swedenborg. It's all humans, all the way up, all the way down. It's all persons. You have to deal with things as persons, not as things. There are no things in the inner world. That is such a revolution in IFS. We deal with all of these parts as people—fully dimensional, 360-degree people.

Jonathan: And here you have this man in a wig from 200 umpteen years ago saying, "Well, they're all people in there."

Chelsea: When I think about somebody reading this book, I hope it's as cool for people as it was revolutionary for me to be learning about IFS for the first time. This blob that was my inner traumatized experience—like I'd just hit up against it and nothing really helped it resolve—then suddenly, I had pathways and I could make inroads. Everything was then opening up, and things were shifting around and getting rearranged, and I can feel the difference. There's access, there's movement, and progress in a way that just was never possible before in any kind of therapy that I had tried. I love the thought that somebody reading this book could be hearing the idea that you have parts, and all these other principles. Somebody could have that click moment and suddenly feel like they're able to have this freedom and agency in their life that they didn't have before.

Religious Belief versus Experience

Bob: I have one last proposition I want to have you check out with Swedenborg. One of my favorite people on the planet is Tanya Luhrmann, the Stanford anthropologist. She says the great mistake of academia is that they consider religion to be about beliefs. Religion is primarily about experience, and beliefs are secondary or even tertiary to the experiences people have. That's what makes them religious. She said, with this in mind, that porosity of mind is the fundamental substrate of all religion, because it's what allows you to have these experiences of spirit. So would Swedenborg agree that experience is primary in religion rather than doctrine?

Jonathan: He absolutely agrees that it's not all about doctrine. In fact, he has a great passage where he explains how Lot's wife turning to a pillar of salt is because she turns from love back toward doctrine. That's what freezes her into a pillar of stone (*Secrets of Heaven* 2454–2455). It's pretty awesome. He uses words like "how you live your life," which is related to experience. He doesn't express it in exactly those terms, but it's very much about how "religion is all about how we live, and the religious way to live is to do good" (*Life* 1).

I grew up with that same thought: that religion equals a belief system. It's teachings. For him, religion is a "doing" word; it's a practice, but not in a strictly ritualistic way, rather in how you live your life. It's how you treat people. He differentiates between the word religion and the word church. He'll use the word church for a body of teachings, but religion is what you're doing, how you're loving.

You need to connect the dots to get that over to experience. But it's not hard. It's definitely doctrine being a second—absolutely second—fiddle.

Chelsea: I'm so intrigued by Tanya Luhrmann's pinpointing experience, because, again, we talked about the eighteenth century having a resistance to feelings, and that's carried over into our times. Swedenborgian traditions have also been allergic to feeling. They're comfortable if you say belief, and practice, and how you live. But oh wait, if there's feelings involved in that, we don't want to go there. Messy feelings.

The Biblical story that's coming to my mind is the whole story of Jacob and Esau, these twins. Swedenborg describes the birthright. Esau, he says, corresponds to the will, to this feeling level, and Jacob is the understanding. Jacob steals the birthright of Esau. Jacob is the sense that the understanding is what's really important. You think it's what rules the show, but the gist of the story is that it only appears that way, when it's really the other way. Love, this feeling, and the will, is what's really primary (Genesis 25–33, *Secrets of Heaven* volumes 4–6).

Jonathan: It's trickery to suggest that truth has that upper position. Jacob keeps doing it by tomfoolery and deception.

Chelsea: So the image that comes to my mind is when they meet again. Jacob is coming back to Esau to make amends, and he's afraid. He's terrified. It's similar to Joseph's brothers because he knows he's done something bad to Esau. I did some bad things to you. You have every right to punch me in the face, but I'm coming to ask your forgiveness.

Jonathan: He sends, like, 400 people ahead of him. Flocks and goats and raisins and bunches of grapes and figs and dates.

Chelsea: And then Esau just hugs Jacob, and they weep—there's that grieving again. It's just this embrace.

So Swedenborg would say, yeah, the will comes first. Our intellect is really a secondary thing. But I think they've sort of sanitized the word will. I think you could make the argument that that's experience. That's all the feeling. But of course, if you do that, you lose some control. We can't be letting people trust their own hearts and experience! It would be mayhem!

Bob: I'm hearing you equate will with doing, with practice, with experience, and then you finally get hooked up to feelings over there; it sort of snuck in the back door and hoped they wouldn't notice.

Jonathan: Swedenborg uses the term experience hundreds of times. A lot of what he's talking about is his experience. He's not expecting other people to believe his experience. But the way that he presents it is, he says, "I've been convinced beyond the shadow of doubt by my experience" (see *Last Judgment* 9:9). So experience is a big word to him. It's the substrate of his whole revelation! But I think some people mistakenly think, "Oh, well, I should believe him because he experienced it." And he's pretty big on the idea of, no, does it make sense to *you?* You have to go through your own process with it. The idea of experience is huge to him. A lot of what was going on was that he was experiencing these things that to other people are just dry syllogisms about this equals that.

Chelsea: It's all about his spiritual experiences. That's what we are referencing all the time. He packs his spiritual experiences even into his Biblical exegesis because he is like, this is the real deal.

He says in *Secrets of Heaven* 68 that "I realize many will claim that no one can talk to spirits and angels as long as bodily life continues, or that I am hallucinating, or that I have circulated such stories in order to play on people's credulity, and so on. But none of this worries me; I have seen, I have heard, I have felt."

He lands it by saying *felt.*

So that's his definition of what's real: I've seen it. I've heard it. I've felt it.

Bob: I want to add a suggestion that might bridge his experience, doing, will, and practices to our feelings about emotions: Eugene Gendlin's concept of the felt sense.[89] He would have people go into their bodies. He said, you'll experience something in the trunk of your body. You will have a felt sense there, which is a physical sensation combined with some kind of emotional reality, some living sense of something. And that might be like an intermediary thing you could go to, to bridge between Swedenborg using the word experience: felt sense, and then you're at emotions.

Chelsea: I love that you brought that up because it's not like, "Oh, I've got a pinched nerve, so I'm feeling some tingling in my thigh." There's a sense, but then there is this emotional feeling that is this alive bridge.

Jonathan: A word Swedenborg uses a lot to describe things is "affection." Some of his use of the word affection is about emotion. He uses the word emotion quite a bit too. It's obvious that he thinks that takes precedence over the mere cerebral world that the Enlightenment was talking about so much.

Chelsea: So we're talking about felt sense and that's where you get to emotion, from will and practice and life, and living. Remember that love and wisdom are distinguishably one. Earlier I was saying, what is truth, really? It's reality. It's what you're feeling. Like this whole idea that truth is anything apart from love is a fabrication. That's where you end up battling in dogmas and doctrine and all this stuff. We just went through this whole path of will leading to felt sense. But if felt sense is

---

89 Eugene T. Gendlin, "The Experiential Response," *Use of Interpretation in Treatment* (1968): 208–227.

reality, then that's truth. And so we've come full circle. Truth is feeling. There is no separateness there.

Jonathan: Truth is the form of love. It's just the form that love takes.

Closing Thoughts

Jonathan: I just wanted to say that I have felt a very nice kind of eternity in these conversations. I really don't want it to stop. It's been so fun. I treasure that feeling.

Bob: I've really enjoyed both of you a great deal. It's been a wonderful pleasure. Very exciting and very deepening for me. I'm really grateful.

Chelsea: I am so grateful to you both for engaging in these conversations. It is a dream come true for me. I hope they help people, and I look forward to whatever comes next.

BIBLIOGRAPHY

Aurelius, Marcus. *Meditations*. New York: Penguin, 2015.

Barrett, Frederick S., Matthew W. Johnson, and Roland R. Griffiths. "Validation of the Revised Mystical Experience Questionnaire in Experimental Sessions with Psilocybin." *Journal of Psychopharmacology* 29, no. 11 (2015): 1182–1190.

Bergquist, Lars, ed. *Swedenborg's Dream Diary*. Translated by Anders Hallengren. Royersford: Swedenborg Foundation, 2024.

Brach, Tara. "Meditation, Psychedelics, Mortality: A Conversation with Tara Brach and Roland Griffiths." Tarabrach.com, January 18, 2023. https://www.tarabrach.com/meditation-psychedelics-mortality-conversation/.

Brazelton, Thomas Berry, and Bertrand G. Cramer. *The Earliest Relationship: Parents, Infants and the Drama of Early Attachment*. Reading, MA: Addison-Wesley, 1991.

Brewer, Judson. *Unwinding Anxiety: New Science Shows How to Break the Cycles of Worry and Fear to Heal Your Mind*. New York: Penguin, 2022.

Chödrön, Pema. *When Things Fall Apart: Heart Advice for Difficult Times*. Boulder: Shambhala Publications, 2000.

Chomsky, Noam. "Deep Structure, Surface Structure, and Semantic Interpretation" in *Foundational Issues*, vol. 1 of *Semantics: Critical Concepts in Linguistics*. Edited by Javier Gutiérrez-Rexach. United Kingdom: Routledge, 2003.

Clarke, Isabel. *Madness, Mystery and the Survival of God*. Ropley: O Books, 2008.

Climacus, John. *The Ladder of Divine Ascent*. Translated by Colm Luibheid and Norman Russell. New York: Paulist Press, 1982.

Corbin, Henry. *Swedenborg and Esoteric Islam*. Translated by Leonard Fox. West Chester: Swedenborg Foundation, 1995.

Deahl, Martin, and Michael Andreassen. "Psychiatric Colonialism, PTSD and the Western Psychiatric Diagnostic Tradition . . . Is One Man's

Food Another Man's Poison?" *International Journal of Social Psychiatry* 70, no. 1 (2024): 36–39.

Dias, Brian G., and Kerry J. Ressler. "Parental Olfactory Experience Influences Behavior and Neural Structure in Subsequent Generations." *Nature Neuroscience* 17, no. 1 (2014): 89–96.

Dronkers, Nina F., Maria V. Ivanova, and Juliana V. Baldo. "What Do Language Disorders Reveal About Brain–Language Relationships? From Classic Models to Network Approaches." *Journal of the International Neuropsychological Society* 23, no. 9–10 (2017): 741–754.

Duran, Eduardo. *Healing the Soul Wound: Trauma-Informed Counseling for Indigenous Communities*. New York: Teachers College Press, 2019.

Eck, Allison. "Altering Perceptions on Psychedelics." *Harvard Medicine*. Spring 2022. https://magazine.hms.harvard.edu/articles/altering-perceptions-psychedelics.

Eckhart, Meister. "Sermon Fifty-Seven." In *The Complete Mystical Works of Meister Eckhart*. Translated by Maurice O'C. Walshe, 295–299. New York: The Crossroad Publishing Company, 2009.

Eliade, Mircea. *The Forge and the Crucible*. Translated by Stephen Corrin. London: Rider & Co., 1962.

Ellenberger, Henri F. *The Discovery of the Unconscious: The History and Evolution of Dynamic Psychiatry*. New York: Basic Books, 1970.

Erickson, Milton H. *The Collected Works of Milton H. Erickson*. Vol. 3. Edited by Ernest Rossi, Roxanna Erickson-Klein, and Kathryn Rossi. Phoenix: Milton H. Erickson Foundation, 2008.

Erickson, Milton H. "The Use of Symptoms as an Integral Part of Hypnotherapy." *American Journal of Clinical Hypnosis* 8, no. 1 (1965): 57–65.

Falconer, Robert. *The Others Within Us: Internal Family Systems, Porous Mind, and Spirit Possession*. N.p.: Great Mystery Press, 2023.

Falconer, Robert. *When You're Going Through Hell . . . Keep Going: Trauma, Healing, Spirit, and Internal Family Systems*. N.p.: Great Mystery Press, 2024.

Fernández, Alejandro Pérez, Manuel Carreiras, and Jon Andoni Duñabeitia. "Brain-to-Brain Entrainment: EEG Interbrain Synchronization While Speaking and Listening." *Scientific Reports* 7, no. 1 (2017): 4190.

Fuchs, Eberhard, and Gabriele Flügge. "Adult Neuroplasticity: More than 40 Years of Research." *Neural Plasticity* 2014, no. 1 (2014): 541870.

Gazzaniga, Michael S. "The Split Brain in Man." *Scientific American* 217, no. 2 (1967): 24–29.

Gendlin, Eugene T. "The Experiential Response." *Use of Interpretation in Treatment* (1968): 208–227.

Gilman, Io Y., and Kendall I. Shields. "At Harvard, Psychedelic Drugs' Tentative Renaissance." *The Harvard Crimson*. February 19, 2022.

https://www.thecrimson.com/article/2022/2/19/psychedelics-tentative-renaissance/.

Hesse, Hermann. *Steppenwolf*. Translated by David Horrocks. United Kingdom: Penguin, 2012.

Hodge, David R., Gordon E. Limb, and Terry L. Cross. "Moving from Colonization toward Balance and Harmony: A Native American Perspective on Wellness." *Social Work* 54, no. 3 (2009): 211–219.

Katie, Byron, and Stephen Mitchell. *Loving What Is: Four Questions That Can Change Your Life*. New York: Harmony Books, 2002.

King, Kristin. "Reading What the Writings Say They Cannot Say." *New Church Life* Vols. CXIX–CXX, nos. 8–9 (August–September 1999): 345–360, 393–410.

King, Lester S. "Cases of the Reincarnation Type, Vol 1: Ten Cases in India." *The Journal of the American Medical Association* 234, no. 9 (1975): 978-978.

Lang, Bernhard. Introduction to *Heaven and Hell*. West Chester: Swedenborg Foundation, 2000.

Leeson, Peter T., and Jacob W. Russ. "Witch Trials." *The Economic Journal* 128, no. 613 (2018): 2066–2105.

Lewis, Clive Staples. *A Grief Observed*. Grand Rapids: Zondervan, 2001.

Liotti, Giovanni, and Paul Gilbert. "Mentalizing, Motivation, and Social Mentalities: Theoretical Considerations and Implications for Psychotherapy." *Psychology and Psychotherapy: Theory, Research and Practice* 84, no. 1 (2011): 9–25.

Llinás, Rodolfo R. *I of the Vortex: From Neurons to Self*. Cambridge: MIT Press, 2002.

Luhrmann, Tanya Marie. *How God Becomes Real: Kindling the Presence of Invisible Others*. Princeton University Press, 2020.

Luhrmann, Tanya Marie, Kara Weisman, Felicity Aulino, Joshua D. Brahinsky, John C. Dulin, Vivian A. Dzokoto, Cristine H. Legare et al. "Sensing the Presence of Gods and Spirits Across Cultures and Faiths." *Proceedings of the National Academy of Sciences* 118, no. 5 (2021): e2016649118, https://doi.org/10.1073/pnas.2016649118.

Nelson, Thomas O. "Consciousness and Metacognition." *American Psychologist* 51, no. 2 (1996): 102–116.

Nichols, Michael P., and Richard C. Schwartz. *Family Therapy: Concepts and Methods*. New York: Gardner Press, 1984.

McGilchrist, Iain. *The Master and His Emissary: The Divided Brain and the Making of the Western World*. New Haven: Yale University Press, 2019.

Odhner, Carl Theophilus. Annals of the New Church: With a Chronological Account of the Life of Emanuel Swedenborg. Vol. 1, 1688–1850. Bryn Athyn: Academy of the New Church, 1904.

Odhner, Chelsea. "The Danger of Enjoying Evil and the Gothenburg Heresy Trial." Produced by Chelsea Odhner. *Inside Off The Left Eye*,

May 23, 2021. Podcast, MP3 audio, 55:04. https://inside-offthelefteye.simplecast.com/episodes/the-danger-of-enjoying-evil-and-the-gothenburg-heresy-trial.

Odhner, Chelsea. "When Swedenborg First Spoke to Spirits from Other Planets." Produced by Chelsea Odhner. *Inside Off The Left Eye*, January 17, 2021. Podcast, MP3 audio, 42:19. https://inside-offthelefteye.simplecast.com/episodes/when-swedenborg-first-spoke-to-spirits-from-other-planets.

Odhner, John Durban, and Kurt Nemitz, trans. *Emanuel Swedenborg's Diary, Recounting Spiritual Experiences During the Years 1745–1765*. 4 vols. Bryn Athyn: General Church of the New Jerusalem, 1998–2013.

Odhner, Sarah. "Emanuel Swedenborg | GCED | Childhood 1688–1709." YouTube video, 11:26. September 6, 2016. https://www.youtube.com/watch?v=3O4vhrqdpjk.

Off The Left Eye. "The Spiritual Link Between the Human Brain and Consciousness." *Swedenborg and Life*. YouTube video. 26:32. November 16, 2020. https://www.youtube.com/watch?v=Iu8VeM1DmoA, 4:51.

Prechtel, Martín. *The Smell of Rain on Dust: Grief and Praise*. Berkeley: North Atlantic Books, 2015.

Rose, Jonathan S., dir. *Spirit and Life Bible Study*. Episode 90, "Why Does the Second Coming Involve Sorrow?" Aired May 9, 2012, (mp3) http://640422ec8536d2c2516d-e7819cbb798e5e645cb0f80bf20efc9a.r74.cf2.rackcdn.com/120509SecondComingSorrow.mp3

Rose, Jonathan, S. Introduction to *The Shorter Works of 1763*, by Emanuel Swedenborg, 15–107. Translated by George Dole. West Chester: Swedenborg Foundation, 2020.

Rose, Jonathan S., Stuart Shotwell, and Mary Lou Bertucci, eds. *Emanuel Swedenborg: Essays for the New Century Edition on his Life, Work, and Impact*. West Chester: Swedenborg Foundation, 2005.

Schwartz, Richard C. Foreword to *The Others Within Us*, by Robert Falconer, xiii–xx. Great Mystery Press, 2023.

Schwartz, Richard C. *No Bad Parts: Healing Trauma and Restoring Wholeness with the Internal Family Systems Model*. Boulder: Sounds True, 2021.

Schwartz, Richard C., and Martha Sweezy. *Internal Family Systems Therapy*, 2nd ed. New York: The Guilford Press, 2020.

Scott, Derek. "IFS, Grief and Loss." IFSCA. Accessed November 2, 2024. https://ifsca.ca/videos/ifs-grief-and-loss/.

Scott, Derek. "Self-Led Grieving: Transitions, Loss and Death." In *Innovations and Elaborations in Internal Family Systems Therapy*, eds. Martha Sweezy and Ellen L. Ziskind (Routledge, 2017), 90–108.

Sigstedt, Cyriel Odhner. *The Swedenborg Epic: The Life and Works of Emanuel Swedenborg*. New York: Bookman Associates, 1952.

Stephen, Michele, and Luh Ketut Suryani. "Shamanism, Psychosis and Autonomous Imagination." *Culture, Medicine and Psychiatry* 24, no. 1 (2000): 5–40.

Stephenson, Craig E. *Possession: Jung's Comparative Anatomy of the Psyche*. New York: Routledge, 2016.

Stevenson, Ian. "Cases of the Reincarnation Type, Vol. IV, Twelve Cases in Thailand and Burma." *The Journal of Nervous and Mental Disease* 173, no. 1 (1985): 63.

Stevenson, Ian. *Reincarnation and Biology: A Contribution to the Etiology of Birthmarks and Birth Defects*. Westport: Praeger, 1970.

Suzuki, Daisetz Teitaro. *Swedenborg: Buddha of the North*. West Chester: Swedenborg Foundation, 1996.

Swedenborg, Emanuel. *Divine Love and Wisdom*. Translated by George F. Dole. West Chester: Swedenborg Foundation, 2003.

Swedenborg, Emanuel. *Divine Providence*. Translated by George F. Dole. West Chester: Swedenborg Foundation, 2003.

Swedenborg, Emanuel. *Heaven and Hell*. Translated by George F. Dole. West Chester: Swedenborg Foundation, 2000.

Swedenborg, Emanuel. *Last Judgment / Supplements*. Translated by George F. Dole and Jonathan S. Rose. West Chester: Swedenborg Foundation, 2018.

Swedenborg, Emanuel. *Life / Faith*. Translated by George F. Dole. West Chester: Swedenborg Foundation, 2014.

Swedenborg, Emanuel. *New Jerusalem*. Translated by George F. Dole. West Chester: Swedenborg Foundation, 2016.

Swedenborg, Emanuel. *On the Divine Love and the Divine Wisdom*. Translated by Samuel Worcester and revised by John C. Ager. In vol. 6 of *Apocalypse Explained*, translated by John C. Ager, revised by John Whitehead, and edited by William Ross Woofenden. West Chester: Swedenborg Foundation, 1994–1997.

Swedenborg, Emanuel. *Other Planets*. Translated by George F. Dole. West Chester: Swedenborg Foundation, 2018.

Swedenborg, Emanuel. *Secrets of Heaven*. Vols 1–6. West Chester: Swedenborg Foundation, 2008–2023.

Swedenborg, Emanuel. *Secrets of Heaven*. Vols 7–8. Translated by Lisa Hyatt Cooper. Royersford: Swedenborg Foundation, 2024.

Swedenborg, Emanuel. *Secrets of Heaven*. Vols 9–16. Translated by Lisa Hyatt Cooper. Forthcoming.

Swedenborg, Emanuel. *Survey / Soul-Body Interaction*. Translated by Jonathan S. Rose and George F. Dole. West Chester: Swedenborg Foundation, 2022.

Swedenborg, Emanuel. *The Economy of the Animal Kingdom, Considered Anatomically, Physically, and Philosophically*. Translated by Augustus Clissold. 2 vols. Bryn Athyn: Swedenborg Scientific Association, 1955.

Swedenborg, Emanuel. *The Economy of the Animal Kingdom, Considered Anatomically, Physically, and Philosophically, Transaction III.* Translated by Alfred Acton. Bryn Athyn: Swedenborg Scientific Association, 1976.

Swedenborg, Emanuel. *True Christianity.* 2 vols. Translated by Jonathan S. Rose. West Chester: Swedenborg, Foundation, 2010–2011.

Swedenborg Society. *Double Thoughts.* London: Swedenborg Society, 2010.

Swiney, Sherry. "The 'That's a Lie' Program." Keyholejourney Blog. July 21, 2016. https://keyholejourney.wordpress.com/2016/07/21/the-thats-a-lie-program/.

Van Dusen, Wilson. *Emanuel Swedenborg's Journal of Dreams: The Extraordinary Record of the Transformation of a Scientist into a Seer.* Translated by J. J. G. Wilkinson. New York: Swedenborg Foundation, 1986.

Van Dusen, Wilson. *The Presence of Other Worlds: The Psychological and Spiritual Findings of Emanuel Swedenborg.* West Chester: Swedenborg Foundation, 2004.

Van Dusen, Wilson. *The Presence of Spirits In Madness: A Confirmation of Swedenborg in Recent Empirical Findings.* New York: Swedenborg Foundation, 1972.

Weller, Francis. *The Wild Edge of Sorrow: Rituals of Renewal and the Sacred Work of Grief.* Berkeley: North Atlantic Books, 2015.

INDEX

ABOUT THE PUBLISHER

The Swedenborg Foundation is an innovative multi-media nonprofit publisher dedicated to expanding the reach and understanding of Emanuel Swedenborg's writings, making Emanuel Swedenborg's thought more widely known and freely available to all. Since its inception in 1849, the Foundation has evolved from a simple publishing house into a multimedia hub of education and enlightenment. The Swedenborg Foundation bridges the gap between spiritual ideas and modern issues through works which engage the intersection of spirituality and other fields.

All the books we publish are made possible by the generous support of our donors. Connect with us at www.swedenborg.com to support this and other publishing projects, check out our membership community, and to purchase and freely access Swedenborg's writings.

ABOUT THE AUTHORS

CHELSEA ROSE ODHNER is a multifaceted professional bridging spiritual scholarship, creative expression, and holistic healing. As Vice President of Publishing for the Swedenborg Foundation and a trained Internal Family Systems practitioner and bodyworker, she brings a unique interdisciplinary approach to understanding human experience. Her work spans writing, music, and spiritual content strategy, including her original spiritual music album "Confident Hope."

Trained in yoga philosophy and interfaith dialogue, she works to highlight important intersections in the areas of spiritual growth, psychological understanding, and creative expression. Odhner is dedicated to translating complex spiritual concepts into practical, transformative tools for personal growth. She works one-on-one with people as a licensed massage therapist and certified coach via her practice at locusofhealing.com.

ROBERT FALCONER is a pioneering therapist and international educator in Internal Family Systems therapy. He brings over five decades of transformative psychological expertise and a heartfelt commitment to healing and understanding the complexity of human experience. Falconer has authored several influential books, including *Many Minds, One Self*, co-written with IFS founder Richard C. Schwartz. Falconer's book *The Others Within Us* is a groundbreaking work which centralizes "porosity" as a key component to healing.

He is a respected international trainer who has led workshops in many countries, including Europe, Pakistan, Mexico, China, Canada, Australia, and Japan. Falconer champions a holistic view that recognizes the inherent spiritual nature of psychological healing. Falconer remains an active teacher and thought leader. His work challenges Western therapeutic paradigms and advocates for a more comprehensive understanding of human consciousness. More information about him and his work can be found at robertfalconer.us.

JONATHAN S. ROSE, PhD, is a scholar and translator of the works of Emanuel Swedenborg. As Series Editor of the New Century Edition translation of Swedenborg's theological works, he has dedicated his career to making Swedenborg's teachings accessible through meticulous translation and research. Dr. Rose has authored works including *The Message of Love Behind the Ten Commandments* and *Swedenborg's Garden of Theology* and been the host of the Spirit and Life Bible Study. He was also a tenured professor, innovative researcher who developed Latin analysis software, and curator of the Swedenborgiana Library.

Beyond his scholarly pursuits, Dr. Rose is also an accomplished musician who explored spiritual themes in his eclectic gospel album "Clear Shining after Rain." An ordained minister and former college chaplain, Rose has a passion for exploring the therapeutic potential of Swedenborg's teachings, inspired by innovative psychologists like Wilson Van Dusen, Raymond Moody, and Jerry Marzinsky. In his work, he aims to help people know and understand Swedenborg's works so that they can connect with heavenly inspiration and healing.